W9-CAV-496

THE COMPLETE IDIOT'S GUIDE® TO

Retirement Planning

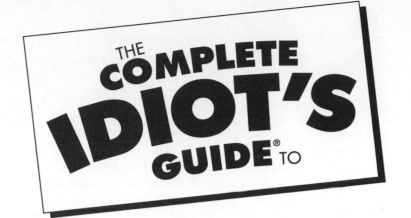

THE
COMPLETE
IDIOT'S
GUIDE® TO

Retirement
Planning

by Jeff J. Wuorio

ALPHA

A member of Penguin Group (USA) Inc.

For Judy, Meghan, and Nathan, for patience and understanding above and beyond the call.

ALPHA BOOKS

Published by the Penguin Group

Penguin Group (USA) Inc., 375 Hudson Street, New York, New York 10014, USA

Penguin Group (Canada), 90 Eglinton Avenue East, Suite 700, Toronto, Ontario M4P 2Y3, Canada (a division of Pearson Penguin Canada Inc.)

Penguin Books Ltd., 80 Strand, London WC2R 0RL, England

Penguin Ireland, 25 St. Stephen's Green, Dublin 2, Ireland (a division of Penguin Books Ltd.)

Penguin Group (Australia), 250 Camberwell Road, Camberwell, Victoria 3124, Australia (a division of Pearson Australia Group Pty. Ltd.)

Penguin Books India Pvt. Ltd., 11 Community Centre, Panchsheel Park, New Delhi—110 017, India

Penguin Group (NZ), 67 Apollo Drive, Rosedale, North Shore, Auckland 1311, New Zealand (a division of Pearson New Zealand Ltd.)

Penguin Books (South Africa) (Pty.) Ltd., 24 Sturdee Avenue, Rosebank, Johannesburg 2196, South Africa

Penguin Books Ltd., Registered Offices: 80 Strand, London WC2R 0RL, England

Copyright © 2007 by Jeff J. Wuorio

All rights reserved. No part of this book shall be reproduced, stored in a retrieval system, or transmitted by any means, electronic, mechanical, photocopying, recording, or otherwise, without written permission from the publisher. No patent liability is assumed with respect to the use of the information contained herein. Although every precaution has been taken in the preparation of this book, the publisher and author assume no responsibility for errors or omissions. Neither is any liability assumed for damages resulting from the use of information contained herein. For information, address Alpha Books, 800 East 96th Street, Indianapolis, IN 46240.

THE COMPLETE IDIOT'S GUIDE TO and Design are registered trademarks of Penguin Group (USA) Inc.

International Standard Book Number: 978-1-59-257692-0
Library of Congress Catalog Card Number: 2007930860

09 08 07   8 7 6 5 4 3 2 1

Interpretation of the printing code: The rightmost number of the first series of numbers is the year of the book's printing; the rightmost number of the second series of numbers is the number of the book's printing. For example, a printing code of 07-1 shows that the first printing occurred in 2007.

Printed in the United States of America

Note: This publication contains the opinions and ideas of its author. It is intended to provide helpful and informative material on the subject matter covered. It is sold with the understanding that the author and publisher are not engaged in rendering professional services in the book. If the reader requires personal assistance or advice, a competent professional should be consulted.

The author and publisher specifically disclaim any responsibility for any liability, loss, or risk, personal or otherwise, which is incurred as a consequence, directly or indirectly, of the use and application of any of the contents of this book.

Most Alpha books are available at special quantity discounts for bulk purchases for sales promotions, premiums, fund-raising, or educational use. Special books, or book excerpts, can also be created to fit specific needs.

For details, write: Special Markets, Alpha Books, 375 Hudson Street, New York, NY 10014.

Publisher: *Marie Butler-Knight*
Editorial Director: *Mike Sanders*
Managing Editor: *Billy Fields*
Acquisitions Editor: *Tom Stevens*
Development Editor: *Michael Thomas*
Senior Production Editor: *Janette Lynn*
Copy Editor: *Amy Borrelli*

Cartoonist: *Andrew Sides*
Cover Designer: *Bill Thomas*
Book Designer: *Trina Wurst*
Indexer: *Brad Herriman*
Layout: *Chad Dressler*
Proofreader: *John Etchison*

Contents at a Glance

Part 1:   **Retirement Basics**   1

   1 Retirement Has Changed   3
*Learn what's new with retirement and what that means to
you as you look toward your own.*

   2 Who's Retiring Now?   15
*It's time to update your notion of just who's retiring out there
and what they're doing with themselves.*

   3 Your Retirement Goals—A Self-Assessment   27
*Want to know if you're really the retiring type? If, so, when
might be the best time to hang up your working shoes? The
answers are here.*

   4 The Issue of Money—A First Look   39
*Determine how much is "enough" savings for retirement,
learn ways to calculate your retirement needs, and consider the
importance of proactivity and inflation.*

   5 Where Might the Money Come From?   51
*Good question! Maybe from personal savings, company pen-
sions, Social Security, life insurance, or, more likely, a combination of sources.*

   6 The First Part of the Plan: Basic Financial Steps   63
*Here, we tackle the importance of monitoring your spending
and keeping your debt in check.*

Part 2:   **Where the Money Comes From**   75

   7 On the Job   77
*The changing face of company-sponsored retirement, from
defined benefit plans to 401(k)s.*

   8 Social Security   91
*A look at the storied government retirement program, from
its inception to what you can expect to receive once you retire.*

   9 Let's Hear It for IRA!   103
*An overview of the Individual Retirement Account, including
an examination of the latest version of the IRA—the Roth.*

  10 The Basics of Investing, Part One: Mutual Funds   115
Using mutual funds to save for your retirement.

11 The Basics of Investing, Part Two: Stocks   129
The lowdown on stocks and what they can do for you, from the various types you can buy to strategies to build a solid portfolio.

12 The Basics of Investing, Part Three: Bonds and GICs   143
Bonds and guaranteed insurance contracts—potentially important additions to your retirement plan.

Part 3:   **Timing Is Everything**   **157**

13 If You're Young   159
The importance of getting started early and sticking with a plan over the long haul.

14 Midway to Retirement   171
There's still time to take action if needs warrant it. Gauge where you are and whether you need to change your strategy.

15 Ready to Retire!   183
How to set up and oversee a funding strategy for your retirement.

16 Making Sure It Lasts Long Enough   195
Budgeting ideas, lifestyle adjustments, and other steps you can take to keep your nest egg in top-notch shape.

Part 4:   **Key Financial Concerns**   **207**

17 The Tax Man—Older but Still Around   209
Ways to save on taxes before you retire, and ways to trim your tax bill during retirement.

18 Health Insurance   221
Gauge your health insurance needs and shop for the best, most affordable coverage you can find.

19 Retirement Communities and Long-Term Care
Insurance   233
Some ideas on retirement communities and assisted living, as well as information on long-term care insurance.

20 Other Insurance Issues   245
The role of life insurance and other types of insurance, including insurance you don't need.

21 Estate Planning   257
The basics of estate planning, including wills, living wills, trusts, and other vehicles.

Part 5:   **When It's Not Enough**   **267**

22 Retiring on a Shoestring   269
Some ideas to help make ends meet, from trading down your home to reverse mortgages.

23 Retire—Then Go to Work   279
Decide if after-work retirement is right for you and, if so, how you can best market yourself.

24 Alternate Living   291
Explore some new housing and community concepts.

Appendixes

A Glossary   303

B Retirement Planning Worksheets   311

Index   325

Contents

Part 1: Retirement Basics   **1**

1 Retirement Has Changed   **3**

What's Changed?..4
Longevity...4
Retirement Age Has Changed...5
More Retirement Choices..7
   Continuing to Work...*8*
   Starting a Business...*9*
   Serving on Boards of Directors.......................................*9*
   Doing Volunteer Work..*9*
   Participating in Organizations and Clubs.....................*10*
   Going Back to School...*10*
What This Means to You..10
New Challenges Mean New Strategies.............................11

2 Who's Retiring Now?   **15**

Just Who the Heck Are All These Retirees? 16
   The "Average" Retirement Age....................................*16*
   What Else Is It About Them?.......................................*17*
How's Their Health?..19
   Chronic Conditions...*19*
   Mental Health...*20*
Where Are They Living?...21
How They Afford Retirement...23
But Are They *Really* Affording Retirement? 24

3 Your Retirement Goals—A Self-Assessment   **27**

Retire? Says Who?...28
   Are You the Retiring Type? A Checklist.......................*28*
   The Example of Walter Zweifler...................................*29*
When to Retire..30
   Factors to Consider...*30*
   Don't Just Let Retirement Happen...............................*31*
Should Couples Retire at the Same Time? 32
Is Early Retirement Right for You?...................................33
An Issue of Lifestyle...34

Where to Retire?..35
    Staying Put..*35*
    Relocating..*36*

4 The Issue of Money—A First Look   **39**

How Much Is Enough?..40
How Much Will You Need? How to Calculate It......................40
Where You Are Now Matters..43
Get the Message? Get a Jump on Things!...............................45
Understanding Inflation..45
Another Key—Steady Income 46
Money—The End All to Retirement?....................................47

5 Where Might the Money Come From?   **51**

Getting to Know the IRA 52
Other Savings Programs 53
Workplace Programs 54
Social Security 55
    Retirement Benefits..*56*
    Spousal Benefits..*57*
    Survivors Benefits..*57*
    Disability...*57*
Life Insurance and Annuities..58
    Life Insurance...*58*
    Annuities...*59*
Reverse Mortgages 60
The Importance of a Broad Plan..61

6 The First Part of the Plan: Basic Financial Steps   **63**

Keep an Eye on Your Spending...64
The Perils of Credit Card Debt 66
Other Ways to Cut Your Spending 68
    Pay Down Your Mortgage..*68*
    Refinance Your Mortgage *69*
Put All Those Savings to Use 70
    Rule One—Pay Yourself First *70*
    Where to Stash Your Savings *71*
    Less Access, Better Returns *73*

Part 2:   **Where the Money Comes From**   **75**

7   **On the Job**   **77**

The Changing Face of Company-Sponsored Retirement..........78

Defined Benefit Plans 79

Cash Balance Plans.. 81

Pension Equity Plans 81

Defined Contribution Plans..82

401(k) Plans... 82

Other Options 84

Keoghs and Variations on the Theme..............................85

Keogh Plans.. 85

Money Purchase Plans 86

Profit Sharing Plans 86

Other Options 86

Individual (or Self-Employed) 401(k)s 86

SIMPLE IRA.. 87

Simplified Employee Pensions...87

Whatever You Do, Do Something 88

8   **Social Security**   **91**

A Little History Lesson 92

How the System Works 93

How Much Will I Get?.. 94

The Written Statement.. 96

When Should You Start Receiving Benefits? 96

The Late Retirement Boost 98

The Life Expectancy Game 99

Other Programs Under the Social Security Banner 100

Benefits for Your Spouse 100

Benefits for Survivors 100

Disability Coverage.. 101

Will It Be Around? 101

9   **Let's Hear It for IRA!**   **103**

A Short History Lesson 104

IRA's Many Charms 105

Some IRA Limitations 106

Roths—Another IRA Option... 106

How to Choose 108

To Convert or Not? 109

Some Caveats...110
    Moving IRA Funds Around *111*
    How to Invest Your IRA Assets *112*

10 The Basics of Investing, Part One: Mutual Funds   **115**
Mutual Funds—an Overview 116
    How They Work *116*
    Advantages and Drawbacks.....................................*117*
Overview of Major Fund Types 118
    Aggressive Growth Funds *118*
    Growth Funds *118*
    Growth and Income Funds *119*
    Index Funds..*119*
    Small-Cap, Mid-Cap, and Large-Cap Funds *119*
    International Funds *120*
    Sector Funds *120*
    Socially Responsible Funds *120*
    Real Estate Investment Trusts (REITs) *120*
Factors to Consider When Choosing a Fund 121
    Performance *121*
    Risk...*121*
    Expenses *122*
    Portfolio Turnover *122*
    Loads *123*
    Taxes *123*
    Closed-End vs. Open-End Funds...............................*123*
    Fund Size *124*
    Management *124*
Where to Find All This Information 124
    The Prospectus *124*
    Financial Publications *124*
    Fund Screens *125*
Buying a Mutual Fund 125
    Brokerage Houses...*125*
    From the Funds Themselves *126*
    Investment Minimums...*126*
How to Track Your Fund 126
Some Ideas on Portfolios for Retirement.........................127

11 The Basics of Investing, Part Two: Stocks — 129

Stocks—What They Are 130
  Types of Stock..*130*
  Stock Exchanges: Where Stocks Are Traded..............*131*
Selecting Stock 132
  Some Basic Steps...*132*
  Where to Find the Numbers—The Balance Sheet......*133*
  Putting This All Together—Ratios for Analysis *134*
  Technical Analysis *136*
  Analysts *137*
  Stock Screens *138*
How to Buy Stock 138
  Traditional Full-Service Brokerage House *138*
  Discount Brokers..*139*
  Deep Discount..*139*
Some Stock Strategies 140
  Dollar-Cost Averaging..*140*
  Value Averaging *140*
  Limit Orders *140*
  Stop Loss Orders *141*

12 The Basics of Investing, Part Three: Bonds and GICs — 143

Bonds—What They Are 144
Types of Bonds 144
  Corporate Bonds..*144*
  Treasury Bonds *146*
  Zero Coupon Bonds *147*
  Municipal Bonds *147*
  International Bonds *148*
How Bonds Make Money 148
The Risks of Bonds 149
How to Shop for Bonds 150
  Full-Service Brokerage Houses *150*
  Discount Brokerage Houses *150*
  Direct Purchase Plans *150*
Speaking of Diversity—Bond Mutual Funds 151
  What to Look for in Bond Funds..................................*152*
  How to Follow a Bond...*152*
Guaranteed Investment Contracts (GICs) 153
Where Bonds and GICs Fit in Your Retirement Program 153

Part 3: **Timing Is Everything** **157**

13 **If You're Young** **159**

Time Equals Opportunity 160
Risk Tolerance—There's the Rub 161
Risk Tolerance—A Quick Quiz 162
   Primary Objective *162*
   Investment Returns *162*
Finding the Long-Term Mix That's Right for You 164
Another Way to Tackle Risk Tolerance 165
Max Out to the Max 166
Hit the Autopilot 167
Job Shopping? Ask About Retirement 168
Don't Turn a Blind Eye to IRA 169

14 **Midway to Retirement** **171**

How Do You Stack Up? 172
Gauging Where You Are 173
What If You're Ahead of the Curve? 175
   Should I Cut Back on the Amount I'm Saving? *176*
   What's Wrong with Having a Bit More? *177*
   Making Adjustments *177*
Choose: Your Retirement or Other Goals (Like a
   College Education) 181

15 **Ready to Retire!** **183**

Gauging Where You Are 184
   First, Add It All Up *184*
   Putting It Together *186*
Withdrawing Money (While Continuing to Invest
   What Stays Behind) 187
The 4 Percent Withdrawal Rule 187
Making Adjustments 188
   Investing After You've Retired *188*
   Try to Beat Your Withdrawal Rate *189*
   What Rate of Return Do You Need? *190*
How to Withdraw Funds 191
If Need Be, Get Some Help 192

16 Making Sure It Lasts Long Enough   195

   Review Your Position Regularly 196
   Adjust Your Portfolio 196
   Budget Adjustments 198
   Travel on the Cheap 199
   Manage Your Debt 201
   Other Steps to Help Your Nest Egg Last 202
   Avoiding Scams...204

Part 4: Key Financial Concerns   207

17 The Tax Man—Older but Still Around   209

   Is It That Important? 210
   What You Can Do Before Retirement...211
      Consult a Tax Professional...211
      Convert a Conventional IRA to a Roth—or Open One 211
      Diversify..212
   Taxes and Social Security 213
   Ways to Trim Taxes After You Retire..214
      Schedule Another Meeting with a Tax Professional 214
      Take Minimum Distributions Whenever Possible 214
      As a General Rule, Tap Your Roth IRA Last 214
      If You Have Them, Cash in Taxable Assets First and Try
         to Spread Them Out 215
      Handle Company Stock Carefully 215
      Don't Itemize Your Tax Deductions 215
      Don't Overlook Medical Expenses 215
      If Warranted, Challenge Your Property Tax Assessment 216
      Move to a Tax-Friendly State 216
   Working and Taxes..217
   Tax Resources 218

18 Health Insurance   221

   Why It's So Important 222
   Types of Insurance..222
      Fee-for-Service 223
      Managed Care...223
   Evaluating Your Health Insurance Needs 224
   Holding Down Your Health Insurance Costs...............................225

Special Situations..226

If You're Self-Employed.............................*226*

If You Lose Your Job................................*227*

If You Retire Early.................................*227*

Medicare 228

How to Enroll.....................................*229*

How to Choose What's Right for You *230*

Supplemental Insurance 231

19 Retirement Communities and Long-Term Care Insurance   233

Retirement Communities—An Introduction 234

How to Choose the One That Meets Your Needs 235

Individual Services...............................*235*

Group and Community-Based Programs and Services *235*

Questions to Ask *236*

When a Nursing Home Is Necessary.....................237

Paying for Nursing Home Care *238*

Enter Long-Term Care Insurance *239*

Is It Worth It? *240*

How to Shop for Long-Term Care Insurance *241*

20 Other Insurance Issues   245

The Role of Life Insurance...............................246

Do You Need It? *246*

How Much Coverage Do You Need?...................*246*

Types of Coverage 248

Term Life Insurance..............................*248*

Cash Value Life Insurance........................*249*

Choosing Between Term and Whole Life.............*251*

Disability Insurance—Often Overlooked, Always Crucial 252

Other Forms of Insurance................................254

Umbrella Insurance *254*

Vision and Dental Insurance......................*254*

Insurance You Don't Need................................255

21 Estate Planning   257

The Basics of Estate Planning 258

First Steps *258*

Your Beneficiaries...............................*259*

Other Ways Estate Planning Helps *260*

Writing a Will 261

Living Wills 262
Trusts 263
Preplanning/Prepaying a Funeral 265
The Importance of Professionals 266

Part 5:   When It's Not Enough   **267**

22   Retiring on a Shoestring   **269**
Just How Tight Are Things? 270
Cutting Back 270
Consider Working Part-Time 271
Work a Bit Longer 272
Manage What You Have Carefully 273
Trading Down 274
Reverse Mortgages 275
Home Equity Loans 276
Look Beyond Money 277

23   Retire—Then Go to Work   **279**
How to Decide If You Need to Go Back to Work 280
Where to Begin Looking 281
How Much Do I Want (or Need) to Work? 281
What Do I Want to Do? 282
What Sort of Specific Skills Can I Offer an Employer? 282
Start Your Search 282
Marketing Yourself 284
Upgrade and Hone Your Resumé 284
Improve Your Skills 285
Learn the Art of the Interview 286
Keep an Eye Peeled for Age Discrimination 288
Start Your Own Business 289
Effects on Social Security and Medicare 289

24   Alternate Living   **291**
Staying Where You Are—With a Difference 292
Senior Co-Ops 292
Senior Cohousing 294
Shared Housing 296
The ECHO Option 297
Choosing an Affordable Place to Live 299
Living Abroad 300

Appendixes

A   Glossary   303

B   Retirement Planning Worksheets   311

Index   325

Introduction

Retirement is on the way. And how your finances stack up by the time you retire will go a long way toward determining the sort of retirement you're able to enjoy.

Unfortunately, far too many of us approach retirement ill-prepared. Either we've simply not saved enough or what we have managed to put away has been stored in the wrong places. Even worse, some of us go so far as to ignore the issue of retirement planning completely.

This book is designed to address those and other challenges. Starting with the basics, I'll walk you through every important element that pertains to building a financially solid retirement. I address just how much you'll need to save to enjoy the retirement you wish, along with savings and investment strategies to help you reach those financial goals. I'll even offer tips and advice to help you check to make certain you remain on track.

But we'll also discuss other important elements to a financially secure retirement, including health and long-term care insurance, housing, Social Security, and others. Hopefully, you'll learn about elements and options pertaining to retirement that you haven't heard of before.

Among the varied material that makes up this book, two dominant themes emerge. First and foremost, the old stereotypes many of us have about retirement are fast fading into oblivion. Replacing them are retirement choices and options that may have seemed completely far-fetched a generation ago.

The other issue is the importance of proactivity. Just as retirement has changed, so has the need to approach it aggressively and with a solid knowledge base. Moreover, the earlier you start thinking about your retirement, the more fulfilling your retirement is likely to be. With this book in your hands, you've taken a critical first step toward that objective.

How This Book Is Organized

This book is presented in five parts:

In **Part 1, "Retirement Basics,"** you'll get your first glimpse into the world of retirement. Not only will you get a sense of some of the salient elements of retirement, you'll also enjoy a fresh glimpse into just who's retiring and what they're doing. From there, we'll help you decide just what sort of retirement might suit you best as well as initial steps to take toward that goal.

Part 2, "Where the Money Comes From," moves us into the actual mechanics of putting together a retirement funding program. I'll cover company-sponsored retirement plans, Social Security, and individualized savings programs. From there, we'll cover more specific financial elements and how they may fit your particular situation, including mutual funds, stocks, bonds, and other choices.

Part 3, "Timing Is Everything," takes a chronological look at the retirement funding continuum, starting with what you can do at a young age to begin planning your retirement. Next, we'll look at the importance of monitoring your progress as you get close to retirement, followed by strategies and ideas to help your retirement savings last as long as you need it to.

Part 4, "Key Financial Concerns," hits on a variety of specific financial topics that can have a significant impact on the quality of your retirement. Issues include taxes, health and other forms of insurance, long-term care, and other elements that can be addressed in a variety of ways, both before and during retirement. The part winds up with an overview of estate planning and the role it plays in protecting your savings and other assets.

Not every retirement is perfect. **Part 5, "When It's Not Enough,"** explores the issue of inadequate savings and steps you can take to counteract a lack of cash. Strategies include trading down, working after retirement, and a variety of alternate living arrangements that are not only cost-effective but may offer valuable social connections to boot.

Retirement Planning Features

Not surprisingly, certain parts of our discussion warrant additional attention. To make sure nothing gets lost in the shuffle, we've included four special boxes throughout the text highlighting key points, terms, and other details.

Retire Right_____

These point out special tips and tricks to help you toward your retirement financial goals.

Golden Years Gaffes_____

Here, we highlight potential problems and pitfalls that anyone looking toward retirement can encounter—and, of course, ways to head them off.

def•i•ni•tion

These boxes contain explanations of financial and legal terms.

Retirement Reality

Facts and other tidbits about retirement that may surprise you.

Acknowledgments

Thanks to Fran Berman for her terrific help in tracking down details, facts, and insights. Finally, thanks to my agent, Marilyn Allen, for her ongoing friendship and invaluable guidance.

Special Thanks to the Technical Reviewer

The Complete Idiot's Guide to Retirement Planning was reviewed by an expert who double-checked the accuracy of what you'll learn here, to help us ensure that this book gives you everything you need to know about planning for your retirement. Special thanks are extended to Glen Clemans.

Glen Clemans is a financial advisor in Lake Oswego, Oregon. He specializes in retirement planning and has been an advisor for over 20 years.

Trademarks

All terms mentioned in this book that are known to be or are suspected of being trademarks or service marks have been appropriately capitalized. Alpha Books and Penguin Group (USA) Inc. cannot attest to the accuracy of this information. Use of a term in this book should not be regarded as affecting the validity of any trademark or service mark.

Part 1

Retirement Basics

Part 1 provides a solid foundation for the planning and execution of a solid retirement strategy. You'll get your first glimpse into the world of retirement as well as a sense of where you'll best fit when the time comes to join that community. Not only will you get an idea of some of the salient elements of retirement, you'll also learn just who's retiring and what they're doing (the news will likely surprise you). From there, I'll help you decide just what sort of retirement might suit you best as well as initial steps you can take toward that goal.

Retirement Has Changed

In This Chapter

- ◆ The story behind the numbers
- ◆ Why have things changed?
- ◆ Greater longevity
- ◆ Different retirement choices
- ◆ New challenges, new strategies

Look up the word *retire* in the dictionary. Webster's offers this definition first: "To go away, retreat, or withdraw to a private sheltered or secluded place."

Now, look a bit further down and find the definition for retired: "That has given up one's work, business, career, etc., because of advanced age."

No offense intended to Mr. Webster, but, to paraphrase an old advertising line, this isn't your father's retirement any more. Retirees are hanging up their working shoes with greater flexibility and choice than any prior generation in history. Gone are the days of mandatory retirement at age 65. Today's retirees are just as likely to retire at age 50 as they are at 75.

Gone, too, is the stereotype of retirement—playing golf, gardening, or simply doing little if anything at all. Retirement today can mean any number of things—travel, volunteer work, going back to school, even beginning a second career.

But that breadth of opportunity brings with it greater responsibility—the responsibility that each of us has to consider our retirement options prudently, and, from there, to map out the best possible financial plan to meet those objectives.

That's what this book is all about. And, here in the first chapter, we'll introduce you to some of the realities of today's retirement, along with some topics that are closely intertwined with that and the challenge we all face to make our retirement years the best they possibly can be.

What's Changed?

Perhaps an easier question to ask with regard to retirement is what has *not* changed. As we will see, very little remains the same when it comes to your post-working years. And the way things are trending, there's little likelihood that that sweep of change is going to diminish anytime soon.

Longevity

To grasp the significance of just how much retirement has changed, it's helpful to turn the clock back a bit—say, roughly 100 years. At the beginning of the twentieth century, retirement was almost unheard of. The reason: fairly few people lived—and worked long enough—to get to the point to retire. In 1910, life expectancy was a modest 50 years. Couple that with an average "retirement" age of 74, and it's easy to see that most people worked to the day they died.

How small was the retirement population back then? According to ElderWeb.com—a website that addresses long-term care topics—only 1 percent of the entire population could be considered "retired."

By 1940, although life expectancy had increased to 61, average retirement age was still 70. Translated: only 5 percent of the population was classified as retired. An increase, but not exactly a groundswell of retirees looking to fill free time with fulfilling pursuits.

By 1970, life expectancy was up to 67, although the average retirement age was 65—on average, a scant two years to enjoy all you had worked for (don't spend it all in one place). Total retirement population: 10 percent.

By 2000, life expectancy finally broke through the 70-year mark (73), and the average retirement age continued to fall (62). Taken together, that meant that 15 percent of the American people were retirees.

In the year 2007, according to the Social Security Administration, there are nearly 36 million Americans aged 65 and over. A male child born today can expect to live until nearly 75; a newborn girl, almost to 80. In fact, those statistics are somewhat skewed when you look at an older age baseline. If a man makes it to age 50, from there he can expect to live until 77 or so; women can look forward to their 81st birthdays. According to some, the numbers are even greater—according to the Society of Actuaries, a 65-year-old couple in reasonable health has a statistical life expectancy of age 90.

Projections hold that those numbers are only going to continue to grow. By 2030, more Americans will be over the age of 65 than under 18. In fact, statistics suggest that many people today can expect to spend a third of their lifetime in retirement.

That places us in the heart of an interesting dynamic—one that's changing the very face of America. It's a force born of opposite directions—as the average American lives longer and longer, the average retirement age continues to fall.

> **Retirement Reality**
>
> The numbers become even more interesting the older you get. Make it to 65, and you can expect to live until 83. In fact, the fastest-growing segment of the overall population is those aged 85 and up—the so-called "older old."

Retirement Age Has Changed

The old rule of thumb had it that, like it or not, you retired at age 65 (actually, a bit older—in 1950, the average retirement age was 67). The reasons behind that were simple. Workers received full benefits from Social Security at age 65. On top of that, defined benefit plans offered at a broad range of workplaces also introduced full benefit eligibility at 65. In fact, some went even further by cutting off credit for service once an employee hit 65, effectively discouraging you from working any further to benefit your retirement.

Now, however, the average retirement age has fallen to 62. Many people retire in their 50s and even younger.

Why? A lot of it has to with changes in retirement-related legislation as well as shifts in the way retirees were paying for their retirement.

First off, Social Security introduced early retirement at age 62. Here, you were eligible for a portion of the full benefit you would receive at age 65 (more on this in Chapter 8).

A number of pieces of legislation also contributed to shifts in the age at which many people retired, including the following:

◆ In 1978, Section 401(k) was added to the Internal Revenue Code, creating the now popular 401(k) retirement plan. In a nutshell, the plan allowed workers to defer income into retirement plans tax-free. More specifically, the plans do not specify a retirement age.

◆ The introduction of the Individual Retirement Account (IRA) also opened up the possibility of earlier retirement for many people. IRAs allow withdrawals penalty-free beginning at age 59 $\frac{1}{2}$. IRAs were strengthened further with the debut of the Roth IRA in 1999 (more about IRAs in Chapter 5).

> **Retirement Reality**
>
> Even as more people retired early, other pieces of legislation strengthened older workers' rights to remain on the job. For instance, the Age Discrimination in Employment Act was amended in 1978 to prevent employment discrimination for people up to age 70.

Changes in corporate policy also sweetened the possibility of retiring sooner than age 65. From the mid-1970s into the 1980s, defined benefit plans consistently lowered the age at which a participant could receive benefits. More specifically—according to the Monthly Labor Review, 50 percent of defined benefit plans in 1974 offered unreduced benefits at age 62. By 1983, some 80 percent allowed employees to retire with full benefits at 62. Moreover, the number of plans allowing early retirement at age 55 rose from 76 percent to 85 percent during the same time period.

Simple fact: more people are retiring earlier than what was once considered "normal." Further, people are also retiring earlier than they expected to. According to the Cornell Retirement and Well Being Study—which took in more than 600 participants and tracked them over a period of several years—many people included in the first wave of interviews said they anticipated retiring at age 60 or 61. However, later in the study, participants had actually retired at an average age of 59.

More Retirement Choices

It's clear that certain financial incentives made retirement—particularly early retirement—more appealing and possible for a greater number of people.

But that's not the only driving force behind the decision to retire. In its work, the Cornell Retirement and Well Being Study asked participants to identify the reasons they retired. By an overwhelming number, both men and women said they wanted to retire "to do other things." More specifically, 70 percent of the men gave this reason, 69 percent of the women.

Other findings for women:

- Financial incentives: 40 percent
- Sufficient income: 38 percent
- Spouse retired: 38 percent
- Older worker policy: 24 percent
- Poor health: 24 percent
- Didn't like work: 24 percent
- Didn't get along with boss: 22 percent
- Family health issue: 21 percent
- Not appreciated: 19 percent
- Job ended: 7 percent

For the men:

- Financial incentives: 62 percent
- Sufficient income: 45 percent
- Didn't like work: 33 percent
- Older worker policy: 22 percent
- Didn't get along with boss: 19 percent
- Not appreciated: 17 percent
- Family health issue: 16 percent
- Job ended: 13 percent
- Spouse retired: 9 percent

A few interesting patterns crop up in these responses. One is the importance of finances. Although not at the top of the list, both men and women consistently cited the role of sufficient funds as a reason behind their decision to retire. By the same token, although one third of the men said they didn't care for their jobs, negative reasons such as poor health or restrictive employment policies were relatively minor.

But the telling number in the study is the 70-some percent of both men and women who said they retired because they wanted to do other things and pursue other interests.

It's fairly safe to assume several usual suspects within that mix. These would certainly include time for travel, family, friends, hobbies, and other like activities that may have gotten short shrift during years spent working.

But as the age at which many people retire has changed, so too have the activities and pursuits that many retirees are pursuing, including ...

- Continuing to work in some manner.
- Starting a business.
- Serving on boards of directors.
- Doing volunteer work.
- Participating in organizations and clubs.
- Going back to school.

Continuing to Work

According to the Cornell study, roughly two out of five people reported working for pay in some fashion after they formally retired from another form of full-time employment. The percentage of men working after retirement was significantly higher than women—49 versus 39 percent. On average, retirees worked roughly 30 hours a week for 43 weeks out of the year.

Reasons behind the decision to work in some manner are rather eye-opening. Nearly 9 out of 10 people said they wanted to work "to keep active." Other responses: "had free time" (73 percent); "to maintain social contacts" (68 percent); "desire for additional income" (63 percent); "not ready to retire" (58 percent); and "to maintain their profession and professional contacts" (56 percent).

What's particularly interesting among those responses is what is not cited that often. Only about two in five participants said they worked because they *needed* the additional income.

Technology is another factor that's boosting retirement work activity. Rather than going to an outside office to continue working, more retirees are able to work from home using a computer and Internet connections. That also lends greater flexibility as to where they choose to live when they retire.

Starting a Business

Working after retirement doesn't necessarily mean going to work for someone else. Equally popular is the option of starting a business. Of the participants in the Cornell study, half of the people who continued to work after retirement were self-employed.

Often, a new business affords an opportunity to pursue an interest completely different from what a retiree did when he or she was working. According to New Directions, a consulting firm for senior executives, many retired business people are starting small businesses as varied as alpaca farms and lighthouse items sales operations. But no matter the business, retirees consistently cite the enjoyment of more flexible hours and a renewed sense of purpose behind their decision.

Retire Right

If you're thinking about starting your own business, SCORE is a group of retired business executives who offer would-be entrepreneurs free advice and guidance. Go to www.SCORE.org.

Serving on Boards of Directors

There is a growing demand for retired executives to serve on various forms of boards of directors. According to the 2003 Spencer Stuart Board Index, 12 percent of new outside directors were made up of retired executives. That's double the number from only five years prior to that.

Doing Volunteer Work

A high level of activity doesn't necessarily mean paid compensation. Retirees are also flocking to a broad variety of volunteer work. According to the Cornell study, nearly half of all participants said they were doing some form of volunteer work—either through a formal commitment or just "helping out" in some manner. Additionally, some 42 percent of married couples said they performing volunteer work together.

Nor is that a minor commitment. Retirees on average said they devoted more than 20 hours a month to volunteer activities (although the average time per month drops to 12 hours if the retiree was also holding down some type of employment.)

Participating in Organizations and Clubs

Retirees are definitely joiners. More than half who took part in the Cornell study said they were active in some sort of club or organization, including social, sporting, and religious groups.

Going Back to School

A growing number of retirees are using their free time to pursue something that, in their earlier years, they may have merely suffered through—schooling.

Going back to school when you don't have to can be a pure joy. Many retirees go back to school at all levels, earning everything from Bachelor's degrees all the way up to doctorates. Many schools offer specialized programs and fee structures to make their offerings attractive and affordable. (Even better, if you're of a certain age, many schools waive the required SAT in order to enroll!)

Retirement Reality

Smith College in Northampton, Massachusetts, offers the Ada Comstock Scholars Program. It's designed to make college possible for women who might otherwise not attend college or who had an earlier education sidetracked for some reason. Among Ada's recent graduates: Anne Martindell, who received her Smith degree at age 87.

What This Means to You

There's no doubt about it—retirement and much, if not all, connected to it has undergone an upheaval in the past 20 years. And, in terms of your own plan for retirement, that means both good news as well as some challenges that prior generations of retirees didn't really encounter.

On the plus side, we're living longer and enjoying better health, and, as a result, we're getting much more out of retirement than our elders did.

As we've seen, too, there's a greater freedom of choice for each of us to decide what constitutes retirement. Gone are the days when retirement by definition meant bingo, bland food, and a level of general inactivity that slowly slipped toward physical and mental erosion. Retirees are doing everything these days, from traveling to starting a business to returning to school to finish a degree or work on a new one.

But alongside those advantages have come a new set of challenges. First, one of the foremost issues is longevity—since we're all living longer, we all have to be able to afford that longer life span (and to make it both enjoyable and fulfilling, however we wish to define those criteria). It's a simple fact—the longer you live, the more expensive it's likely going to be.

Moreover, the financial element of retirement isn't nearly as automatic—or as largely out of our hands—as it used to be. Not too long ago, Social Security and company pension plans—one developed, managed, and funded exclusively by your employer— were the two-legged financial bedrock for many retirees. You worked, the money was put away for you automatically and, one day, you hung up your working shoes and started receiving monthly checks (sadly, often against your wishes).

Now, with the advent of defined contribution plans—where you're the one making the financial calls, so to speak—the issue of how successful a retirement we're able to enjoy has been placed squarely in our laps. Add to that the exploding number of self-employed people and the spread of personal savings vehicles such as Individual Retirement Accounts, and the question of how to map out and execute a successful retirement funding program is placed directly on our shoulders—more so than any other generation in history.

But as we've also seen, it's not just a question of money—it's also an issue of what you want that money to allow you to do. Retiring with a pile of money, but with little notion of what you want to do, can be as frustrating and limiting as a cash-strapped retirement.

New Challenges Mean New Strategies

What all this boils down to is the imperative of planning—and, from there, consistent execution of that plan. Without a thoughtful strategy in place and the means to follow through on that plan, the notion of retirement becomes a far more haphazard proposition than it needs to be.

Golden Years Gaffes

We'll cover this more in Chapter 2, but a common disappointment among current retirees is a perceived failure to have adequately planned their retirement.

As we proceed through the topic of retirement, we'll be going into comprehensive detail about the specific steps that comprise an effective, thoughtful plan. But let's start with a few more global thoughts that will be helpful to bear in mind:

◆ **A plan is essential.** As we've discussed in this chapter, the responsibility for mapping out and executing a financial plan for retirement is increasingly an issue of personal responsibility rather than an employer "taking care" of retirees. With the ball so squarely in your court, it's critical that you approach that duty with a plan that takes into consideration both your goals for retirement as well as the reality of your situation.

◆ **Your plan needs to take in more than just financial considerations.** Money is critical to retirement, but so is an idea of how you intend to spend your time at something that's rewarding and enjoyable—not mere filler. So, don't overlook retirement planning topics which, at their bottom line, have little or nothing to do with money.

◆ **If possible, start early.** Again, we'll tackle this in some detail in subsequent chapters, but if you're relatively young, it never hurts to think about your retirement and begin to act on an overall strategy. It gives you the best chance to put together the best financial package possible, allows for adequate time for any necessary adjustments along the way, and, if nothing else, can help ease some of the pressures that can accompany planning for your retirement.

◆ **It's never too late to catch up.** By the same token, you may be a somewhat older person with little in the way of retirement planning or resources in place. Don't panic—you may not have as much time as your younger colleague mentioned above, but there's always time to think about your retirement—and from there, build and execute a program that can help you catch up in a hurry.

◆ **Keep an eye on things.** You may think you have the most thoughtful, comprehensive retirement plan around. That may be so, but be sure to monitor your progress. Few are the retirement plans that prove successful from a "set it and forget it" approach. Know where you are—and where you're going—at every step along the way.

◆ **Don't be afraid to adjust things as need be.** Circumstances change, as do your goals and wishes. As you proceed toward retirement, don't be gun-shy about making adjustments, be it to the financial makeup of your plan or your long-term objectives. Nothing to do with your retirement needs to be cast in stone.

◆ **Enjoy the experience.** Granted, a fulfilling retirement mandates responsibility and planning—more so than prior generations may have had to take on. But the good news is that, with greater financial resources, better health, and the prospect of greater longevity, the very notion of retirement is a good deal more inherently positive and appealing than it may have been in the past. Treat it seriously, but don't forget to enjoy it to the hilt—both in planning it and, ultimately, living it to the full.

> **Retirement Reality**
>
> A recent survey by the American Association of Retired Persons found that two out of three people aged 50 and over see their phase of life as time to begin a new chapter and to set new goals. In other words—a beginning, and anything but an ending.

The Least You Need to Know

◆ Retirement is a relatively new phenomenon. Barely a century ago, only a small fraction of workers actually "retired."

◆ You can expect to live a longer life than your parents or grandparents—and, as a result, spend more time in retirement than they might have.

◆ Retirement now means a greater number of choices than ever before, from continuing to work in some capacity to returning to school.

◆ Retirement now also means greater individual responsibility—our responsibility to ourselves to think carefully about retirement and plan with equal care.

◆ Be holistic in your retirement planning. Address financial and nonfinancial issues with equal attention.

◆ Approach retirement as a fresh new phase in your life, rather than the end of a prior way of life. Embrace the varied opportunities and promise that retirement can hold for all of us.

Who's Retiring Now?

In This Chapter

- ◆ Who's retiring?
- ◆ Are they in good physical health?
- ◆ Where are they?
- ◆ Do they make ends meet?
- ◆ How do they make ends meet?

In Chapter 1, we looked at a variety of ways in which retirement has changed—for the better and otherwise. Now we'll turn our attention briefly—and more specifically—to the growing number of people who occupy that space in life known as retirement.

We'll take a look at who they are, where they are, and how they are—in terms of their finances as well as other elements that can impact a successful retirement, such as health and self-satisfaction.

There will be a fair number of statistics, numbers, and other research findings in this chapter. Take them as you will—as you'll see, when it comes to retirement, who you ask often dictates the answer you're going to get in terms of data and statistical patterns.

But all these numbers are both important and helpful. For one thing, they will give you a glimpse into the population group that you will likely be joining one day. But equally important are the trends and issues that these numbers raise—issues and challenges that you will do well to know about and, as a result, plan for accordingly as we continue into other areas of the book.

Just Who the Heck Are All These Retirees?

As we discussed in Chapter 1, retirement has undergone a radical transformation over the past couple of decades. The very notion of there being a "retirement"—however that might be defined or what comprises it—is far more rooted in a culture where, not very long ago, people kept working up until the day they headed off to the pearly gates.

But that doesn't bring us any closer to the first salient question of this chapter: who makes up the retiree community today. Unfortunately, there's really no one definitive answer or description because, as we have seen and will continue to see, retirement is what the individual makes of it. And that unto itself defies generalization.

But we can get an idea from various sources.

The "Average" Retirement Age

First: just what is the "average" retirement age these days? Again, it depends on who you ask—federal statistics suggest that the average age of retirement is somewhere in the vicinity of 62.

Other sources differ. Recently, the brokerage house Merrill Lynch conducted a study of the *baby boom* generation.

def•i•ni•tion

For those who've heard the term and are unsure just what it means, **baby boomers** refers to people born in a flourish of family boosting activity that followed World War II and continued into the 1960s.

According to that survey, the average "boomer" expected that he or she would retire around the age of 64—some two years later than government numbers indicate.

Still other sources offer a different perspective. The American Association of Retired Persons (AARP) found in a recent survey of older Americans that some 70 percent of people who had not yet retired said they expected to work well into their retirement years, or never retire at all.

Bottom line: there is no bottom line when it comes to the "average" age of the retirement population. By all accounts, the numbers are simply far too skewed to pinpoint any one age—or for that matter, age range—when an older person decides to stop working.

But that confusion raises a central point, one that we will continue to emphasize throughout this book. Just as there is no one "right" or "consistent" age at which you should retire, nor is there one right or consistent way to retire—be it in a financial sense or any other sense for that matter.

That means retirement these days is all about varied opportunity and promise, rather than some sort of pigeonholed, predestined fate. And we'll see all the more of that the more we explore the millions of people who are closing in on retirement or have already retired.

> **Retirement Reality**
>
> The Federal Bureau of Labor Statistics projects that 17 percent of the country's workforce will be aged 55 and older by 2010—four points higher than just a decade earlier.

What Else Is It About Them?

This discussion also illustrates another central point. To a certain extent, the age at which people retire—or expect to retire—is secondary to other details concerning the retiree population. According to the Merrill Lynch study:

- ◆ Most people who expect to retire at 64 also anticipate beginning an entirely new career or job.

- ◆ But it's not an either/or sort of situation. Many retirees say they see their lives as a balance between work and leisure rather than one or the other exclusively.

- ◆ By continuing to work longer, boomers say they expect to be "younger" longer than prior generations. In other words, they don't yet consider themselves "old" and, as a result, are looking forward to new opportunities and possibilities in their lives.

- ◆ However focused they are on their own retirement, retirees are not self-centered. The Merrill Lynch study said retirees are also very focused on their parents, their children, and their communities.

- ◆ Women will play a greater role in retirement than ever before. Married retired women are more than six times likely to share responsibility for savings and investments than their mothers' generation.

Retirement Reality

Professor Nancy Morrow-Howell of Washington University in St. Louis nicely sums up the dynamic of expanding choice in retirement. She calls it "productive aging."

◆ Women and men have differing expectations of retirement. Men are looking forward to less work, more leisure time, and greater time with family and friends. Women, on the other hand, anticipate the possibilities of an "empty nest" and commensurate opportunities for career development, personal growth, and greater involvement in their communities.

Other sources chime in with other telling statistics:

◆ According to the U.S. Department of Health and Human Services, older women outnumber older men by some 6 million (20.8 million versus 14.8 million).

◆ More than half (54.7 percent) live with their spouse. By contrast, 30.8 percent live alone, says Health and Human Services.

◆ Age and money are not the only determining dynamics of the retirement population. According to a Department of Health and Human Services report, minority groups will comprise slightly more than one quarter of the older population by 2030, up from 16 percent in 2004.

◆ Consistent with the Merrill Lynch study, Health and Human Services reports that some 400,000 grandparents aged 65 and older had primary responsibility for grandchildren who lived with them. Overall, 671,000 grandparents aged 65 or older maintained homes in which grandchildren also lived.

◆ The longer you wait to retire, the happier and more satisfied you're likely to be. A study by the National Academy on an Aging Society found that, among other things, workers aged 60 and older were more likely to be better educated, and better off in health and finances than people who retired between the ages of 51 and 59.

◆ Still, more often than not, retirement means happiness and satisfaction. According to the Cornell Retirement and Well-Being Study mentioned in Chapter 1, retirees say they are "completely satisfied" with life more often than workers who are still in their primary career jobs (more about this in the next section).

How's Their Health?

Financial stability isn't the sole determining factor in enjoying a fulfilling and productive retirement. Not surprisingly, health and overall physical well-being also occupy important roles—and, in turn, connect with other important planning elements.

Just how healthy are today's retirees? By one standard of measurement, rather robust. According to the Cornell study, the average survey participant rates their overall health as an 8 on a scale of 0 to 10 (0 being the lowest health rating and 10 being the highest).

The news is even better than a mere snippet. Most participants in the study reported that their health remained at the same level—or even improved as they got further into retirement. By the same token, roughly one third of study participants said they experienced "minor" declines in health over the space of several years.

In fact, when studying the topic of energy levels, retirement seems to have a decidedly positive effect. Using the same scale when rating overall quality of health, participants ranked their energy at an average of 7.5. That's an improvement from the 7.2 level that the average participant estimated when they were still working prior to retirement. In particular, newly retired moved the most from low energy levels to high energy levels (4.5 in pre-retirement to 6.0 after they retired).

This seems to confirm a trend we have discussed at some length. Rather than viewing retirement as a period of slowing down, retirees are approaching their post-working years with energy levels that likely wouldn't be contained by whittling or a meandering game of shuffleboard. Retirement is increasingly about possibility, and retirees are hitting the ground running.

Chronic Conditions

But the news on the health front is not uniformly positive. According to Health and Human Services, most older persons are dealing with at least one chronic condition (and, in fact, are facing several conditions concurrently). Among the most frequently occurring conditions among the elderly:

- Hypertension (49.2 percent)
- Arthritic symptoms (36.1 percent)
- Heart disease (31.1 percent)

- Cancer (20 percent)

- Sinusitis (15.1 percent)

- Diabetes (15 percent)

Retirement Reality
Poor health doesn't necessarily translate to an increased mortality rate. Those who died while taking part in the Cornell study were divided equally between persons in good health and those whose health was below par.
Being in good health in retirement means more than longevity. It also means continued physical dexterity and mental sharpness—attributes that retirees who wish to continue to work in some way need to maintain.

Interestingly enough, particularly when compared with life expectancy statistics, women were more likely to be in poor health than men (32 percent versus 22 percent of men in the Cornell study).

Not surprisingly, that makes necessary health coverage another important component among the retirement population. According to a study by AARP, 75 percent of people approaching retirement said the timing of their actual retirement depended in large part on when they would be eligible to receive retiree health benefits and coverage for prescription drugs. If you doubt the importance of suitable health coverage in retirement, participants in the AARP study rated that higher in importance than being able to access payments from a retirement savings program (71 percent).

Mental Health

As a group, retirees' bodies are in pretty good shape—and, by some accounts, are becoming more so all the time.

But what about another part of the equation—emotional and mental health?

Here, as is the case with physical well-being, retirees tend to be in rather good shape—and, for that matter, for the same apparent reasons. According to the Cornell study, participants early in the study showed very low symptoms of depression—3.9 on a scale of 0 to 36. By contrast, only roughly 1 in 10 people taking part in the study showed any symptoms of depression.

Like physical health, those results improve as people move further into retirement. The Cornell study reported lower scores among people who reported some signs of depression when they were interviewed several years later.

Retire Right _____

Why the lower rates of depression the further people got into retirement? One possible explanation is that, since so many work in some capacity and, at the same time, enjoy that work more than they did prior to retirement, they're generally happier. So if your pre-retirement job wasn't all that stimulating, you'll do well to find something you enjoy.

Just how happy are today's retirees? Pretty doggone happy. In a rather lopsided result, some 97 percent of all study participants in the Cornell research said they were usually or always happy. By roughly the same margin (95–96 percent) participants also said they were completely or mostly satisfied with their lives.

All this comes with a decidedly ironic twist. While retirees are generally healthy and happy in retirement, most retirees in the Cornell study said they wished they had planned more for their retirement than they did. Although much of that planning has to do with the financial side of things, other elements entered into a perceived lack of preparation, including leisure activities, family needs, and where the optimal place to retire might be.

Reading this book, just imagine the jump you're going to have on that entire process, from money to mental and physical well-being.

Where Are They Living?

Overall, retirees are physically and mentally happy. Just where is all this happiness happening?

Not surprisingly, the retirement population tends to concentrate in several areas of the United States. According to the 2004 census, some 52 percent of persons aged 65 and older lived in the following nine states:

- California (3.8 million)
- Florida (2.9 million)
- New York (2.5 million)
- Texas (2.2 million)
- Pennsylvania (1.9 million)

Additionally, Ohio, Illinois, Michigan, and New Jersey each had more than one million people aged 65 or older.

Of that group, Florida's senior population made up the largest percentage of the overall population in the state (16.8 percent.)

Equally interesting are those areas of the United States where the 65-and-over population has undergone significant growth. Here they are in order of greatest growth from 2000 to 2004:

- Nevada (up 58.1 percent)
- Alaska (47.9)
- Arizona (30.9)
- New Mexico (26.4)
- Colorado (22.2)
- Delaware (22.2)
- Utah (22.1)
- Idaho (20.9)

For every state with a balmy year-round climate, another with a decided four-season environment wasn't too far removed in appeal to retirees—evidence that, when it comes to choosing a retirement destination, sun and warmth are not the only considerations.

What, in fact, may play a greater role in retirement destination is where someone happens to live when they retire. During the year 2004, according to census data, only some 4 percent of older persons moved (as opposed to more than 14 percent for people aged 65 or younger).

Retirement Reality

Poverty remains a real problem for seniors in many states. Mississippi reported a senior poverty level of 17.2 percent. Arkansas, Texas, and South Carolina also reported high poverty rates among older residents.

But the question of where to retire is not purely a domestic one. An increasing number of retirees are opting to retire outside the United States. For instance, the American-born population of retirees is growing in nearby countries such as Mexico and Panama (both of which have established governmental policies geared to attracting U.S. retirees, from the overall cost of living to exemption from property taxes).

Golden Years Gaffes

Retiring overseas doesn't necessarily mean a one-way trip to Xanadu. Check out Chapter 24 for additional discussion as well as some caveats.

How They Afford Retirement

Much of what you may have heard about the financial element of retirement focuses on the importance of personal savings—those steps that you take on your own to build a nest egg to fund the retirement you hope to have.

The reality, however, is a bit different, at least so far as today's retirees are concerned. First and foremost is the dominant role played by Social Security. According to testimony provided by the Brookings Institution to the House Committee on Ways and Means, Social Security accounted for more than half of retirement income for roughly 70 percent of people over the age of 65. Even more striking: it is the only source of retirement income for one quarter of people above the age of 65.

Nor, in many cases, are personal savings picking up any of the slack. According to Survey of Consumer Finances data, two thirds of families headed by a worker aged 55 to 64 had less than $88,000 in retirement savings just a few years ago.

To put that in greater perspective: that $88,000 would be enough to purchase an annuity (a guaranteed funding contract we'll cover in greater detail in Chapter 5) that would pay a mere $653 every month.

What about the third leg of the funding "stool"—company pensions? As we will see later, the notion and function of company pensions have shifted drastically in recent years—away from purely company-funded programs to defined contribution programs where employees are far more actively involved.

Golden Years Gaffes

Some additional perspective: that $653 a month replaces just 15 percent of a median household income of $53,400. If that sounds like you, plan on additional income sources to make up the difference.

The good news is that the percentage of workers participating in some form of pension plan has been constant—roughly 50 percent over the past 25 years. But a potential problem is linked to the increase in defined contribution plans where, in lieu of a guaranteed flow of money into a retirement account, an employee's retirement nest egg can be affected by poor choices of how to invest the account or, even worse, failure to participate at all.

> **Golden Years Gaffes** _____
>
> As of 2006, two out of three workers were employed by private companies that offered no pension plan whatsoever.

But Are They *Really* Affording Retirement?

Okay, after all the statistics, analysis, and postulating from any number of sources, the question is begged: are most Americans affording retirement? Or, perhaps more appropriately, do they have sufficient financial assets to enjoy the sort of retirement they want or planned to have?

It's a question with a variety of answers, some seemingly conflicting. On the one hand, some studies suggest that current retirees have rather substantial assets. One, prepared by AARP's Public Policy Institute, found that current retirees have a median wealth of $448,000. Persons nearing retirement were slightly better off at $520,000.

In fact, as of the writing of this book, a rather controversial study was released that argued, in effect, that Americans might be saving too much for retirement—and, in so doing, needlessly denying themselves things that they could rightfully afford during their working years.

The study by a group of economists at the University of Wisconsin and research performed elsewhere suggested that Americans were in far better shape financially than they might have assumed. The reason, they maintain: misleading and self-serving advice from financial advisers, not to mention financial calculators provided by brokerage firms and others which, in the researchers' eyes, provide grossly inflated estimates of just what people need to retire comfortably.

But there's ample evidence to counter those claims of needless savings. In addition to increased longevity and potential obligations to offer financial support to other family members, critics of the study point out the prospect of daunting medical expenses for current and prospective retirees. According to financial services provider TIAA-CREF, the average 55-year-old who plans to retire at age 65 can expect to spend more than $200,000 in medical expenses that are not covered by Medicare.

Troubling results from other sources also offset those rather glowing numbers. First is the rather paltry average savings in retirement accounts cited earlier—a mere $88,000 for households where the head of the house was between 55 and 64.

Still another disquieting statistic is poverty levels among elderly persons. Although, as we will see in Chapter 8, Social Security was introduced to combat widespread poverty among the elderly, the problem persists to this day. According to the federal Department of Health and Human Services, about 3.6 million elderly persons (nearly 10 percent) were below the poverty level in 2004. An additional 2.3 million (6.7 percent) of the elderly were classified as "near poor," meaning their income was close to what could be construed as the poverty level.

Those numbers become more discouraging as you break them down further. While 1 of every 12 elderly white persons was considered poor in 2004, that number leaps to 23.9 percent for elderly African Americans. Elderly Hispanics (18.7 percent) and Asians (13.6 percent) also showed significant poverty levels.

So where do all these statistics—some in decided conflict—leave us? One position that would be rather hard to argue in favor of is that Americans, as a group, are socking away too much money for retirement. Not only do numbers indicating paltry savings levels and poverty suggest otherwise, it's not a question of the money simply going to waste if, by chance, someone saves "too much." That can then be turned into charitable giving or a substantial estate for heirs (an issue we will cover in Chapter 21).

What seems the most reasonable conclusion is that, while many Americans are, in fact, doing a decent job saving for retirement, others simply are not. As the Brookings Institution report to the Congress concluded: "There is wide variation in retirement savings and many families are accumulating substantial assets that will be enough to ensure a comfortable retirement. But it is safe to say that at least one third of families are not adequately prepared for retirement, according to a number of studies by economists."

Now that you have a sense of the scope and variety of the group that you will most likely be joining one day, let's get started to make certain you hook up with the very best part of that group—those whose financial situation for retirement is secure.

The Least You Need to Know

- Although the average age for retirement has come down in recent years, Americans are continuing to retire at a variety of ages.

- For the most part, American retirees are healthy and happy.

- Health insurance is critical. Many retirees timed their retirement to ensure they would have medical coverage.

- Americans are not retiring exclusively to warm-weather climates. Statistics suggest they tend to stay where they are when they retire.

- Most Americans rely on Social Security as their primary retirement funding source.

- Estimates hold that as many as one third of American families are not saving enough for retirement.

Your Retirement Goals— A Self-Assessment

In This Chapter

- ◆ Not everyone needs to retire

- ◆ When should you retire?

- ◆ For couples—retire together or separately?

- ◆ How about early retirement?

- ◆ Lifestyle issues

- ◆ Where should you retire?

Up to this point, we have covered a number of elements relating to retirement—who's retiring, when they retire, where they're retiring to, and other topics.

Now, however, it begs the question: with all this talk of retirement, do you know for a fact that you really want to retire in some way, shape, or form?

It is by no means a given that you're cut out to retire. Nor should you feel some sort of mandate that you have to retire.

But, if you do want to retire (and many, if not most of us, do), it's critical to start mapping out basic goals and objectives. We'll cover that in this chapter as well.

Retire? Says Who?

This might seem a bit odd coming from a guide to retirement, but the fact remains: not everyone needs to retire—or, for that matter, should.

Are You the Retiring Type? A Checklist

The fact that some people choose not to retire—in whole or in part—and are perfectly happy with that decision makes it important that you know for certain that you are, in fact, the kind of person suited to retirement. It's a difficult topic to tackle and, in many cases, there are simply no definitive answers. But, to help you out, work your way through the following questionnaire to get a sense of where you come out on the issue of retirement:

- ❏ To me, work is fun.

- ❏ I have yet to land what I would consider a "dream job."

- ❏ I find it challenging to occupy myself when I'm not working.

- ❏ I would rather face mandatory retirement rather than having to make the choice myself.

- ❏ I often take work home for nights and weekends.

- ❏ When I describe myself to others, I always include my job as part of the description.

- ❏ I like to have things mapped out in advance rather than improvising on the fly.

- ❏ My colleagues are the people I most often do things with outside of work.

- ❏ I often work more than I really have to.

- ❏ When I'm not working, I often find myself thinking about work.

This is not a scientific exercise by any stretch of the imagination. However, if you agreed with more than, say, five of these statements, it's a reasonably good bet that you're not exactly chomping at the bit waiting for retirement to kick in.

The Example of Walter Zweifler

Walter Zweifler is CEO of Zweifler Financial Research. He also happens to be 74 years old and has absolutely no plans to retire. He lists his reasons:

- ◆ You can share your experience with younger colleagues.

- ◆ You can keep your mind and body in top shape. When it comes to your brain—use it or lose it.

- ◆ The money you earn can be given to worthy charities and contribute to a better world.

- ◆ If you like what you are doing, it's fun to keep doing it.

- ◆ If you don't like the way your endeavors have migrated over the years, staying active allows you to make positive changes in how things are done.

- ◆ You will be much more efficient than you were at 30 or 40. You will do more and accomplish more.

- ◆ It gives you the opportunity to provide a second chance to someone who made a mistake but has real talent.

- ◆ You will not outlive even the most generous accumulation of net worth. Making a mistake and overearning is a great problem to have to deal with!

Walter's thoughts illustrate a powerful truth—there is certainly nothing wrong or unusual in not wanting to retire. For him and countless other people, working provides a variety of benefits that supersede a mere paycheck. Activity, a sense of involvement, and an ongoing interest in challenging yourself all argue for staying with a job or form of employment regardless of what age you happen to be.

But if retirement appeals, it's essential to recognize the importance of those same sorts of values, only in a different setting. Put another way, if you get a sense of achievement from work, you need to find a parallel way of getting that same feeling when you retire. Same pleasure, different environment.

Retirement Reality
One thing to bear in mind about the debate over whether to retire or not is that, historically speaking, retirement was unknown for much of human history. Consider such historical figures as Benjamin Franklin, Grandma Moses, and others who maintained a "work" schedule well into their later years. The fact is, in the long history of mankind, if you were healthy, people didn't suddenly reach a particular age and simply stop doing what they were doing. Our definition of "retirement" is a fairly new phenomenon.

When to Retire

Okay, so you've read Walter's thoughts and decide they don't match your situation (or you skipped them completely—you're that certain that retirement is right for you). In any event, you know for a fact that sometime in the future, you're going to want to retire.

That begs the question: when's the right time to do it? Like so many issues having to do with retirement, that is a very individualized question—one with few definitive answers.

Factors to Consider

Naturally, there is the issue of money. You'll certainly need adequate finances to retire in the fashion that you wish. Since we'll be covering that topic in exhaustive detail in subsequent chapters, we'll toss money out of the discussion for the time being.

So how do you know just the right time to retire? For many, 65 certainly seems to be some sort of magical number. There is a certain amount of empirical support, however—retiring at 65 allows for greater Social Security benefits than an earlier retirement (we'll hit this in more substance in Chapter 8). And naturally enough, three more years of work allows you to save more on your own and accrue a more substantive pension from your job.

But deciding when to retire should be more than just a matter of money. Much of the decision depends on what you want to do after you retire. If, for instance, you hope to travel, start a brand-new avocation, or volunteer for a worthwhile cause, you'll certainly want adequate time to immerse yourself in your new life and enjoy it to the full.

Another consideration is your health. Granted, as we get older, we're all naturally more susceptible to a greater variety of illnesses and physical limitations. If all you plan to do is sit out on the back porch whittling for the next 20 years or thereabouts, diminishing physical capability may not be all that much of an issue. But if your plans take in more active pursuits (and compared with a knife and piece of wood, they certainly ought to!), you'll want to be in adequate shape to get the most out of them. That, too, should enter into your thinking as to when the optimal retirement target might be.

Some people who have retired also say that they just knew when the time was "right" for them to retire. Perhaps they had achieved sufficient financial stability or had attained certain benchmarks in their career. For whatever reason, many say that they just knew when it was time to shift gears and do something else. Not particularly scientific, but one that many attest to.

An equally important factor to consider in the question of when to retire is its impact on others, including family members—spouses and partners in particular. Consider the following scenario: you've spent the better part of your life living with someone else, only some 40-hours plus of every week of that lifetime is spent apart. Now, at the drop of a hat, one is home all the time. Perhaps the other one is as well; or perhaps the other one continues to be gone for that 40-hour weekly commitment.

If you think that's a recipe where the potential for sparks to fly is very real, you're very much on target. Retirement doesn't exist in a vacuum. It affects everyone around you, from family to friends to former work colleagues. That makes it essential to factor in those relationships when considering when the right time to retire might be—as well as the potential impact that your retirement might have on those relationships.

It's essential to discuss your retirement plans with anyone who may be affected by them to a significant degree. See how they feel about your retiring at a certain date. Ask them if they think it's a good idea. Explore ways that your relationship may be affected by retirement—for the good as well as the bad.

Don't Just Let Retirement Happen

Although the issue of when to retire can be somewhat dicey to work out, experts agree that it's essential to have something to retire to. One of the biggest potential pitfalls to retirement is letting it happen and hoping that something, somehow, will appear to engage you for the remaining years of your life. Don't let that happen to you—when planning the financial elements of your retirement, don't spare any detail as to just what all that money is going to do for you in terms of continuing a fulfilling, rewarding life. The two go hand in hand toward building the retirement you would genuinely wish to have.

 Golden Years Gaffes

Not having a retirement goal is a pitfall. By the same token, don't retire to get away from something. Stopping work because of, say, a failed marriage or a major problem at work starts your retirement on a negative footing. And you may have little in the way of planning to reverse that unfortunate start.

Should Couples Retire at the Same Time?

The question of timing naturally leads to a follow-up issue—should married couples and other partners plan to retire at the same time?

Not to sound like a skipping CD, but this is yet another retirement-related issue where the jury is largely out. Some studies have suggested that couples who time their retirement at the same time do, in fact, experience greater happiness and satisfaction after they retire. Other research suggests there is no correlation between marital happiness and the timing of the retirement of the two partners.

So is it a good idea to time your retirement for the same target? On the one hand, it can be a boon to planning—since you're both going to be "free" at roughly the same date, you can better map out precisely what you'd both like to do. Additionally, since the first couple years or so of retirement can be very much viewed as a learning experience—one in which you're encountering new challenges, new realities, and other issues—it can be helpful to have a partner in the same "classroom" at the same time.

On the other hand, retiring at the same time can merely double whatever challenges and potential frustrations that crop up. Lack of activity, focus, and even outright boredom can become all the more crippling if one—or both—partners are experiencing those feelings at the same time. Those can be exacerbated by two people tapping into financial reserves that may support one person but be strained by two.

While the issue of retiring at the same time may boil down in large part to a question of finances—particularly if there are differences in age with a resulting impact on the amount of Social Security benefits—it's also important for couples to sit down proactively to discuss the emotional, social, and psychological effects of retiring at the same time. Discuss the issue of marital roles. What will you expect from your partner? Would you want to spend all of your time together or use a common retirement date as a springboard for joint activities as well as those you may pursue on your own? Solicit feedback from family members and friends. This sort of frank discussion will help you determine whether a common retirement date has more advantages than potential drawbacks.

Retire Right _____

One strategy to bolster a marriage after one or both retire: renew your vows. That can further the feeling of starting a new phase of your life afresh.

Is Early Retirement Right for You?

Now, let's push the time frame a bit forward. What about the possibility of retiring early—years before the "usual" target range of 60 to 65?

If anything, the question reinforces the importance of many of the issues we've already discussed. First is money—not only do you have less time to accumulate sufficient funds to retire, you're likely going to be around a good deal longer than you might be under more conventional circumstances. That means your money has to last you that much longer. In subsequent chapters, we'll be covering the mechanics of determining how much money is needed to retire—including scenarios for those interested in hanging up their working shoes long before 60 or so.

Finances aside, what's the key to an early retirement that is every bit as fulfilling as it is early? Plan, plan, and plan some more. Just as is the case with someone looking to retire at age 62, someone with their eye on 45 (or even earlier) needs to have something substantive to retire to. In one sense, this is a terrific opportunity. Rather than being able to earmark 20-some years or perhaps a bit more to a fresh pursuit, early retirement gives you a chance to potentially invest decades in some pursuit or activity. That, in turn, opens up a greater range of possibilities, from starting a second career (such as teaching) to starting your own business or nonprofit and having the time to build it up to a substantial level.

One consideration that sets planning for early retirement apart from other sorts of retirement—besides money—is the issue of what captivates you now. Put another way, is there something in your life now—your working life—that so encompasses your interest and energy that you would dearly love to devote much more to it if you had the opportunity?

Granted, that's an issue that also affects "conventional" retirement, but it becomes all the more important if, by retiring early, you're going to have that much more time on your hands. Several experts interviewed for this book pointed out the importance of a current passion in building a successful early retirement—rather than retiring and then trying to decide what to do. If you have something now that completely draws you in, then an early retirement—if it's feasible from other aspects—may be the ideal vehicle to make it blossom and grow.

> **Retirement Reality**
>
> *Far Side* cartoon creator Gary Larson retired from the strip a number of years ago—in large part, to devote more time to the study of jazz guitar.

Retire Right

One expert consulted for this book never really used the term "retirement." Rather, he always called it "the next chapter." That can be a handy and beneficial way to approach your thinking. Rather than leaving something, you're merely turning a page and starting on something fresh—something that you've given a good deal of thought to.

An Issue of Lifestyle

Another central question in beginning to think about your retirement is deceptively simple: just how do you want to live in retirement?

On the surface, that may seem rather straightforward. You'll want to be happy, satisfied, engaged, and a host of other positive characteristics. But, taken a step further, what aspects will help contribute to helping you achieve those goals?

As is readily apparent, money can play a significant role in determining the sort of lifestyle you lead. For instance, anyone who wishes to travel extensively but lacks the financial means to do so may find it challenging to live the sort of retirement they envisioned.

But it goes even further than that. As we get into the meat and potatoes of the financial aspect of planning your retirement, the question of lifestyle will crop up constantly. In a nutshell, it boils down to three salient issues:

- Do you wish to pursue a lifestyle in retirement that's roughly comparable to the life you lived prior to retirement?

- Would you prefer a more affluent lifestyle?

- Would you be satisfied with a lesser lifestyle—not necessarily spartan by any means, but perhaps simpler and less costly?

Taking these three choices into consideration involves a variety of issues. First off is finances. Aiming for a comparable or more affluent lifestyle will mandate a more substantive retirement nest egg (and, perhaps, more years working to attain it). By the same token, a simpler lifestyle, while less appealing to some people in some aspects, does have its points—perhaps easier to manage, not to mention likely less time working away to accumulate sufficient finances.

That said, in beginning to consider retirement, it's important to prioritize—at least in a preliminary manner—just what you want in your retirement life (and those things you can do without). For example: if you now own a power boat, will you want to keep it in retirement (and, with it, the expense of maintaining and storing it)? If you want to travel, does that mean in a fancy RV or with a tent tossed into the back of the minivan you already own? Is that expansive house you live in now really necessary later on, particularly with your children grown and on their own (more about this in the next section)?

You get the idea. In planning for the finances that drive your retirement, think realistically about what you genuinely value and what may be a bit more superfluous. Not only can that contribute to the sort of retirement you want, it also gears your financial planning toward the appropriate goal.

Think, too, about other elements having to do with lifestyle—those that are significantly less tied to finances. These are the activities of retirement—those pursuits and other happenings that can genuinely characterize the quality and fulfillment of your retirement.

As we noted earlier in the section on early retirement, you may already have an activity or avocation in mind that you really want to dive into upon retirement—perhaps a sport or a hobby such as painting or music. But, even if you feel what you already plan on will be sufficient, it never hurts to at least be aware of some other pursuits that many in retirement have found both provocative and fulfilling. If you need a refresher, refer back to our discussion on retirement activities in Chapter 1.

Where to Retire?

One final element to the process of retirement self-assessment has to do with where all the wonderful things you plan for retirement are going to happen. We'll be covering the specifics of housing in the final chapter of this book, but for now, let's toss out a few ideas and parameters that might be helpful to consider long before any firm decisions need be made.

Staying Put

On the one hand, staying put where you are now does, in fact, have some powerful arguments on its side. For one thing, there's a comfort level. You know the community, you know the people, your friends are nearby, and, for the most part, you have a reasonable level of expectation of the ins and outs of daily life.

There are, however, potential downsides as well. First, you may be looking to make a clean break in retirement—that unto itself may mandate a completely new setting. You may simply be bored with where you are and ready for a change. You may be tired of the weather, traffic, or a host of other elements.

It can be helpful to draw up a list outlining both the positives and the drawbacks of your current living setting. Consider how involved you are in the community. Do you make friends easily? Do you value the health care you currently receive? These and other questions may, at the very least, offer a hint as to whether staying or going might be the better option.

Retire Right _____

As is the case with most everything to do with retirement, finances can also play a role in your relocate/don't relocate decision. Simply put, it costs money to pull up stakes and head off down the road—a financial commitment you may not be willing or able to make. On the other hand, as we discuss below, you may be moving to a spot that's a good deal less expensive to live than where you are now. Over the long haul, that may end up saving you money.

Relocating

If the notion of relocating to somewhere else proves, at the very least, worthy of some consideration, it's important to incorporate a variety of factors into your thinking. That way, you can make a balanced choice that doesn't overlook any critical element.

Thinking about relocating? Consider these issues:

♦ Crime rate

♦ Climate (particularly extremes, such as hurricanes, tornadoes, snowstorms, etc.)

♦ Available health care

♦ Cultural amenities

♦ Outdoor recreational possibilities

♦ Housing costs

♦ Other living expenses, from property taxes to the cost of groceries and other services

♦ Shopping

- Proximity to educational opportunities (nearby colleges and universities)

- Transportation amenities (airport, train station)

- Proximity to major metropolitan areas (if the location is fairly small or rural)

- Proximity to churches and other places of worship

Feel free to toss any additional thoughts you may have into the mix. The more comprehensive, the more thoughtful the decision and the more likely a satisfying choice.

To help you get a fix on the sort of target communities that may match the parameters you have in mind, there are any number of excellent books on retirement relocation (search Amazon.com for a complete listing). They detail the pluses and drawbacks to a variety of retirement destinations and provide comprehensive information to help you get a better feel for any place you may be considering. Additionally, *Where to Retire* magazine can also be a useful resource for retirement location hunters. Go to www. wheretoretire.com for more information.

Once you've zeroed in on a prospective retirement destination or two and compiled a list of pluses and minuses, hedge your bets a bit: go back and compare what you found with your current location. It may serve to reinforce your decision to relocate; on the other hand, it may bolster a choice to stay put.

 Retire Right

When the time comes to retire and you decide to relocate, do yourself a favor: rent a place to live a few months before you commit to buying a home of some sort. You can do all the research in the world, only to have reality prove different. Make certain your spot is all it's cracked up to be before you get in too deep financially.

The Least You Need to Know

- Don't assume that everyone is cut out for retirement. Evaluate who you are and what you want to determine if retirement is right for you.

- Think carefully about when you might want to retire. Of course money's a factor, but there are other things to consider—such as the effect on family and friends.

- If you and a spouse or partner are considering retiring at the same time, be sure to talk everything out to make sure that it's genuinely in both your interests.

- Considering early retirement? Great—just make sure you'll have enough to fill what likely will be a lengthy retirement.

- Start giving some thought to your retirement lifestyle. How important is it that you maintain a comparable standard of living?

- Think carefully, too, about the issue of relocation. Don't just choose a place for its sunny, balmy climate. Consider a variety of factors to make certain that any place you choose to relocate fits your needs in every way possible.

Chapter 4

The Issue of Money—
A First Look

In This Chapter

- ◆ What exactly is enough?
- ◆ Calculating your retirement needs
- ◆ The necessity of being proactive
- ◆ Understand inflation
- ◆ The importance of steady income
- ◆ Is money the make or break to retirement?

As you no doubt already know, money is a central element to a happy and fulfilling retirement. For many of us, there's no getting around that truth. Even those of us who live a rather spartan lifestyle with simple needs will require some sort of nest egg to pay whatever expenses we accrue as part of day-to-day living.

That raises a basic issue—how much is enough? As we'll discuss later, that depends on a variety of factors: your current lifestyle, where you are in terms of your retirement savings, and just what you plan to do in retirement, among a number of others. But variables aside, it's important to gain a fairly concrete sense of just what your financial requirements are going to be—and from there, the best way to devise and execute a plan to reach those goals.

An equally important part of this chapter will be perspective—more specifically, stressing the importance of money but pointing out that it is just one part of planning and enjoying a fulfilling retirement. Put another way: money's important, but it doesn't have to be a do-or-die proposition. In that sense, we'll be taking a two-pronged approach to the topic of money. We'll be stressing the role it undoubtedly plays, but not necessarily placing it on an all-or-nothing pedestal.

How Much Is Enough?

The question of how much money is enough to afford retirement is akin to asking how much air you need to breathe. The answer is the same for both questions: it all depends on the individual. Although the expenses involved—housing, food, and other costs—may be the same, what you will need in retirement depends on a number of factors specific to you.

While that may seem to make perfect sense, there are others who argue that there *is* a hard-and-fast barometer for gauging how much you'll need to retire. Some may say that you'll need roughly 80 percent of your pre-retirement income to maintain the same lifestyle after you retire. Others are a bit less optimistic, pointing out the eroding influence of inflation—that, they say, mandates 100 percent of pre-retirement income to live comparably after retirement. Still a third camp says that it costs you less not to have to earn a living (no commuting, business wardrobe, and the like). That means you can be reasonably comfortable on a mere 60 percent of what you earn now.

Whatever side of the debate you agree with, the fact that the question even exists illustrates that there really is no definitive answer. There are simply too many variables. But it also points out the importance of figuring out what's going to work for you. And that's just what we will do in the next section.

How Much Will You Need? How to Calculate It

You can get a reasonable sense of what you will need for retirement by running a few numbers.

On the most simple level: say you now live fairly comfortably on $80,000 a year. Taking a cautious strategy, let's now say you'll need 80 percent of that money to retire on. That works out to $64,000 a year.

But there's likely more to it than just that. For one thing, much depends on what sort of retirement you envision. On the one hand, you may need considerably less money than you do now to enjoy a satisfying retirement (as we get older, many of our wants and needs become much more simple). On the other, expenses in other areas may increase (medical care and prescriptions, for instance, become a greater financial obligation as we age).

Another way to gain a sense of how much you'll need is to look at the financial formula from the opposite end. Rather than looking at the money you have coming in, focus instead on where it goes. Start the process by tallying up where you spend your money now. Map out a list of every expense you can think of, from your mortgage all the way down to more discretionary spending.

From there, apply the same math you did when figuring your income. For instance, let's say you earn $80,000 a year but your expenses amount to $70,000. Factoring in the same 80 percent we used earlier shows that you will spend $56,000 every year in your retirement. That's an $8,000 annual difference between the income calculation we worked out earlier—a substantial disparity.

As if you needed any more, there are other variables on top of all of this. For one thing, there's the issue of how long you have until you actually retire. Not only will that likely affect your income—assuming your pay increases over that time period—but your standard of living may also increase. Put another way—how you live now may really not be the most accurate indicator of how you will likely live in retirement. How you live at the point of your retirement may be a far more telling barometer.

Then there's the issue of inflation. We will cover inflation in more substantive detail later in this chapter, but for now, suffice it to say that inflation boosts both your income as well as the cost of the goods and services you purchase with that money. Depending on how long you have until retirement, that means it's important to factor in the likely effects of inflation—both in terms of the money you will have in hand as well as the cost of living.

Okay, so what's the best way to work out how much you'll need? Short answer: you need to take income, spending, and inflation into account. We will do that using the following worksheet and accompanying table.

> **Retirement Reality**
>
> Annual inflation runs somewhere in the neighborhood of 3 to 4 percent. That may not seem like a great deal, but it adds up—particularly over a long period of time. To illustrate: say a couch costs $1,000 today. That same piece of furniture will cost nearly $1,500 with 4 percent inflation—a 50 percent overall hike—in a mere 10 years.

Retirement Expenditures

Examples

1. Current annual income _____ $70,000

2. Current spending _____ $60,000

3. Spending at Retirement _____   80 percent

4. Yearly Living Costs _____ $48,000
   (multiply #2 by #3)

5. Time until retirement _____   15 years

6. Annual growth rate   3 percent

7. Inflation Factor _____   1.56
   (refer to the following table and multiply by #4)

8. Estimated annual living _____ $74,880
   costs at retirement

Annual Growth Rate

Years to Retirement	3%	4%	6%	8%	10%	12%
5	1.16	1.22	1.34	1.47	1.61	1.76
10	1.34	1.48	1.79	2.16	2.59	3.11
15	1.56	1.8	2.4	3.17	4.18	5.47
20	1.81	2.19	3.21	4.66	6.73	9.65
25	2.09	2.67	4.29	6.85	10.83	17.00

The table above may seem complicated, but it really is only a formula that takes into account the effect of inflation and time on money. Looked at another way: if something costs a certain amount now, this chart lets you calculate how much that same item will be with various sorts of inflation rates and time periods. In the case of the example that we worked out, the assumption was a 3 percent annual inflation rate with 15 years until retirement.

Although this formula cannot possibly delineate your requirements down to the precise penny, it does offer a telling view of the financial requirements of retirement. Just glance at the numbers—with the scenario we worked out, you will need $74,000 a year to maintain your current lifestyle. Given a 15-year span until you retire, that means you will need $4,000 a year more than you earn now—at a time of your life when your working days will likely be completely over! Even more intimidating, if inflation comes in higher than the 3 percent we factored in, that makes your financial requirements even steeper.

Where You Are Now Matters

All these numbers may seem like something of a downer. On the surface, they can be. Depending on how you wish to live and other issues, retirement can be a genuinely pricey consideration.

But it is not an impossible task—far from it. Ironically enough, one reason that retirement planning is a very achievable goal is one of its greatest challenges—time.

You no doubt recall how we discussed the effect of time on the cost of goods and services—an essential factor is mapping out a retirement plan. But time, to quote Mick Jagger, is also very much on your side.

On a simplistic level, the longer you have until you retire, the greater the opportunity for increased savings. Being able to save $5,000 for 10 years means $50,000. A 15-year time frame pushes that amount to $75,000.

But there's more to it than that. What you can do with the money you save can also differ. As we will get into in greater detail in Chapter 13, the longer your time frame, the more aggressive you can afford to be with how you invest your savings. And because of *compounding* over time, that can add up to a substantial difference in how much money you're able to carry into retirement.

def•i•ni•tion

Another factor that boosts the return on money you save or invest is known as **compounding.** For those who have heard this term but aren't really sure what it means, compounding means your money earns money and, from there, keeps growing larger. For instance: $500 with a 10 percent return becomes $550 at year's end. Another year at 10 percent becomes $605 (10 percent of $550 rather than the initial $500).

The advantages of compounding don't end there. For one thing, the longer the time frame, the longer compounding has time to work. In the example we offer in the previous sidebar, $500 earning 10 percent a year comes out to $1,296 in 10 years. Boost that to 20 years, and you can pocket $3,363—more than $2,800 than what you started with.

Another way compounding works in your favor is its use in planning your retirement goals. Let's go back to the exercise we did earlier when we determined an annual retirement income goal of $74,000. If you had nothing saved to date—but had some 20 years prior to your retirement—you would have to invest roughly $6,000 and earn approximately 12 percent annually to reach that $74,000 target (granted, this is just for one year, but you get the idea).

Retire Right _____

There are a host of online calculators that let you set a financial goal and, in turn, let you play with various scenarios to figure out how much to save and at what rate of return. One terrific place with a battalion of handy calculators is Bankrate. com (www.bankrate.com).

Notice one assumption we just made in the preceding scenario—that you had saved nothing up to this point. That is yet another critical factor in determining where you are and what you have to do in the future. The bigger the financial base from which to build, the greater the likelihood of a result that allows for a satisfying and fulfilling retirement.

Consider the following situations. The first one involves a 45-year-old man who hopes to retire in 15 years. Trouble is, he's yet to save anything at all toward that goal. That makes his objective of saving for retirement a good deal more challenging than it need be. In fact, using the $74,000 annual income target we used earlier, he would have to set aside $200 every month for 15 years and earn 9 percent interest every year to fund just 1 year of retirement—not an insurmountable goal by any means, but still, funds sufficient for just 1 year of retirement.

Now let's take up a slightly different scenario. Another 45-year-old, eyeing a retirement age of 60—only here our subject has already set aside $20,000 in retirement savings. He, like our somewhat less prepared friend, can also save $200 a month and expect a 9 percent return. The result: $149,129, more than double than the first example.

The message here is simple, yet powerful. The more you have already saved not only puts you in a better position to achieve your retirement goals, it also lessens the ongoing financial obligation. Not to suggest that it's a good idea to save less for your retirement if you have the means to do more, but it can certainly take some of the pressure off.

Get the Message? Get a Jump on Things!

Building a solid retirement plan means little if you don't act on what you work out. That not only means setting up a regular program of savings and investing toward retirement, but also getting started with the program as early as you possibly can.

The situation we offered in the prior section—one involving no retirement savings and another with a modest amount—provides a vivid picture of the importance of being proactive. However powerful the image, bear in mind that our little exercise only involved saving for one single year of retirement. Saving for an entire retirement puts it into a more realistic light. And with people living longer—and commensurately planning to do more with that additional time—the importance of ample savings becomes all the more imperative.

The bottom line: start saving for your retirement as early as you can. As we've documented, the effects over time can be remarkable. And, just as important, starting early can mitigate much of the stress that many people encounter when thinking about their retirement. Not only do you have a long period of time in which to meet your financial goals—and, as a result, personal objectives as well—the amount of money that's absolutely necessary to earmark becomes less of a burden. The longer the time frame, the longer even a modest amount of money has to work on your behalf.

Note: we'll cover savings strategies and other issues for young people just starting to plan their retirement in Chapter 13.

Retirement Reality

If you're relatively young—say, in your 20s or 30s—the idea of starting a retirement funding program may seem alien to you. Well, here are some numbers that might well change your mind. If you're 25 now and want to retire by age 60, putting aside a modest $100 a month at 7 percent interest totals more than $176,000 by the day you hang up your working shoes.

Understanding Inflation

Inflation is one of those terms that all of us hear on a regular basis—and, just as frequently, misunderstand or misinterpret. As we pointed out earlier in this chapter, inflation is the effect of rising prices on your purchasing power. Usually expressed in terms of percentages, inflation in the United States has hovered in the vicinity of 3 to 4 percent in recent years.

What does that mean in practical terms? If you have $1 to spend on a particular item or service, that dollar will actually be able to buy only 97 cents worth at the end of the year if inflation is running at 3 percent.

Retire Right

If you're interested in working through various scenarios that document the effects of inflation, have a look at the inflation calculator at www.westegg.com/inflation. Plug in a dollar amount, enter two dates, and it shows what a dollar amount in the past would translate to in the future due to inflation. Example: $100 in 1960 equals nearly $250 by 1980. Ouch.

The calculator we cite in the accompanying sidebar illustrates an important truth about inflation. While 3 percent a year may seem piddling, inflation can make big inroads into your retirement nest egg over a long period of time. To illustrate: say you have $500,000 in retirement savings in 1980. Translate that to the year 2000, and you would have had to save more than $1,143,000 to enjoy the same purchasing power. Moreover, with factors like that at play, it's little wonder that costs for housing, food, medical care, and other necessities have exploded in recent years.

Retirement Reality

Okay, here's a bit of news to counter all these intimidating statistics. While 3 to 4 percent inflation may be rather painful, it's nothing compared with the early 1920s, when inflation topped a horrific 20 percent.

The simple message here is that inflation is a major player in planning out the financial nuts and bolts of your retirement. And, while we'll work out scenarios that take inflation into account in a rather specific capacity, the bottom line is that it's genuinely hard to save too much when it comes to funding your retirement. With inflation constantly chipping away at its value, money today becomes considerably less valuable in the future. So it's solid thinking to always try to sock away as much as possible.

Another Key—Steady Income

On the surface, the basic financial challenge of retirement is to save as much as you possibly can for what you define as your needs. That's true—if enough money is on the table, it betters your chances for having the sort of retirement that you want (and, for that matter, deserve).

But there's an interesting wrinkle to that. Studies have found that retirees with a traditional pension—one that guarantees them a monthly check for the remainder of their lives—tended to have happier, more fulfilling retirements than others with other sorts of vehicles, such as a 401(k).

Why? Obviously, there's a sense of security associated with a guaranteed form of income. It's also reassuring that a set amount of money will arrive on a regular basis, rather than having to decide on your own how much to withdraw from a retirement account (and hoping that you're not draining down your money at too fast a rate).

Even better, studies document that the most satisfied and fulfilled retirees have both sorts of funding vehicles—a steady source of income plus a cache of cash. Here, you get the best of both worlds—a reliable income source to meet many of your ongoing financial obligations as well as a ready supply of savings, possibly used for less delineated costs ranging from medical care to a spur-of-the-moment vacation.

Unfortunately, "traditional" company pensions are becoming less and less common, what with companies opting more often for 401(k) plans, not to mention a boom in small businesses and other forms of self-employment. That, in turn, means fewer circumstances involving a regular, guaranteed check.

But there are ways to adjust. One way is to set up an automatic withdrawal program from a 401(k), IRA, simplified employee pension, or whatever vehicle might hold your retirement savings. It's not a bottomless well, of course, but it is reliable—a key to a happy retirement with as few financial worries as possible.

Another option is to buy an income annuity. This choice, which we will get into in greater detail in Chapter 5, basically involves investing a lump sum with an insurance company or other financial concern. In turn, the company agrees to pay you a fixed payment every month for the rest of your life.

It may seem trivial, but mapping out a steady income stream is an important element of the financial component of your retirement. It also shows that there are some heady psychological aspects associated with the finances of retirement—a topic which we delve into in the next section.

Money—The End All to Retirement?

Okay, now it's time to put the brakes on just a bit as we conclude this chapter. Throughout, we have been discussing the importance of money—how much you will need, how to calculate that, the effects of inflation, and a number of other introductory topics all having to do with the finances of retirement.

Make no mistake—all that's very important. But it does beg the question: however critical finances are to retirement, are they necessarily the make or break to a fulfilling, satisfying retirement?

Like so many other issues having to do with retirement, that depends in part on the person asking the question. If, for instance, your plans for retirement are, shall we say, rather capital dependent—you want to travel extensively, maybe build a luxurious second home or have other cost-heavy notions—then, yes, much of your retirement may depend on how much you have socked away in savings.

But, on second thought, maybe we're posing the wrong sort of question. Rather than asking if money makes for a happy retirement, it's more useful to wonder if it has to be that way—if money, at least, necessarily has to play the overriding role that it often does?

Here, the answer would likely be a resounding *no*. Granted, money is important, but it is not, by definition, the only factor in a happy retirement. As we've discussed, it's important to gauge how much money you'll need to fund the retirement you hope for and, from there, map out a plan to gain that objective.

Golden Years Gaffes

Think a little bit of extra cash automatically assures you of a happier retirement? Not so. A recent study at the University of Wisconsin–Milwaukee found that an additional $10,000 saved for retirement only increased the chances for a happy retirement by a scant 1 percent.

But be wary of changing parameters. Ron Manheimer, executive director of the North Carolina Center for Creative Retirement, notes that far too often, persons planning for retirement set a goal, only to meet it, exceed it, and, from there, set a new arbitrary financial goal. And so on, causing needless stress and worry. As Manheimer puts it, "It's a matter of meaning, not just money. It can't simply be a question of having a lot of money."

So it seems clear that a happy retirement doesn't simply turn on adequate cash, however important that may be. What else goes into a happy retirement? Here's a checklist that may broaden your thinking somewhat:

❏ Have a plan in place—one that takes in more than just financial issues.

❏ Stay active, but not too active. Research has shown that excessive activity in retirement can be just as detrimental as too little to do.

❏ If possible, choose when you retire. Persons who have to retire due to physical limitations, downsizing, or other factors outside of their control are less likely to be satisfied as those whose retirement date was of their own choosing.

❑ Have a wide range of social support and networking, including both family and friends. Isolation can be a major cause of unhappiness in retirement.

❑ Set different priorities. Now that you no longer are working, look for and appreciate other things in life. As Manheimer of the North Carolina Center for Creative Retirement puts it: "It's a chance to enjoy the world for what it is."

❑ Accentuate the positive. It may seem trite, but those who look on the bright side have a happier retirement than those who see retirement as a string of hurdles and challenges.

❑ Give it time. Look at retirement as a work in progress. Research suggests that older retirees enjoy themselves more than younger ones. So give retirement enough time to evolve into what you truly want it to be.

> **Retirement Reality**
>
> For those of you who may unfamiliar with the thoughts of the Greek philosopher Aristotle, here's his list of those elements that comprise happiness: noble birth, many friends, good friends, wealth, good children, many children, good old age, health, beauty, strength, stature, athleticism, good reputation, honor, luck, and virtue. Notice money's in thero, but it's far from the only thing.

The Least You Need to Know

◆ Gauge how much money you may need in retirement. Sixty to 80 percent of your current income is a reasonable guesstimate.

◆ Don't just focus on money coming in. Get a sense of where your money goes now—and what your spending might be like come retirement.

◆ Start saving for retirement early. It allows you more time to accumulate a substantial nest egg. Starting early can also lessen the stress associated with saving for retirement.

◆ Take inflation into account in your planning. The longer you have until retirement, the more expensive goods and services will be.

◆ Consider a form of steady income, such as an annuity. This, too, can lessen the stress of making your money last.

◆ Keep money in its proper perspective. Yes, it's important, but it's by no means the only component of a happy, fulfilling retirement.

Chapter 5

Where Might the Money Come From?

In This Chapter

- ◆ IRAs
- ◆ The importance of personal savings
- ◆ Pensions and other workplace programs
- ◆ Social Security
- ◆ Life insurance and annuities
- ◆ The importance of a broad plan

Up to this point, we've discussed at some length the importance of having sufficient funds to live the sort of retirement you wish. No getting around it—money's an important element to retirement, no matter how frugally you plan to live.

But just as important is the issue of sources—put another way, where will the money come from and where will you keep it as you prepare for retirement?

In this chapter, we'll introduce you to a variety of retirement funding vehicles. We'll provide a quick overview of their various features, their advantages and drawbacks and how, taken individually or used as a package, they can work to build a solid financial retirement package. And, in subsequent chapters, we'll go into additional detail regarding how to invest in them, finding the sort of risk tolerance that's right for you and other issues related to using these vehicles as effectively as possible.

Getting to Know the IRA

For many people planning for retirement, an IRA is a central element. Formally known as Individual Retirement Accounts, they've been around since 1981, providing a solid vehicle with which to build a financial base for retirement.

Basically, an IRA is a savings vehicle—but with added advantages. It allows you to save money on a tax-deferred basis for your retirement. An IRA is exceedingly simple to set up—while you can still do it with as little as a single-page form, you can now establish IRA accounts online in a matter of minutes.

Another great feature of an IRA is its flexibility. Once you have money in an account, you can pretty much do what you want with it, at least from an allocation point of view. You can invest in mutual funds, stocks, bonds, money markets—there's a broad range of options from which to choose. You can even opt for a managed IRA fund, which, over time, automatically shifts its investment mix as you near retirement.

There are other advantages as well. Depending on your circumstances, you may be able to deduct your contribution (more about this in Chapter 9). And no matter if the contribution is deductible or not, your money grows on a tax-deferred basis until you begin to withdraw it after you retire.

Even better, there are now two IRAs from which to choose—the traditional IRA and the Roth. The primary difference is in tax treatment. While you may be able to deduct traditional IRA contributions, a Roth offers no up-front deductibility. However, proceeds from a Roth may be withdrawn tax-free after you retire (a traditional IRA is taxed).

For more details about IRAs—including how to choose between a traditional IRA and a Roth, whether IRA conversion is a good idea or not, and other issues—check out Chapter 9. But for now, know that an IRA is a powerful retirement weapon—one that you should consider adding to your arsenal.

Other Savings Programs

Some fairly grim news emerged as this book was being written. According to the Federal Reserve Board, Americans had recorded the lowest savings rate since the years of the Great Depression. Phrased in statistical terms, the savings rate for 2006 was a negative 1 percent—meaning that Americans, as a whole, were spending more than they were setting aside in savings.

There are various theories as to how this all happened. Ready access to credit cards, home-owner refinancing (with resulting extra cash in hand), low interest rates, and a general emphasis on consumer satisfaction (translation: greed?) have all been cited for the troubling trend.

> **Retirement Reality**
>
> The last time a negative savings rate occurred was in 1932 and 1933—the very heart of a worldwide depression.

But this is not the entire story. Savings rates have been dropping for decades, but this is not necessarily because people are saving less. As 401(k)s came into being and have gained in popularity, they have replaced traditional savings accounts as the vehicle of choice for most households. Since 401(k)s don't count on the government statistics, it makes it look like we are not saving.

Still, not only does this raise serious red flags for all Americans, it's particularly worrisome to retirees. The time of the savings news coincided with a wave of baby boomers, some 78 million people, turning age 62. That has economists concerned that, as a whole, people are simply not saving enough to adequately fund their retirement.

Granted, we have all sorts of terrific savings vehicles, such as IRAs and 401(k)s, to help us save for retirement. And, rightly or not, many people approaching retirement are relying on the value of their investment portfolio and appreciating value of their homes to help fund their retirement as well.

But it also points out a powerful truth: we need to save more. And, notwithstanding Roth IRAs, Keoghs, and every sort of more formal investing and savings vehicle, that can boil down to the importance of saving on your own.

On the surface, you may respond with an impossible shrug of your shoulders—you're already saving in your 401(k) or Simplified Employee Pension where you work and, besides, you haven't an extra penny left to set aside. Maybe, maybe not. First off, when you have a moment, have a look at Chapter 6, which details some budget and savings strategies. Once you're done, you may be pleasantly surprised at how much money suddenly appears out of nowhere.

What you might uncover may seem small at first glance but, given sufficient time and discipline, even modest amounts of money can build into something substantial. To illustrate: putting away a relatively modest $25 a month at 5 percent interest for 20 years gets you $10,374. Bump up either the amount saved or the interest rate, and that amount becomes that much greater.

The downside, of course, is that conventional savings don't offer any tax advantages, such as the tax-deferral features of an IRA or a 401(k). However, unlike those and other vehicles, your cash in conventional savings is readily available—touch money in an IRA or 401(k) before a certain age or outside of certain extenuating circumstances, and you're socked with penalties.

Not so with savings that you set up on your own. Unless the money is locked into a CD (and even there you can get at it, albeit with some form of penalty), it's there for you to use as necessary. Not only can that be handy to meet routine, expected expenses, it's particularly important for the unexpected—medical bills, fender benders, and other unanticipated costs that cause considerable financial mischief for those who are unprepared.

In Chapter 6, we go into detail about the various options you have for stashing your savings. But for now, don't overlook the importance of augmenting other retirement vehicles with plain old saving on your own.

Retire Right

Think you'll have a hard time setting aside extra savings on your own? Relax and let your credit card handle it. There are about 50 cards available that automatically take a portion of what a customer spends with the card and puts it into a savings account.

Workplace Programs

The role and function of retirement plans where you work are changing. In the old days, you worked, you retired, and based on how long you were there and other factors, you received a pension in the form of a monthly check for the rest of your life.

Granted, those sorts of programs are still around, although they're fast being replaced by a variety of retirement funding options—many of which mandate your participation as an employee to a far greater level than the old pension system ever did.

Here's a quick overview of some of the programs you'll likely encounter where you work:

◆ **Defined benefit program.** The old workhorse. You work for a company for a certain number of years, retire and, based on your salary and length of employment, receive a pension. How you take that can vary. Some opt for a regular monthly check, while others take a lesser regular amount in exchange for a guarantee that, should they die, their surviving spouse will continue to receive payments.

◆ **Defined contribution plans.** Increasingly popular, they require the employee's active involvement in the program. By far the most popular is a 401(k) plan. Here, money is automatically deducted from your salary before you take possession of it. From there, the money is put into an investment vehicle of your choosing, including mutual funds, company stock, and other options. As we'll discuss in great detail in Chapter 7, this offers tax advantages and tax-deferred growth on everything you put into the 401(k) account.

◆ **Profit sharing.** Your company promises to pay you a yearly amount. Although the name suggests a connection to profits, it's really at the discretion of an employer, regardless of performance. Somewhat unpredictable, as good years can bring large profit sharing rewards, while down years may mean little or nothing.

◆ **Employee stock ownership.** Also known as ESOPs, employees may buy company stock with little or no commission costs (the company may also buy it on their behalf). Again, there's a close tie to the performance of the company. If things go well, the stock value will likely increase. If things head south, so can the value of the stock you own.

◆ **Stock bonus.** Akin to profit sharing, except that you receive proceeds in the form of stock rather than cash.

The advantages and drawbacks to each of these options are varied—worthy of the careful consideration they will receive later. But, for many, workplace retirement planning is the bedrock of their overall retirement program—one that mandates careful thought and consistent execution.

Social Security

We all know what this is, at least in a rudimentary sense. And, admittedly, we've all been somewhat nervous about its financial solvency.

Here, in this brief introduction, we'll cover some of the basics of Social Security as well as dispel some needless misinformation that may cloud your understanding of how it will fit into your retirement funding program.

> ### Retirement Reality
>
> Social Security, formally known as the federal Old Age, Survivors, and Disability Insurance program, was signed into law by President Franklin Roosevelt in 1935. At the time—the heart of the Great Depression—one out of every two senior citizens lived in poverty.

We will be covering Social Security—and how you can access the system to your best advantage—in exhaustive detail in Chapter 8. However, following are some of the major components of the overall program:

Retirement Benefits

This is the largest, and certainly the most widely known, element of the Social Security system. Throughout your working life, you make contributions to the Social Security system. When you retire, you receive monthly Social Security benefits based on earnings over the course of your working career.

How much you will get depends, in essence, on how much you earned. The more money you earn over a longer period of time, the more money you can expect to receive come retirement. The Social Security Administration considers your earnings over the course of more than 30 years, takes inflation into account, then works out a yearly average. From there, a percentage of that amount represents your monthly benefit.

Okay, everyone asks the question—how much can I expect to receive? Here's a simple scenario—say you're 50 years old and plan to retire in 15 years at age 65. You now make $100,000 a year. A rough guesstimate of your Social Security benefits puts your post retirement monthly benefit at $1,937 in today's dollars.

The earliest you can begin receiving Social Security Benefits is age 62. You become formally eligible once you have accumulated 40 *work credits*.

Retire Right

Want to work out your own scenario? The Social Security Administration has a quick online calculator at www.ssa.gov/planners/calculators.htm. There, you can get a rough idea of what you can expect to receive based on your earnings and projected retirement date. You can also take inflation into account. In the above scenario, inflation-adjusted dollars amount to a monthly benefit of $3,337.

def•i•ni•tion ─────────────────────────────
> **Work credits** are based on a year's employment. You earn four credits for every year you work. Theoretically, then, you are eligible for Social Security benefits after 10 years of work.

Spousal Benefits

We mentioned earlier that we would briefly touch on Social Security benefits that receive a good deal less attention than the conventional monthly benefit. Spousal benefits are one such benefit. Spouses who do not work are also qualified to receive Social Security benefits beginning at age 62. Overall benefits amount to 150 percent of what someone retiring on their own might receive.

The reasoning? Simple. Even if one spouse doesn't work, Social Security recognizes the reality that it costs much more for two people to live than just one. Hence the larger benefit, no matter if the second spouse works or not.

The benefits are all the more attractive if both spouses are employed. Here, the spouse is eligible to receive benefits based on his or her earnings or half of your benefit—whichever is larger.

Survivors Benefits

Another nice feature of Social Security is that you don't have to be around for your family to benefit from the program. Survivors insurance pays monthly benefits to surviving spouses, children, and even parents (if they're deemed to be financially dependent on you). In some instances, even ex-spouses are eligible. With a retired married couple, the smaller of the two checks drops off when one person dies. Like conventional benefits, survivors benefits are calculated based on your average earnings over the course of your working life. We'll get into the specifics of what sorts of survivors receive what sorts of benefits in greater detail in Chapter 8.

Disability

We're all going to die at some point (unless, of course, someone's discovered something rather significant that they're not sharing with the rest of us). But here's a bit of reality that's less well known—studies suggest that a 20-year-old has a roughly 3-in-10 chance of becoming disabled sometime before he or she reaches retirement age. And that means no income coming in whatsoever.

Fortunately, Social Security addresses this issue as well. The definition of disability is that you are incapable of performing any sort of substantive work for at least a year. Once you meet this definition of disabled, you will continue to receive disability benefits for as long as you are disabled.

Again, you ask—how much does that come to? It depends on how much you make and for how long you have been earning it. Here's a rough example for a 50-year-old who started out with a rather modest wage scale and now earns $100,000 a year. Rough monthly disability estimate: $2,064, taking inflation into account.

Retire Right

Again, Social Security online offers a nice calculator that lets you figure how much disability benefit you may be entitled to. Check it out at www. ssa.gov/retire2/AnypiaApplet. html.

Life Insurance and Annuities

Life insurance and annuities are two more potential sources of retirement income. Whether they are a good choice for you, however, depends on the particulars of your circumstances.

Life Insurance

On the surface, the issue of life insurance as a source of income in retirement runs headfirst into an age-old financial maxim—as a rule, if you need life insurance, buy *term life insurance* and invest the difference.

def•i•ni•tion

Term life insurance is the most simple—and affordable—form of life insurance. You take out the policy, pay the annual premium, and you're covered. No cash value, nothing more than basic coverage. **Whole life insurance** is different primarily in that it also offers a cash value to the owner of the policy.

For many people, cash value (also known as *whole life*) insurance is unnecessary. If all you're interested in is the coverage, term is cheaper and far more straight-forward.

However, there are some instances when cash value life insurance can play an effective role in a retirement funding program. Some possible scenarios:

- You are contributing the maximum amount to your primary sources of retirement income, such as an IRA or 401(k) where you work.

- You have a substantial estate and any additional form of tax advantage may be helpful.

◆ You're concerned about what your health might be when you near or are in retirement and may face challenges renewing term life insurance.

◆ The thought of "conventional" investing makes you jittery and you are attracted to a vehicle that is far more conservative than, say, stocks or mutual funds.

If cash value seems at least worthy of some of your attention, here's a primer. Cash value life insurance combines the protective element of all sorts of insurance with a savings mechanism. Cash value premiums are set for the life of the policy and invariably start out higher than premiums mandated by term coverage.

Part of whole life's premiums pay for the actual insurance protection, while the remainder goes into a reserve account. The reserve serves two functions. One is to meet increasing insurance costs as the policy owner ages. The reserve also builds up a cash value through two separate means: a "guaranteed" interest rate and an additional return generated from insurance company investments.

If the use of life insurance seems appealing, we cover the topic in complete detail in Chapter 20.

Annuities

Another option that, in effect, involves paying for something now in exchange for a benefit down the road is an *annuity*.

To begin with, there are two primary sorts of annuities insofar as when you begin to receive payments. One, an immediate annuity, begins making payments almost immediately (usually within about 30 days of setting up the annuity). The other is known as a deferred annuity—this involves a longer time frame, as you buy the annuity and begin to receive payments sometime in the future.

def•i•ni•tion

An **annuity** is basically a financial contract. You buy an annuity with the guarantee that the company—usually an insurance company—will provide a series of regular, fixed payments in exchange.

There are also two primary forms of annuities when it comes to how the company selling the annuity handles the money you give it. The more conservative choice is a fixed annuity. This, which the company usually invests in bonds or mortgages, provides a stable, if modest, rate of return.

The other option is a variable annuity. Here, you have your choice among several more aggressive investment options, including stock, bonds, and money market portfolios. The payout potential is much greater but is also subject to more volatility, particularly if you opt for choices such as stock portfolios or mutual funds.

No matter which sort of annuity appeals to you, one feature that's universally attractive has to do with taxes. All money in any annuity grows on a tax-deferred basis (although there is, of course, a tax consequence once you begin to take payments).

However, it's important to bear in mind some significant caveats with regard to annuities. For one thing, many impose a nasty "surrender charge"—sometimes upward of 10 percent of the principal—if you cash out the policy or move it to another company within the first five years of the contract. There are also ongoing fees for maintaining an annuity (usually in the vicinity of $20 to $30 a year). On top of that, there will be asset management fees, which can amount to 2 percent or more of the value of the annuity each and every year.

Like other options, annuities are best suited to prospective retirees who have already maxed out more viable forms of retirement savings, such as a 401(k) where they work. Also, they can be a nice complement to other savings strategies for people who are looking for relatively safe choices as well as a reliable source of income for retirement.

Retire Right

When buying any sort of insurance product, be sure to investigate the financial stability of the company behind the product. Two places that rate financial stability of companies are Standard and Poor's (www.standardandpoors.com) and A.M. Best (www.ambest.com).

If the idea of an annuity of some sort seems appealing, shop aggressively. Cost and fee structures can vary considerably from one company to another, which, in turn, can affect how expensive the annuity is to own. Additionally, be sure to check the financial stability of the company selling the annuity. You don't want to sink thousands of dollars into an annuity, only to have the issuing company go the way of mood rings before you receive any money. Also, annuity income, even from a variable annuity invested in mutual funds, is classified as ordinary income. This is generally taxed at a much higher rate than mutual fund dividends and capital gains.

Reverse Mortgages

Most of us look at our home as a form of financial obligation—one that involves a monthly mortgage payment to pay down the overall amount we owe on the property.

However, your home can also become an income source, once you retire. This is due to a product known as a reverse mortgage.

Here, the entire dynamic of payment is reversed. Rather than your cutting a monthly mortgage check, a reverse mortgage involves a contractual arrangement with a bank involving the equity in your home. Effectively, you convert some of that equity to cash and, as a result, receive a regular monthly payment based on the overall size of the reverse mortgage.

Actually, there are several payout options. While many retirees opt for the security and predictability of monthly payments, you can also choose a lump sum payment. Interest rates vary—some are fixed, while others are variable.

Ultimately, the reverse mortgage becomes due when you die or sell the home. The money due on the reverse mortgage is then subtracted from the proceeds from the sale of the home.

The downside is that reverse mortgages can prove expensive in a variety of ways. First, there are closing costs and other expenses associated with obtaining the loan. And interest costs—and their effect on just how much your home is ultimately worth—can accrue quickly.

Retire Right _____

The Home Equity Conversion Mortgage (HECM) is the only reverse mortgage available that is insured by the federal government. These offer the most generous loan amounts available and the most flexible payback options. Further information is available at www.hud.gov/offices/hsg/sfh/hecm/hecmhome.cfm.

The Importance of a Broad Plan

There may seem to be a great many choices to sort through when it comes to mapping out where money for your retirement might come from. That's both a positive as well as a challenge—broad choices mean broad opportunity, but mandate careful research and choices on your part.

It also illustrates that, with few exceptions, funds for retirement will likely come from several sources, including a program where you work, Social Security, and any additional savings you're able to put together on your own.

That said, when planning for your retirement, be sure to take varied funding sources into account and, if need be, adjust certain parts of your plan accordingly. For instance, if you expect to receive a certain level of benefit from Social Security, you know just how much you'll have to make up in other areas to reach your financial goals.

It also makes sense from a risk management standpoint. For example, if your 401(k) at work is in particularly aggressive investment choices, balance that with more conservative choices in other areas, such as an IRA.

The bottom line is the importance of a broad plan—one in which individual elements work in conjunction with others to provide solid growth, security, and, ultimately, the finances you'll need to enjoy your retirement however you see fit.

The Least You Need to Know

- ◆ IRAs—either in traditional form or the Roth variant—offer terrific opportunities to save for your retirement on a tax-deferred basis.

- ◆ Defined benefit plans are still in place in many companies. Here, you work for a certain number of years and the company pays you an after-retirement benefit based on your salary, length of employment, and other factors.

- ◆ Defined contribution plans such as 401(k)s are becoming increasingly popular. If your company offers one, use it. You'll save on taxes and your money will grow tax-deferred. Your company may even offer a match.

- ◆ Social Security will be an important part of your retirement. Take the time to have an idea of what you might expect.

- ◆ Cash value life insurance and annuities offer tax advantages to fund your retirement, although you should max out other funding options first.

- ◆ Reverse mortgages are another possible retirement funding source. But they can be expensive to put into place and, over time, can cut substantially into the overall value of your home.

Chapter 6

The First Part of the Plan: Basic Financial Steps

In This Chapter

- ◆ Watch where your dollars go
- ◆ Debt: retirement enemy number one
- ◆ Other strategies: pay off your mortgage, refinance, and other ideas
- ◆ Smart savings strategies

In a way, planning a satisfying and rewarding retirement is like planning a meal. You can devise a menu, invite the guests, and map out a host of amenities to make sure everything goes as pleasantly as possible.

But part of that process is setting the table—the place where everything is going to happen. If the table is poorly set, even the most sumptuous meal may seem like cheap takeout.

The same goes for your retirement. You can know when you're going to retire, plan on how you hope to retire, even have a specific retirement

Retire Right

There are a number of money management software programs available that can make the job a great deal less challenging. They allow you to set up a budget, track spending, watch your savings grow, and other chores. They can make getting a handle on money basics a good deal easier.

destination in mind. But until you get some basics in place, even the most comprehensively mapped-out retirement may encounter unnecessary snafus and challenges.

In this case, it comes down to a few financial basics—the preliminary steps that not only make your current life all the more enjoyable but set the stage for your retirement—to put you in the best position to devise and execute a retirement plan that's right for you. Taken unto themselves, they're not particularly challenging or involved. But, left ignored, they can undercut an otherwise solid retirement road map.

Keep an Eye on Your Spending

It goes without saying that, to save money for a happy and fulfilling retirement, you first need the money to save. No quantum physics there. For many of us, that happens automatically to a certain degree. For instance, if you have a 401(k) savings plan where you work, you may have funds withdrawn automatically from every paycheck without your ever having to lift a finger.

But, for many prospective retirees, a single source of funds is often inadequate to underwrite their retirement. Adding in Social Security benefits may still leave many retirees financially short.

That means it's often up to you to augment one element of a retirement funding program with another strategy, such as an Individual Retirement Account. And, to do that, you'll need funds to build up that account.

That makes your spending habits—no matter if you're 25 or 55—an imperative first step toward putting together a retirement program with the greatest chances of success. It makes sense—if your spending is out of control, you simply won't have the necessary funds to put toward your retirement (or, for that matter, toward any other substantial financial objective).

How do you know if your spending and money habits are as solid as they ought to be? Here are a few questions that may point you toward an answer:

◆ Do you find yourself carrying a credit card balance from one month to the next—or worse, growing in size from month to month (more about this in the following section)?

◆ Do you come to the end of the month with little or no money left over once all your necessary expenses have been met?

◆ For substantial purchases, do you find yourself investigating payment plans rather than having sufficient cash on hand to meet the entire expense up front?

◆ Do you have a realistic sense of where your money goes—and why?

These and similar questions may indicate money habits that are not as focused and well thought out as they might be. And, specific to your retirement, it may also suggest a waste of funds that could be earmarked toward your retirement, rather than simply inexplicably flitting off into the cosmos.

The answer for many is setting up and following a budget. That may seem as pleasant as root canal work without anesthesia, but a budget is undeniably the most reliable way of planning where you spend your money as well as knowing just where your money actually goes.

Retire Right _____

One effective way to set up a budget that's right for you is to track your spending for a couple of months. Simply establish a list of fixed expenses as well as discretionary spending and follow the money trail. This is far more effective than trying to set up a budget based on recommended parameters—a certain percentage for food, entertainment, and the like. A budget based on your requirements is bound to be more realistic—and, over the long haul, more effective.

Next, sit down and analyze your money habits. If you've been consistently spending more than your budget allows, this breakdown should offer a comprehensive view of where the holes might be. While some spending is fixed and immune to change—say, a mortgage or car payments—other sorts of discretionary spending can be prime targets for saving. For instance, one less lunch out a week can save $20 or so—that adds up to $1,000 a year (a grand that could be put toward your retirement). Getting books from the library rather than buying them, keeping an eye out for sales, and other strategies, implemented in concert, can reap terrific money-saving benefits.

Retire Right _____

We all know that impulse buying can put a huge dent in even the best mapped-out budget—particularly if it involves a pricey item. One strategy to avoid this: if you see that HD television that you're sure you simply cannot go on living without, give your urge a week or two. Chances are good that, on further reflection, that plain old box you've been staring at these many years will seem more than adequate. (And, if you still feel the need, you can do the prudent thing by beginning to set money aside to buy the television intelligently rather than rushing out to the store, credit card at the ready.)

Two last thoughts on a budget. First, as suggested by the examples given here, it's rare that any of us hits a budgetary home run—that one bit of spending that, unto itself, makes all the difference in our financial well-being. Instead, concentrate on smaller items—they can add up, and often very quickly.

The other point is that mapping out and following a budget before you retire not only frees up cash for your retirement savings, it's also excellent practice for when you do retire. Getting into the habit of following a financial spending plan will become second nature when you're living off what you have saved rather than what you're earning. That, too, can help ensure a happy and fulfilling retirement.

The Perils of Credit Card Debt

For many, the heart of spending issues is credit card use—or, better put, credit card abuse. It's not surprising—credit cards are plentiful, relatively easy to obtain, and often exceedingly generous in the amount of credit they afford their users.

On the surface, that may suggest a wealth of financial potential. Trouble is, that potential far too often morphs into problems. The American Bankers Association reports that the average American household owes $8,000 on credit cards. That would be horrific enough unto itself, but couple that amount with the sting of ongoing interest charges—many of which can easily top 13 percent—and you have a problem that is not only big but also growing constantly.

It's also a rather surreptitious form of growth. Many cardholders only see one number on their monthly statement—the minimum payment. This, which usually represents roughly 2.5 percent of the balance you owe, is the absolute least you have to pay that particular month. In the case of the $8,000 average cited above, that comes to a modest $200. No biggie, right?

Trouble is, paying the minimum is little more than treading water, financially speaking. The minimum basically buys you another month—while interest continues to accrue on the remaining balance. For example, paying the $200 minimum on an $8,000 balance on a 13 percent interest card will take 263 months (nearly 22 years!) to pay off the entire sum.

Even worse, you'll pay nearly $2,600 in interest alone.

How does this all relate to planning your retirement? For one thing, excessive credit card debt is yet another hole draining cash away from your retirement goals. For another, it's a habit you don't want to carry with you into your retirement. Trying to enjoy life on a fixed amount of money can prove downright perilous if interest charges are steadily eating away at your nest egg.

That makes sensible credit card management another retirement prerequisite that warrants your attention. If credit card abuse is of concern to you, here are some strategies to bring it under control—and, in the process, better position you for retirement:

- Don't carry a wallet full of cards. Ubiquitous as credit card offers can be, there's rarely a need to carry more than two cards (one for regular use, the other for emergencies).

- If you have substantial balances on more than one card, choose the one with the highest interest rate and begin paying that down as aggressively as possible.

- If you carry a large balance on a card with a hefty interest rate, another option is transferring the balance to another card—one that often levies no interest charges for as long as a year or so. But, if that appeals, commit to paying down the transferred balance as fast as possible. Sooner or later, interest on the new card will spike—often substantially. This is known as a *teaser card*.

- If you carry balances on several high-rate cards, look into consolidating that debt into one card. That can lower your payments, not to mention making the task of paying down your debt a bit simpler.

def•i•ni•tion

Cards that dangle no interest or low interest for an introductory period are often called **teaser cards**. It's an apt name—interest rates on teaser cards often jump to high levels, often much more expensive than other cards that don't offer the introductory carrot of no interest.

Other Ways to Cut Your Spending

Setting up and following a budget and reigning in your use of credit cards are two powerful ways to get your financial house in order—and, in so doing, free up money that can be set aside for retirement. Many people might assume that these forms of discretionary spending are the primary targets for cost savings.

Not necessarily. Other, more fixed costs can also prove lucrative savings sources, provided you know where to look and what to take advantage of (and what to avoid).

Pay Down Your Mortgage

Owning a home is the most significant financial obligation most of us carry. With regard to planning for your retirement, owing as little as possible on your home is advantageous on several levels. First, paying off your mortgage as quickly as possible eliminates a significant financial load that much sooner. By the same token, should you decide to sell your home at any point—prior to or after retiring—your *equity* will be that much greater. And that means a greater overall profit.

def•i•ni•tion

Equity refers to the difference between the value of your home and the amount you owe on your mortgage. For instance, a $300,000 home with a remaining mortgage of $175,000 results in equity of $125,000.

On the surface, paying off a mortgage that can easily reach into hundreds of thousands of dollars may seem insurmountable. And, in many cases, paying off a mortgage completely is, in fact, unrealistic. But you can pay down a good chunk of the mortgage rather painlessly—and, in the process, save yourself thousands of dollars in interest costs.

Retirement Reality

Surprised at how much even a small extra payment can do to cut both the life of your mortgage as well as the overall cost? It's simple—every conventional payment you make goes to pay both interest and principal. Anything extra goes directly toward paying down the principal—and, over time, cutting both the overall life of the loan as well as the amount owed.

Here's a quick calculation to illustrate how this works. Say you take out a $150,000 30-year mortgage at 6 percent interest. That means a monthly payment of $899. Under that arrangement, paying off the loan over the full 30 years means interest payments totaling more than $173,000—more than the cost of the loan itself!

However, tacking on a modest $50 a month to your payment lets you pay off the loan 4 years sooner—and, in the process, save some $26,000 in interest.

Upping that to an extra $100 per month pays off the loan in only 23 years and saves some $45,000 in interest.

Refinance Your Mortgage

In the not-too-distant past, a mortgage was a far more expensive proposition than it is today. I remember selling a home and taking back a small mortgage to help the buyer afford the property—at the "bargain" rate of 13 percent.

Not so these days. As of this writing, 30-year fixed mortgages are going for less than 6 percent. And that makes refinancing your mortgage worthy of your consideration should you be paying much more than that.

Again, simple math paints a vivid picture. A $200,000 7 percent mortgage runs $1,330 per month. Over the full life of the loan, interest costs total $279,000. By comparison, the same size loan at 6 percent cuts the monthly cost down to $1,199—and over 30 years, saves $68,000 in interest. Find a mortgage even cheaper than that, and your savings are even greater.

A slam dunk? Not necessarily. Much depends on how expensive the refinancing process is—and, in turn, how long you will have to stay in your home for enough savings to accrue to make the deal worthwhile. According to Bankrate.com, the average closing cost for a 30-year fixed $200,000 mortgage was $3,024 in 2006. In the example we provided earlier, that means you would have to stay in your home roughly 23 months to offset the expense of the refinance ($131 saved per month times 23 months).

 Golden Years Gaffes

One misleading aspect to the "average" closing costs is that expenses differ significantly from one area of the country to another—not to mention one lender to another. For instance, in the Bankrate.com survey, New York was at the top of the list in terms of closing expenses—$3,887. Halfway across the country, Missouri checked in with the cheapest at $2,713. So make sure you know your closing costs to make certain the refinance is worth it.

That makes aggressive shopping imperative to determine whether refinancing genuinely makes sense. Be sure to call at least three lenders to compare costs—both in terms of the interest they offer as well as any expenses connected with the loan. Various costs—ranging from title insurance to document preparation fees—may vary considerably. Be certain to obtain a complete list of every cost associated with the refinance. If a number seems unnecessarily high, ask the lender why it's so expensive.

Retire Right _____

Although the cost of refinancing can be substantial, the current era of skinny interest rates can be advantageous to homeowners looking to retool their mortgages. The reason: home refinancing booms when interest rates are low, making the market exceedingly competitive. If you feel a fee or cost attached to a refi is too high—or even completely unjustifiable—lenders hungry for your business may be willing to dicker. So don't assume that closing costs are cast in stone—they may well not be.

Put All Those Savings to Use

Okay, so now you've been able to trim your expenses on any number of fronts. You've got a budget that works, your debt is manageable, and your housing expenses are as modest as anyone could hope for.

Now it's time to consider how to best handle all that cash you've freed up. (For purposes of this discussion, we'll limit the topic to cash management and savings—issues such as investments will be addressed in Chapters 9, 10, 11, and 12. Why does intelligent cash management matter to your retirement? For one thing, like the expenses we've already covered in this chapter, small differences can bring significant rewards. Moreover, cash not only is necessary to pay bills and other expenses, it serves as a stabilizing force for other elements of your financial life. While things such as stocks and mutual funds can rise and fall, cash remains a constant, an element of accessible security.

Finally, knowing how to handle your cash in the most effective manner possible is as important a habit as any you want to develop prior to retirement. Although you may stop working, your money should not. And that means a thoughtful plan of savings and cash management.

Rule One—Pay Yourself First

This bit of advice is somewhat worn, but it bears repeating in terms of smart cash and savings management—pay yourself first. Put another way: treat your savings as every bit as much an obligation as any other bill—in fact, even more so. Putting off saving until other obligations have been addressed often makes saving impossible. By the same token, making it a priority helps ensure that your saving will be both steady and reliable.

Retire Right _____

Here's a great way to turn what once was a liability into an asset. If you've just finished paying off some sort of debt—say, a credit card balance or a car loan—keep making the same payments. Only put the money into savings. After all, if you could afford it while the debt was still in play, there's no reason to stop once the debt is out of the picture.

Other ways to get into the savings habit:

♦ Take advantage of payroll deduction where you work.

♦ Earmark financial windfalls for savings. These can include tax refunds, bonuses, and rebates.

♦ Go monastic. Pick a week every so often and try to cut out all discretionary spending, from lunch out to movie rentals. Save the money you would have otherwise spent. You may surprise yourself with how little you genuinely need.

♦ Break it down. One of the potential discouragements of saving for a particular goal is the size—for instance, a $2,000 HD TV may seem out of the question. Make that less imposing by breaking it down into smaller, more manageable targets—say, $50 a week. That can bring large financial goals into better focus.

Golden Years Gaffes _____

When delineating savings goals, don't overlook the importance of an emergency fund. This is money earmarked for unexpected expenses—everything from a fender bender to a hospital stay. Conventional wisdom says this should be the equivalent of three months' living expenses.

Where to Stash Your Savings

Now that you're in the saving habit, the question is, where's the best place to keep your savings? First off, with apologies to our Depression-era ancestors, your mattress does not qualify. Although the feel of your money that close to you may have been comforting in an era of failing banks, proximity came to the expense of your money doing little more than sitting there.

Still, it did offer one important benefit—ready access. This, in fact, is a central question with regard to where you keep savings and other forms of cash—how often do you need to get to it and how quickly? If ready access is of paramount importance, savings and checking accounts should certainly be at the top of the list.

Unfortunately, keeping your money in a conventional savings or checking account isn't a whole lot better than stuffing the cash into the mattress. While many checking accounts pay no interest whatsoever, as of this writing, conventional interest-bearing checking accounts were averaging a paltry 1.43 percent. Still, there is some good news: as is the case with all bank deposits, your money is insured by the federal government through the Federal Deposit Insurance Corporation (FDIC).

Retire Right

Here's one checking account tip to stash away for when you're actually retired. Many banks offer perks and advantages to customers age 55 and older. These can include free checks, fee-free access to automated teller machines, and possibly better deals on loans. Shop around and compare what's available when the time comes.

Happily, there are alternatives to run-of-the-mill savings accounts. One worth investigating is Internet-based checking and savings accounts. These can pay higher interest than conventional savings (a recent, random glance found several Internet-based banks offering interest of 5 percent or better).

Although it is possible to earn something with these sorts of interest-bearing checking accounts, there are drawbacks. First, many banks mandate substantial minimums to open such accounts (again, a random glance found some minimums as high as $1,500). By the same token, other banks have low minimums to open an account but require that you maintain hefty minimums to avoid monthly fees. For instance, one bank lets you open an account with a skinny $25, but requires an average $1,000 without incurring fees.

Other options that offer quick access to cash:

- **Money Market Deposit Accounts.** These are served up by banks and, like savings accounts, are FDIC insured. They also pay slightly higher interest than conventional savings. The downside is that minimums to open an account can be high and many accounts limit the number of transactions.

- **Money Market Funds.** These are offered by brokerage houses and mutual fund families. Since they invest in relatively safe choices such as government securities, their return is reasonable (as of this writing, money market funds commonly top 5 percent interest). However, they are not FDIC insured.

Less Access, Better Returns

If, by chance, you don't need ongoing access to your money—perhaps you have cash in a checking account and are in a position to stash other funds away for the time being—your options increase, including:

◆ **Certificates of Deposit (CDs).** Offered by banks and brokerage houses, a CD is a form of promissory note—the lender effectively promises to pay you a certain interest rate if you let them hold your money for a specified amount of time. CDs can range anywhere from as short as three months to upwards of five years. The plus is that their returns better money markets—a five-year CD might pay as much as 5 percent interest. The drawback is the commitment—if you redeem the CD before the specified time frame, you'll owe a penalty.

◆ **Treasury Securities.** These are issued and backed by the federal government. They come in various forms, including securities, notes, savings bonds, and other formats. We cover these in greater detail in Chapter 12.

The Least You Need to Know

◆ Set up a budget that can identify money leaks—funds that can be put toward your retirement.

◆ Bring your credit card debt under control. Pay down your existing cards or investigate cards with teaser rates.

◆ Paying down or refinancing your mortgage can also save you thousands of dollars in interest over the long term.

◆ Once you have money to save, investigate your savings options carefully. Don't just consider the return you can get on your savings—think also about how much access you may want to your money.

◆ Consider a budget, debt control, and smart savings a valuable warm-up for your retirement—where smart money habits will go a long way to help ensure a comfortable, satisfying retirement.

Part 2

Where the Money Comes From

Part 2 moves you into the mechanics of putting together a retirement funding program to not only reach your goals, but do so efficiently. I'll cover company-sponsored retirement plans, Social Security, and individualized savings programs. From there, we'll look at more specific financial elements and how they may fit your particular situation, including mutual funds, stocks, bonds, and other choices.

On the Job

In This Chapter

- ◆ Defined benefit plans—traditional and otherwise
- ◆ Defined contribution plans
- ◆ 401(k)s
- ◆ Stock options and other perks
- ◆ Keoghs and variants
- ◆ Simplified employee pensions

For many of us, our workplace is not merely the source of income with which we meet our current living expenses. It's also a primary source of money earmarked for retirement.

That may be a constant, but the makeup of workplace retirement options has changed dramatically. For one thing, retirement choices in the traditional workplace have shifted away from programs where the employer provided the benefits program exclusively. Now, employee participation and choice are more the norm. And that showcases the importance of knowing how the program where you work operates and which choices you should make for the best possible results.

But there's a further dynamic at play. With the rise of entrepreneurs, small businesses, and the self-employed, so, too, have the number of retirement funding options grown.

In this chapter, we'll walk through the various choices you likely face in the retirement program where you work. From there, we'll tackle some guidelines and suggestions to help you make the most of them.

The Changing Face of Company-Sponsored Retirement

An old stereotype still holds with many of us when it comes to pension plans. You work at a company for much of your life. You hit 65, you get a modest farewell meal and a small television (where to put that, who knows?) and, from there, you start getting monthly checks. Moreover, these are checks to which, other than your intelligence and sweat, you have contributed nothing. They're exclusively company-funded.

No more—at least not so exclusively. A few statistics illustrate the shift. According to the federal Bureau of Labor Statistics, roughly one third of all private industry workers took part in a defined benefit plan in 1992–1993—the traditional, time-tested retirement program we just outlined. By the same token, 35 percent took part in a defined contribution plan—a program where the employee contributed in some fashion to his or her retirement and, as such, had a degree of choice and decision in the program.

By 2000, the number of workers in defined contribution plans was relatively unchanged—36 percent. However, the percentage taking part in defined benefit plans had plummeted to a scant 19 percent.

> **Retirement Reality**
>
> According to a 2004 survey by Mercer Human Resource Consulting, 96 percent of employers changed their retirement program in some way in the prior three years. Most also expected additional changes in the future.

Why the change? There are a broad array of reasons—decreased unionization, a rise in part-time workers, among others—but the overriding factor behind the move to defined contribution was a shift of risk. While an employer with a defined benefit program made all the contributions, so, too, did it take on all the risk, such as increased costs due to longevity and investment uncertainty. With defined contribution, employees also took on a share of that volatility (not to mention a share of the financial responsibility for funding the program).

While this may seem to all come down on the side of the employers, employees, too, have benefited greatly. First and foremost is a greater sense of control. While defined benefit plans pretty much took everything out of an employee's hands, defined contribution restores much of that control. As we'll see, depending on the program, you can enjoy establishing just how much you wish to contribute to your retirement (and, to a certain extent, where that money is invested). Moreover, an increasing number of retirement benefit options have become an important element in a company's employee package. Looked at another way: if you want the best people to come work for you, you need to offer a top-quality retirement package. One term to look for here is known as a *qualified retirement plan*.

def•i•ni•tion

A **qualified retirement plan** means the program has to adhere to certain governmental guidelines for tax purposes.

Defined Benefit Plans

In a broad sense, pension plans can be divided into two categories: defined benefit and defined contribution plans. The defined benefit plan is the more traditional, so we'll hit that one first.

In a nutshell, a defined benefit plan is a form of guarantee. You work a certain number of years for a company, you earn a certain salary and, upon retirement, you are guaranteed a monthly check based on those factors. Funds for the program are invested by the company and managed accordingly. In that sense, it's completely hands-off for the employee—all you have to do is work and let the company handle the rest.

> **Retirement Reality**
>
> The first defined benefit program dates back to the mid 1700s in the United States, when a church set up a financial fund to benefit the widows and orphans of deceased ministers.

How much this can come to depends on how long you worked for the company, how much you made, and other factors. However, most employers use one of three methods to determine how much pension recipients will receive:

- ◆ **Flat benefit plans** are the most simple and straightforward. As the name implies, here you receive a set monthly amount based on how long you worked for a company.

- ◆ **Final pay plans** can offer the biggest payout, as they average your salary over the last several years you're employed at a company. After you retire, this average becomes the basis for your monthly benefit, based also on how long you were employed at the company.

- ◆ **Career average plans** are similar to final pay programs, only here it's based on the average of all the years you work for a company.

Retire Right _____

Just how much defined benefit plans translate into actual income will differ. As a general rule, most are designed so that, coupled with Social Security benefits, employees can expect to receive roughly two thirds of their working income after retirement.

Although a regular monthly check is the most straightforward payment option, there are other choices in a defined benefit program. One is a lump sum. Here, you receive all the money due you in a single payment. It is then up to you to handle the money properly to ensure that it lasts for as long as you'll need it.

Although the lump sum option has its advantages—if nothing else, it puts a major financial element of your retirement squarely in your hands—there are critical issues to bear in mind. First, it's essential to roll the money into an appropriate account, such as an IRA. If you take legal possession of the funds in any way, you may be hit with taxes. Additionally, you will need to work out a program of withdrawals to ensure an adequate income for yourself while keeping an adequate amount of money in place to last as long as you'll need it.

Golden Years Gaffes _____

Lump sum distributions have serious and potentially complicated tax implications. Make sure you understand them by talking with your company's human resources department or a tax professional before choosing a lump sum distribution.

If a lump sum doesn't appeal, there are also options for payout programs other than the basic monthly check. This is known as annuity options (see Chapter 5 for annuities you can buy on your own).

As a general rule, the longer the annuity option you select, the smaller your monthly benefit will be. Options include:

- **Joint and survivor.** Here, your spouse or someone else who depends on your income continues to receive pension benefits even if you die. Payments are usually lower than other options, since the assumption is that someone will continue to live for a long time. But it does provide the greatest amount of security.

- **Ten-year certain.** This specifies a 10-year payout program and offers the highest monthly benefit. This may be suited to someone in poor health who may not live longer than 10 years.

- **Ten-year certain/life annuity.** This is something of a hybrid between the monthly check and the 10-year certain. This can pay you monthly amounts for the rest of your life but, if you die before 10 years, your spouse or someone else only receives payments for the rest of the 10-year period.

Cash Balance Plans

Although many companies have opted out of defined benefit programs in favor of some form of contribution-based program, there have been some shifts within defined contribution plans themselves.

One such choice that has taken hold in a number of America's largest employers of late is known as a cash balance plan. This is something of a hybrid, incorporating a defined contribution component into a traditional defined benefit plan.

Like traditional plans, the company makes all contributions to employees' accounts. Likewise, benefits at retirement are based on the balance in those accounts.

But there are differences. For one thing, cash balance plans don't depend on investment returns that can't be predicted. Instead, employers specify a contribution—along with a rate of return on that contribution—which provides a predictable amount when an employee retires. If the investment actually produces less than guaranteed, the employer has to make up the shortfall. But, if returns are better than guaranteed, the excess can be rolled over into subsequent years' benefits. That reduces the cost of the program for the employer.

Since the plan specifies an account balance rather than a monthly payment at retirement, employees have the option of choosing a lump sum payment or an annuity. Additionally, if an employee moves on to another company prior to retirement, assets in a cash balance plan can be rolled into an IRA.

> **Retirement Reality**
>
> As of the writing of this book, one company that shifted away from traditional benefit to a cash balance program was Delta Airlines. The move—affecting all U.S. employees other than pilots—was expected to save the carrier some $500 million.

Pension Equity Plans

Another hybrid—albeit a relatively minor one (as of 2003, pension equity plans covered only 2 percent of defined benefit participants)—a pension equity plan is similar to a cash balance arrangement in that benefits are seen as a lump sum rather than monthly payments. However, while cash balance uses a system based on annual earnings, pension equity is a bit more complicated. Account balances are determined based on age, length of service, and level of salary when an employee terminates service at a company.

Defined Contribution Plans

As we mentioned earlier, defined benefit plans are not the only pension plan offered these days. Increasingly popular are defined contribution plans—in which you as the employee have an active role in choosing how much to save and where those savings go. In that respect, it puts you in the driver's seat when it comes to preparing for your retirement.

401(k) Plans

This is easily the most popular defined contribution plan—and with good reason. It provides a variety of powerful advantages—retirement savings, lower taxes, and the growth potential of a range of investments—within one financial vehicle.

In its essence, a 401(k) lets you save for your retirement by automatically having a certain portion of salary deducted from every paycheck you receive. To be more specific, it is actually deducted before you take possession of the check, which in turn reduces your federal taxable income. The money is then placed in the financial vehicle of your choosing. Depending on how your company plan works, that can take in everything from mutual funds to money markets to company stock. The money then grows on a tax-deferred basis.

If that sounds like a potent lineup, it is. First, consider the tax advantages. If you set aside 5 percent of an annual income of $60,000, that's $3,000 right there that you'll pay no federal taxes on (in the 25 percent tax bracket, that translates to a savings of $750). Set aside more, and your savings jump even more.

From there, the money grows tax-deferred—another plus. We've covered this elsewhere, but tax deferral is yet another powerful ally in your retirement funding program. To illustrate: if you save $500 a month for 20 years at an 8 percent return, you'll receive some $232,000 if you're in the 25 percent tax bracket. Put that money in a tax deferred account, and your payout jumps to $294,000—some $58,000 more.

Another possible advantage to a 401(k) is that your employer may offer a match. This is a contribution that your company kicks in every time you make a deposit in your 401(k). Depending on where you work, this can range from anywhere from 25 cents for every dollar you contribute up to a one-to-one match (with certain maximums).

Speaking of maximums, 401(k)s also let you be rather generous to yourself. Federal guidelines for 2007 allow a maximum of $15,500 in employee contributions every year. Even better, that upper limit will likely be raised in coming years. And the limit is $20,500 if you're 50 or older.

Additionally, 401(k)s often let you choose how to invest your money (unlike defined benefit plans, where the company generally calls the shots). Here, you can tailor your choices to match both your goals and your tolerance for risk. You can choose something as conservative as money market funds all the way up to individual stocks.

However, notice we said "often." 401(k)s can differ greatly as to the range of investment choices they offer participants. According to federal statistics, in 2002, 81 percent of all employees taking part in 401(k)s and similar programs were able to choose how they invested their contributions. Unfortunately, only 5 percent within that group had seven or more investment options.

You can even access your 401(k) without incurring early withdrawal penalties. Many companies allow you to borrow from your 401(k), usually up to half the money you have in the account. You can also get to the money via a "hardship withdrawal." This means any substantial and immediate financial obligation that you cannot pay using any other source, such as medical bills.

Finally, 401(k)s are portable. Unless you're not fully vested (see below) you can roll the proceeds from one 401(k) over into another plan when you change jobs.

Of course, there are drawbacks to 401(k)s. For one thing, there are usually only certain times of the year when you can sign up to participate. Some employers, in fact, can require you to be on the job for a certain amount of time before you join. And, like most any other retirement plan, access the money without any of the exceptions we listed earlier, and you're hit with taxes and penalties.

 Golden Years Gaffes

Although you can borrow from your 401(k), keep that as a last resort. If you leave your job or get fired, you have to pay the money back quickly or else the IRS will treat the money as a withdrawal—meaning taxes and penalties.

Lastly, 401(k)s also have vesting provisions—specifically, the money contributed by an employer under a matching program. In some companies, you have to remain for several years before you're fully vested and, in effect, all the funds in your 401(k) are yours. Other companies have incremental vesting arrangements—20 percent 1 year, 20 percent the next, and so on.

Know, too, there are several sorts of 401(k)s. The most common is the traditional plan. This includes all the usual 401(k) features, including vesting. Another 401(k) is known as a "safe harbor." This is similar to a regular 401(k), except for the fact that an employee is immediately vested in any employer contributions. A third plan is called the simple 401(k) plan. This allows small businesses to set up 401(k)s easily and, as such, is subject to fewer limitations than programs run by larger concerns.

Other Options

Depending on where you work, other options may be available to help you build a financial foothold for your retirement. They include:

- ◆ Profit sharing.
- ◆ Stock bonus plan.
- ◆ Employee stock ownership plan (ESOP).

Profit Sharing

With this program, your company is obligated to kick in a certain amount of money equivalent to a portion of your salary. The downside is that it can be largely performance specific. If the company has a gangbuster year, your profit sharing benefit can be substantial. If, on the other hand, the company stumbles, your profit sharing cut may be zilch.

Stock Bonus Plan

This is similar to a profit sharing plan, only your benefit is in the form of company stock rather than a cash payout.

Employee Stock Ownership Plan (ESOP)

This plan allows employees to buy stock in the company—alternatively, the company may buy stock for employees itself. From there, any appreciation in the stock's value occurs tax-free.

These options can provide a terrific means of further bolstering your retirement nest egg. However, they do carry risks. For instance, if your company offers an ESOP but you have genuine doubts about the firm's long-term financial solvency, you may be wise to steer clear. If at all possible, the volatility of these sorts of programs are best counterbalanced by other retirement savings choices, such as an IRA you start and fund on your own.

Keoghs and Variations on the Theme

Up to this point, our discussion has focused exclusively on employees—people who, in some manner or other, work for someone else.

But, these days, chances are good that you are self-employed or operate a small business with others working for you.

That puts workplace retirement directly on your shoulders. But, as workplace programs have grown and evolved into various forms, so, too, have programs for small businesses and the self-employed increased and matured. Here's an overview of your options.

Keogh Plans

This is the prototypical—and best known—of all choices for small businesses and the self-employed. Named after Eugene Keogh—the congressman who helped push the proposal through Congress—a Keogh is a tax-deferred retirement plan that lets small business owners and the self-employed save money for retirement tax-free. In the case of small businesses, that applies to any employees as well.

One of the most appealing features of Keoghs are their contribution limits. Depending on the specifics of the plan, you are allowed to save as much as 25 percent of your net income—up to $44,000—every year. On top of that, all those contributions are completely tax-deductible. Although proceeds from a Keogh are taxed upon withdrawal, all funds in Keoghs grow on a tax-deferred basis until they're withdrawn.

There are, of course, certain drawbacks and hurdles to Keogh plans. As opposed to other self-employment retirement funding options, such as Simplified Employee Pension plans, Keoghs can be a bit tricky to set up (not to mention often requiring the services of an accountant or some other money professional to help maintain). Moreover, if you have any employees, you're required by law to include them in the plan as well—and to contribute the same percentage that you do to your own account. And, like most every other retirement plan, there are penalties for accessing the money before age $59\frac{1}{2}$.

Keoghs come in two primary forms:

 ◆ Money purchase plans

 ◆ Profit sharing plans

Money Purchase Plans

The beauty of this arrangement is that all contributions are fixed. Limits are 25 percent of net income, up to $44,000. The drawback is that you have a set amount you have to contribute each year, regardless of how much you make in a given year. That, in turn, can limit how much you can set aside—particularly frustrating in profitable years when you can afford to save more.

That boondoggle is addressed with the profit sharing plan.

Profit Sharing Plans

These plans allow for a good deal more flexibility when determining contribution amounts from one year to the next. Although the IRS stipulates that you must have a "definite formula" for allocating contributions, you generally have the freedom to be particularly generous in up years, and rather tightfisted in down years. Like money purchase plans, upper contribution limits are 25 percent of net income or $44,000.

Retire Right

Keoghs are not just for those who run a small business or who work for themselves full-time. You can also set one up if you run a part-time business in addition to other more conventional forms of employment.

Other Options

If a Keogh seems unduly complicated, there are alternatives for small business owners and those who work for themselves.

Individual (or Self-Employed) 401(k)s

These are a nice deal for someone who works on their own and has no plans to bring on any employees in the future. Introduced in 2002, one of its biggest advantages is higher contribution limits—up to $45,000 every year. Unlike Keoghs, it also has a "catch-up" provision which allows for additional contributions for persons aged 50 and older. Finally, setup and maintenance of the program—a real potential snafu with conventional Keoghs—can be considerably less time-consuming and expensive with an individual 401(k). Also, the payroll deduction function is the same as the regular 401(k): $15,500 or $20,500.

The downside of this option is its specificity to those working on their own. So, if personnel expansion plans are in your future, this is not the option to select.

SIMPLE IRA

The name suggests simplicity, but it's actually an acronym for Savings Incentive Match Plan. This is particularly suited to someone whose self-employment income is relatively modest—$30,000 annually or less.

Your income may be small, but the percentage you can contribute isn't. A SIMPLE Plan lets you save upwards of $10,500 a year as of 2007 (you can also tack on 2 to 3 percent of your income). Like other choices, there are catch-up provisions for persons aged 50 and up who want to add some extra muscle to their retirement savings.

That can translate to significant advantages over other retirement options. To illustrate: if you earn the maximum $30,000 a year, you could actually contribute $11,500 to a SIMPLE plan ($10,500 max plus 3 percent of $30,000). That's a sight more than other retirement plans, such as a conventional Keogh (there, your upward contribution limit would be $7,500—25 percent of your $30,000 income).

Simplified Employee Pensions

This retirement funding option warrants particular attention because it is as simple a choice as you can find among other choices—yet offers powerful benefits and advantages.

Simplified Employee Pensions (or SEPs) are something of a hybrid between a Keogh and an IRA. On the one hand, like a Keogh just how much you can contribute is determined by your income. And, it's exceedingly generous—as of 2007, you could contribute as much as 25 percent of compensation, up to a maximum of $45,000 (this amount, by the way, is subject to annual cost of living adjustments for the future). Moreover, like a Keogh, you can also set up SEPs for any employees you may have.

Like an IRA, how you choose to invest a SEP is entirely up to you. You can be as aggressive—stock, mutual funds—or as conservative—money markets, certificates of deposit—as your personal preference and investment goals dictate. Therein lies another plus if you have SEPs for any employees: not only do they have complete freedom of choice as to where they invest their SEP accounts, the burden of making a choice is theirs, rather than yours.

However, despite those crossover points, a SEP has certain advantages over Keoghs and IRAs. First, unlike Keoghs, SEPs are a snap to set up and maintain. And, unlike IRAs and their wash of deductibility provisions, all contributions to SEPs under the maximum allowed by law are fully tax-deductible (and, from there, grow on a tax-deferred basis until withdrawals are made).

SEPs are also exceedingly flexible. You have virtual freedom of choice so far as contributions are concerned—some years you may wish to max out, other years you may wish to bypass any contribution altogether.

Whatever You Do, Do Something

By now, you should be convinced of the critically important role workplace-based retirement programs can play in your overall strategy and approach to retirement—and why it behooves you to fund whatever program may be available to you to the absolute maximum.

But equally important is the conviction to do something. According to the Bureau of Labor Statistics, 85 percent of workers with access to some sort of retirement plan in 2005—be they defined benefit, contribution, or both—actually took part.

On the surface, 85 percent may seem a solid statistic. But what of the other 15 percent? All lucky heirs to opulent fortunes? Or simply misinformed about the importance of taking full advantage of their workplace retirement opportunities?

Let's close with this thought—whatever program may be available to you where you work is every bit as important a piece of your retirement puzzle as any other. If you work someplace where they offer a plan, use it. If you work on your own, be sure to set one up for yourself. If you happen to work in the rare place that does not offer a retirement plan, set one up on your own, such as an IRA.

Whatever you do—be sure to do something. And the sooner you start, the happier and more fulfilling a retirement you will enjoy at the other end of the line.

The Least You Need to Know

- ◆ Most companies are shifting away from defined benefit plans—where the company contributes to an employee's retirement—to defined contribution plans, where the employee contributes and has a more active role.

- A defined benefit plan is a form of guarantee. You work a certain number of years for a company, you earn a certain salary and, upon retirement, you are guaranteed a monthly check based on those factors.

- A 401(k) plan is the most popular form of defined contribution. It saves you on taxes, grows tax-deferred, and your company may match a portion of your contributions.

- Other defined contribution plans include employee profit sharing and programs where the company lets you buy stock in the firm.

- Keogh plans are a popular retirement funding option for the self-employed and small business owner. Although they offer generous contribution limits, they can be complicated to set up and administer.

- A far more simple option is a Simplified Employee Pension. These allow for tax-deductible contributions and tax-deferred growth, but are much simpler to manage than a Keogh.

Chapter 8

Social Security

In This Chapter

- ◆ A brief history
- ◆ How Social Security works
- ◆ What you can expect to get
- ◆ The life expectancy game
- ◆ Other benefits
- ◆ Will it be there?

To say that Social Security has been on the minds of many Americans of late would be as gross an understatement as you are likely to hear. Social Security has been a hotbed of attention, with concerns about the system running out of money, future generations facing lesser benefits as Social Security taps into cash reserves, and other like worries.

A major focal point of this chapter will be to explain what Social Security is (and what it is not), as well as discuss how the system will play a pivotal role in your retirement. In so doing, we'll also try to distinguish between reality and angst-ridden concerns less rooted in the truth. In so doing, we'll try to be as informative as we are reassuring.

A Little History Lesson

One thing that can greatly help our understanding of Social Security—and, in turn, the role it plays in our retirement—is a grasp of the history behind the program.

Social Security was conceived and enacted during the Great Depression. Spearheaded by President Franklin Roosevelt and signed by him into law in 1935, one of the primary goals of the program was to address severe poverty among senior citizens wracked by the effects of the Depression. At the time, estimates held that half of all retirees lived below the poverty level.

The basic methodology of Social Security was to provide a source of income to retired people as well as the unemployed. The program also incorporated a death benefit. The program was underwritten by a payroll tax, paid in part by both employers and employees.

Retirement Reality
Self-employed people are obligated to pay the entire amount that goes to Social Security. They do, however, get a tax break to mitigate the extra expense.

Social Security was actually introduced in 1937. The first Social Security payment was made in 1940 to Ida Mae Fuller of Vermont (who, by the way, went on to collect more than $20,000 in benefits over the course of 35 years).

Needless to say, the program has been adjusted and amended a number of times since its inception. In the latter 1930s, Social Security was broadened so that widowed, nonworking spouses of someone entitled to old-age benefits also became entitled to the same benefits. Orphans also became eligible.

Other additions:

♦ Congress added disability benefits for injured workers in 1956.

♦ Concerned over health-care cost for seniors, Congress established Medicare as an element of Social Security in 1965.

♦ Supplemental Social Security (SSI) was added on in 1974 to help low-income seniors and others with disabilities.

To date, despite some inherent controversy, Social Security remains one of the biggest and most popular social programs ever implemented in the United States. In 2004 alone, nearly 48 million American citizens received some $490 billion in benefits. And there's little doubt that those numbers will continue to grow in the years ahead.

There's also an essential point that needs to be made here in the context of our discussion of Social Security. From its very beginning and throughout its history, Social Security never was and never will be designed to fully underwrite anyone's retirement. These days, that's much too expensive a proposition. Rather, the program was designed to augment other sources of financial support, such as company retirement programs and individual savings. In that sense, Social Security is designed to help, not necessarily solve, the challenge of providing sufficient funds for retirement.

How the System Works

The heart of Social Security is retirement benefits. That, in turn, depends on how much income you earn during the course of your entire working career.

In its most simple form, Social Security tracks your income from the moment you receive your first paycheck to the very last one you endorse before it goes into the bank. The amount of money you're eligible for at retirement is based on this overall earnings total. You can begin to receive benefits at age 62, although they will be reduced (see our definition of normal retirement age below).

That's the system in a simplistic overview. How it really works is a good deal more complex. First, there's a "credit" system involved. You earn four credits for every year that you work. Over the course of your working career, you become eligible for Social Security benefits once you've accumulated 40 credits.

The major factor that determines your monthly post-retirement benefit is not how long you work. Rather, it's how much you earn. Taking the calculation a step further, Social Security takes your earnings for up to 35 years. More specifically, they have a certain maximum that they impose. As of 2006, that was $94,200 per year. Earn anything more than that, and Social Security doesn't take it into account when calculating benefits.

From there, the system adjusts your earnings to account for inflation, then computes a yearly average. Your benefit represents a portion of that average. The lower your income, the higher the percentage; the higher your income, the lower the percentage. Not only does this lend the system an overall sense of balance, the reasoning holds that, the more you earn, the greater your opportunity to save for your retirement. At least in theory, Social Security is less important to your retirement than someone who made less money.

How Much Will I Get?

That naturally begs the question: given my individual circumstances, how much can I expect to receive in Social Security benefits when I retire?

One element that effects how much you can expect to receive is known as full retirement age. For a good portion of Social Security's lifetime, full retirement age was set at age 65. That was the point at which you were eligible to receive full retirement benefits.

Congress adjusted this in the 1980s to implement something of a phase-in system for full eligibility. The following chart outlines the program:

Full Retirement Age

Year of Birth	Full Retirement Age
1937 and earlier	65
1938	65 and 2 months
1939	65 and 4 months
1940	65 and 6 months
1941	65 and 8 months
1942	65 and 10 months
1943–1954	66
1955	66 and 2 months
1956	66 and 4 months
1957	66 and 6 months
1958	66 and 8 months
1959	66 and 10 months
1960 and later	67

Okay, so now you know when the full deal kicks in. How much is that full deal going to come to? Perhaps the easiest and most accurate way to figure that out is to use Social Security's online benefits calculators located at www.ssa.gov/planners/calculators.htm. There, you can use one of three calculators: a quick version to give you a rough estimate with the least amount of input involved; a more detailed calculator that requires you to provide a complete earnings history; and a detailed calculator that provides the most accurate estimate possible (unlike the prior two, this one has to be downloaded).

But, before you make a dash for your laptop, let's run through a few scenarios using the quick calculator. Although these numbers are not designed to be definitive by any means, they should give a rough idea of how much you might expect Social Security to kick in—and, conversely, what you will need to do on your own to adequately augment that income.

Scenario #1: A worker born in 1950, planning on retiring in 2015 at age 65, with current earnings of $40,000 a year can expect to receive $1,138 in today's dollars come retirement. Adjust that amount for inflation, and the news is even better: $1,502 per month.

Scenario #2: Someone born in 1960 who makes $75,000 a year. Here, however, the planned retirement date is the same year—2015—meaning that the worker is opting for retirement early at age 55. That also means he will have to wait some 7 years before he can begin to receive Social Security benefits at age 62 (and at a reduced rate, since someone born in 1960 is deemed "normal" retirement age at 65). Monthly benefit: $1,279 ($2,279 when inflation is taken into account).

Now, let's push this worker out a bit to 2027—the year when full benefits kick in. If he can wait that long, monthly benefits jump to $1,945 (inflated: $3,958).

Scenario #3: A worker earning $100,000 a year, born in 1970, planning on retiring at 67 in 2037. Projected benefit: $2,368 (adjusted for inflation: $6,797).

These varied situations offer a range on insight. First, it gives you an idea of what you may expect. It also illustrates the role of normal retirement age and its impact on what you can expect to receive.

Lastly, it also shows how varied income ranges produce differing results from a percentage point of view. In the first scenario, without taking inflation into account, Social Security is effectively replacing some 34 percent of that worker's annual income. In the second scenario, the worker retiring early only receives some 20 percent of his prior income (this rises to 31 percent). In the third scenario, the highest earner of our group of three receives Social Security benefits totaling some 28 percent of his working life income.

Golden Years Gaffes

Does the situation in scenario #2 argue for waiting until you reach normal retirement age to start to receive benefits? Yes, in some circumstances. It all depends on what other things you have in place. If your full benefit is particularly important, it may behoove you to wait. If you have enough in place, you can afford to retire earlier and take the reduced benefit.

The Written Statement

It's not entirely up to you to find out how much you can expect from Social Security. Since 2000, the Social Security Administration has been mailing Personal Earnings and Benefit Statements to every person aged 25 and up who is participating in Social Security.

Basically, the statement summarizes your earnings to date—literally, from one year to another beginning with the first year you earned a paycheck. It also outlines what you can expect to receive in retirement benefits if you retire at age 62, your normal retirement age date, or at age 70.

Bear in mind that these estimates are very much estimates. For instance, in the statement the IRS says it assumes that your earnings will remain pretty much where they are up until the point you retire. Obviously, anyone who plans on raises and other forms of salary increase can expect greater retirement benefits than the Social Security assumption provides for.

Retire Right _____

If you're less than 25 years old and want to check out your Social Security earnings statement—or you have any questions about any statements you may have already received—contact the Social Security Administration at 1-800-772-1213.

The statement also reports what you can expect to receive in benefits should you become disabled (refer to the section on disability later in this chapter) as well as what various family survivors might expect to receive.

Not only is it important to review the statement to get a sense of what sort of Social Security benefits you may be tracking toward, it's also essential to check the report for any mistakes or outright omissions.

When Should You Start Receiving Benefits?

The scenarios we laid out in the prior section point out something of a quandary for many prospective retirees: when is the best time to start receiving Social Security benefits?

As we've noted, you can start getting checks as early as age 62. But, as we also discussed, the checks will be smaller.

On the other hand, if you wait until normal retirement age, your checks will likely be fewer, but larger (particularly so if you hold out until age 70).

There's no getting around it—if you opt to receive Social Security before you reach full retirement age, the amount of benefit you receive is permanently reduced. More specifically, the reduction translates to $^5/_9$ of 1 percent for every month you retire early—6.67 percent for every year.

Following is a chart that summarizes the impact of early retirement—from six months early up to five years:

Months early	Percentage of Benefits
6	96.67
12	93.33
18	90
24	86.67
30	83.33
36	80
42	77.5
48	75
54	72.5
60	70

Here's how the reduction can work in a payment scenario. Let's assume that, under normal retirement age, you would be eligible for $1,750 a month. You decide to retire eight months early. That would make your benefit percentage roughly 96.2 percent of your total amount (100 percent minus eight times $^5/_9$ of 1 percent). Translated: your monthly benefit is now $1,683, or 96.2 percent of $1,750.

That means it's important to calculate just how much benefit you might receive by opting for smaller checks at an earlier date. On the one hand, although the checks may be smaller, you're likely to get more of them than if you wait. Additionally, if you have plans that mandate a little additional funding—say, a special vacation—it makes sense to trade a little additional income for access to the funds.

On the other hand, if your financial plan depends on receiving every penny you can from Social Security, it's probably wise to hold off until you reach normal retirement age. If nothing else, try to hold off as long as possible. As the chart above illustrates, a year or two can make a significant difference in the size of check you'll eventually receive.

The Late Retirement Boost

There is another side to the formula that affects the size of your Social Security benefit. Rather than retiring before you reach normal retirement age, you can actually boost the size of your benefit if you continue to work beyond normal retirement.

Up until recently, there really was little incentive to work any longer than you had to. As recently as 1990, the government offered a paltry 3.5 percent increase in benefits for every year you continued to work beyond full retirement age. Given that you would receive fewer payments on top of very little benefit, calculations held that many people had to live well into their 90s just to break even.

Recognizing that it simply wasn't working, Congress has since upped the benefit for working past normal retirement. In a nutshell, if you were born anytime after 1943, you can expect to receive an annual bonus of 8 percent in Social Security benefits for every year you work beyond full retirement.

The benefits kick in in other ways. For one thing, the 8 percent bonus doesn't take into account the effects of inflation, further boosting the amount you'll receive. And, on top of that, by working longer, you'll effectively increase the income by which your Social Security benefit is calculated. That increases your monthly check as well.

> ### Retirement Reality
>
> Why the largesse on the feds' part? They certainly recognized the importance of providing retirees with every dollar possible. But offering perks for delaying means they can hang on to your money a bit longer, reducing the strain on the system as a whole.

Like opting for benefits prior to full retirement age, it's important to think carefully about the pluses and potential drawbacks of delaying your benefits. On the one hand, if you know the extra money will come in handy, consider extending the amount of time you work. On the other, working longer, in effect, does cut short your actual retirement time—something that most of us look forward to and which may not be worth a little extra spending money.

There is another option if you want to retire but don't want to forgo the extra windfall of working longer. Retire, but put off when you apply to receive Social Security benefits. Although you won't have any opportunity to boost your benefit by contributing additional income to the Social Security formula, you'll still be entitled to receive the annual 8 percent bonus. However, only do this if other elements of your financial picture are sound enough for you to forgo the additional funds provided by Social Security.

The Life Expectancy Game

Now seems an opportune time to address a central issue having to do with Social Security benefits—and, for that matter, most any other element that affects your retirement planning.

That topic is life expectancy—how long, based on statistical analysis, you can expect to live. That may seem akin to predicting the weather in terms of accuracy—and, to some extent, it is—but it's helpful to at least have a general sense of how long it's reasonable to assume you'll be sticking around. That can make the choice of when to receive Social Security benefits (and other aspects of your retirement's financial planning) a bit less intimidating.

According to the Social Security Administration's most recent statistic, a newborn male has a life expectancy of roughly 74 years. If you're a woman, it's a bit longer—79.

Of course, if you're reading this, chances are rather good that you're somewhere beyond the age of a newborn. And that's where numbers begin to shift in your favor. If, by chance, you're a man age 50, you can expect to live another 27 years. A woman age 50 can expect to make it to age 81.

The numbers improve all the more as you get older. A man hitting the "conventional" retirement age of 65 can expect to live until he's 81. A woman at the same 65 age point has a good chance of living until she's 84.

Should you take those numbers as gospel? Of course not. For one thing, they're averages, taking in everyone from nonsmokers to those with two-pack-a-day habits, from triathletes to people who only run back and forth to the refrigerator. But, look at the numbers and make a mental adjustment based on what you know about yourself. If

Retire Right _____

A complete life expectancy table can be found online at www.ssa.gov/OACT/ STATS/table4c6.html.

you take care of yourself, exercise, and do all the sorts of things you should, you may want to up those estimates a little bit. By the same token, if you treat your body as something less than a temple—or have a family history of disease that has curtailed the lives of relatives—you may want to trim back your expectancy (or, better yet, try to make changes for the better).

From there, apply what you know to your Social Security benefits. If you don't expect an unduly generous life expectancy, you may want to opt for receiving benefits sooner rather than later. On the other hand, if your life expectancy is solid, give serious thought to holding off on receiving Social Security benefits. If you live a particularly long time—and, as a result, drain down other retirement resources—those larger than they might have been Social Security checks may prove to be particularly handy.

Other Programs Under the Social Security Banner

That regular monthly check due you when you retire is certainly the best known—and, for many, the most anticipated—feature of Social Security. But don't make the mistake of assuming that's the length and breadth of your benefits. Far from it.

Benefits for Your Spouse

You work. Your wife or husband never has—and probably never will.

Surprise—your nonworking spouse may also be eligible for benefits under Social Security. Beginning at age 62, a nonworking spouse can begin receiving benefits amounting to roughly half of your benefits. Put another way, between the two of you, you can receive 150 percent of what you would get if you were only receiving your benefit alone.

> **Retirement Reality**
>
> The spousal benefit kicks in for divorced couples as well, provided the marriage lasted at least 10 years and the spouse doesn't remarry prior to age 60.

The news is even better if your spouse works. Under this arrangement, he or she is entitled to benefits based on earnings or 50 percent of your benefit—whichever is larger.

Benefits for Survivors

Not to be macabre, but your Social Security benefits may live on longer than you do. That's because the system also provides benefits for survivors.

> **Retire Right**
>
> Remember the written statement from Social Security you get that summarizes your benefits? It also offers an overview of various survivors' situations and expected benefits as well.

Just how much the benefit comes to depends—as it does with most any other Social Security calculation—on the amount of income you have earned through work credits. The amount also depends on the age of the beneficiaries as well as a family's situation. For instance, widows and widowers age 65 and older are eligible to receive 100 percent of what the deceased worker would have gotten. From age 63 down to 60, the amount is prorated back to some 70 percent of total benefits. However, a widow or widower with a child receives 75 percent, no matter their age.

Disability Coverage

Social Security also provides a form of insurance if you become disabled prior to retirement and are unable to work. The amount of coverage is contingent on the amount of time you have worked. If you qualify, benefits can begin as soon as five months after the disabling injury or illness occurs.

Unfortunately, the guidelines for qualifying for disability benefits can be restrictive. First and foremost, you must be unable to do any sort of substantial work—any work, not merely what you've been trained to do or have done in the past. Moreover, your condition has to have lasted—or be expected to last—at least one year or, even worse, be expected to result in your death.

 Retire Right

The amount you may qualify for in benefits is highly specific to your circumstances. However, you can download a disability benefits calculator at www.ssa.gov/OACT/anypia/anypia.html. Your written statement from Social Security also provides this information.

To apply, you will need to complete an application (this can be done online at www.ssa.gov/adultdisabilityreport). In addition, you will be interviewed in person by a Social Security representative.

If you are denied disability benefits, you have the right to appeal the decision (known as "reconsideration"). Here, your application is forwarded to a disability examiner other than the one who initially turned you down. Unfortunately, the vast majority of reconsidered applications are also rejected.

Will It Be Around?

Okay, now the $64 (make that $74, with inflation) question: What's the financial solvency of Social Security, and will it still be there when the time comes for me to retire?

Here's what we know for certain:

◆ Currently the Social Security Administration estimates there are some 36 million people age 65 or older. Their benefits are being funded by workers and employers currently paying into Social Security.

◆ By 2018, it is estimated that Social Security will, for the first time, begin to pay out more in benefits than it takes in. It is at that point that the system will have to begin tapping into interest paid from Social Security's trust fund to meet its obligations.

That's really all that's certain. Initially, estimates held that the trust fund would be completely exhausted by 2042. However, the Congressional Budget Office recently estimated it would take an additional 10 years for that to happen—at which point the system would only be able to pay 74 cents out of every dollar of scheduled benefits.

Moreover, there are many who argue that the system is by no means damaged—or, at the very least, as broken as many would make it out to be. For instance, the Economics Policy Institute claims that assumptions predicting a breakdown in Social Security are far too pessimistic. Moreover, they suggest that even minor changes, such as broadening the amount of wages and salaries subject to the Social Security payroll tax, would be adequate to address any foreseeable shortfalls.

We're not going to get into the debate of the various proposed fixes for Social Security. What we can do is acknowledge that Social Security is likely to be around for a good long time. And if, in fact, the system does ever encounter real danger, the political clout carried by Social Security would be far too potentially explosive for lawmakers not to act to fix it.

The Least You Need to Know

◆ Social Security should be considered an important element—but not the only element—in your retirement funding plan.

◆ Social Security benefits are based on your earnings. The more you earn, the higher your eventual benefit.

◆ You can begin receiving benefits at age 62. Your benefits, however, will be greater the longer you wait (and work).

◆ Social Security lets you increase your benefit by up to 8 percent per year if you continue to work beyond your full retirement age.

◆ Get to know what your life expectancy might be. It can help you calculate the optimal time to begin receiving Social Security benefits.

◆ Social Security isn't just a monthly check. The program also provides benefits for nonworking spouses, survivors benefits, and disability coverage.

Chapter 9

Let's Hear It for IRA!

In This Chapter

- A little history
- IRA's many advantages
- And his newest, best buddy—Roth
- Choosing between the two
- Should you convert?

By now, you should be getting the strong impression that there are a good many tools in your retirement funding toolbox—all designed to do their part, when used properly and consistently, to help you fund the retirement that you truly desire.

Well, meet one more—actually, two. Individual Retirement Accounts have been around for a while. Sometimes, that sort of long-term familiarity can dull certain charms, making even the sharpest-eyed of us a bit blind.

Don't make that mistake with IRAs. They may not be the freshest kid on the block, but their seniority suggests a staying power borne of flexibility and genuine utility.

But choosing an IRA these days isn't as simple as it used to be. Now, it's imperative to consider the pluses and drawbacks of the varied options available to you—and in turn, to make the best choice that fits naturally into your overall retirement funding strategy.

A Short History Lesson

Our good friend IRA (or, as he goes by in a more formal capacity, Individual Retirement Account) has been around for a good long while. First approved by Congress in 1981, the original IRA let you contribute as much as $2,000 toward your retirement in an account specifically designated for that purpose.

The advantages didn't end there. First off, everyone could deduct their IRA contributions in the year in which they made the contribution. This was the case regardless of whether they had another retirement plan where they worked or not. Additionally, the money grew tax-deferred. That means nary a whiff of tax impact until you began to withdraw the money, which you could do without penalty beginning at age $59\frac{1}{2}$.

If that sounds idyllic, it was—in fact, too perfect, at least in the eyes of Capitol dwellers. Using the moniker "tax reform," Congress in 1986 began to tinker with the IRA. For one thing, the new version mandated strict tax-deductibility parameters—the days when everyone could contribute and deduct their contribution went the way of pet rocks and mood rings. For example: if you were single and you had a retirement plan at your job, you could only deduct any IRA contribution if your yearly salary dipped below $25,000; deductions were phased out between $25,000 and $35,000; beyond $35,000, not a single penny could be deducted.

The result was as scripted as any Hollywood movie. Since deductibility was far less applicable than it used to be, contributions to IRAs dropped like a rock in a pond.

For once, Congress didn't turn a blind eye to a mistake. In 1997, they reinstated higher income levels for deductibility.

That ultimately resulted in two basic guidelines to determine whether you can deduct contributions to a conventional IRA and, if so, how much. The first has to do with whether you're covered by a retirement plan where you work. Federal law asks whether you are an "active participant" in a company-sponsored retirement plan, including profit sharing, 401(k)s, and other options. If you're not, then you can deduct your IRA contribution.

However, even if you are under the auspices of a retirement plan at work, you still may be eligible for at least a partial write-off of your IRA contribution. Here, the litmus test is income. As it stands now, if you're single and earning $52,000 or less, you can deduct your total IRA contribution (you get a partial deduction if you're the head of a household). The deduction for singles is phased out up to $62,000—beyond that, no deduction. Married couples who file their taxes jointly and earn no more than $83,000 annually likewise get a complete deduction. Phaseout occurs up to $103,000, after which the deduction is zapped entirely.

IRA's Many Charms

Deductibility is by no means an IRA's sole advantage.

Contribution levels have been similarly increased. From the initial $2,000 limit, you can now contribute as much as $4,000 to an IRA (one reservation being, if you don't earn that much in a particular year, your contribution is limited to the amount you earn). Additionally, the upper limit is slated to be bumped up to $5,000 in 2008.

Although deductibility is, needless to say, an attractive element of IRAs, you should strongly consider opening one up and contributing to it on a regular basis, regardless of any possible tax benefit (with the possible wrinkle involving a Roth IRA—we'll cover that later in this chapter). One reason, among others, is the IRA's tax-deferred status, which lets you save and earn interest on money in an IRA with no tax impact until you begin withdrawing the money. The thinking here, theoretically at least, is that when you retire, you will likely be in a lower tax bracket than when you were working—hence, less of a tax bite on the withdrawals.

To illustrate: let's say you're 29 years old and plan to retire at age 65. You're in the 25 percent tax bracket. Under one scenario, you invest $2,000 in a taxed vehicle returning 9 percent a year; under a second scenario, you get the same 9 percent return, but are in a tax-deferred IRA. By the time you reach age 65, the taxed investment is worth about $281,000. Not bad, but rather modest compared to the IRA, which is worth nearly $472,000.

> **Retirement Reality**
>
> Contribution levels are a bit more generous for those approaching retirement age. People age 50 and up can contribute $5,000 to an IRA. This is known as a "catch-up" provision—particularly handy if you need to really boost your retirement savings.

> **Retirement Reality**
>
> IRAs require that you have some form of income. The one wrinkle to this is a spousal account. If you are employed but your spouse isn't, you can also contribute to an IRA in his or her name.

Some IRA Limitations

Of course, there are limitations to IRAs. First are early withdrawal penalties. The prevailing rule is simple—take money from your IRA prior to age $59\frac{1}{2}$, and you're socked with a 10 percent penalty. However, there are circumstances when the penalty is waived. For instance, you can access your IRA early if you become permanently disabled. You can also use IRA funds penalty-free to pay particularly high medical expenses.

There are two additional penalty loopholes. Current law says you can withdraw up to $10,000 to help pay for a first home for yourself or other family members. Additionally, there is no limit as to the amount that can be withdrawn to help pay for higher education costs for yourself or other family members.

> **Retirement Reality**
>
> Although there are ways to skirt the early withdrawal penalty, you don't get off entirely scot-free. You're still subject to federal and state taxes on any funds you withdraw.

There are some other rather modest limitations. First, you can no longer make contributions to an IRA once you reach the age of $70\frac{1}{2}$. Additionally, you can't keep money in an IRA indefinitely. Federal law mandates that you begin taking *minimum distributions* at the same $70\frac{1}{2}$ age benchmark.

def•i•ni•tion

> **Minimum distribution** is calculated by dividing the balance of the IRA account by the person's life expectancy (as calculated by the Internal Revenue Service). That amount then must be withdrawn annually from that point on.

There is a flip side to the age issue with regard to an IRA. Although you may be too old to contribute to an IRA, you are never too young. That means, in theory, your 7-year-old daughter who earns spending money walking dogs and serving lemonade to passersby in the summer can, in fact, open her own IRA. And, with what we've discussed about the power of long-term compounding, that can make for a solid start toward funding her own retirement.

Roths—Another IRA Option

When Congress was busy back in the 1990s repairing the mischief it had done to conventional IRAs, they also decided to unveil a new version of the IRA—the IRA Plus, or more commonly, the Roth IRA.

The Roth IRA provides some potentially attractive alternative features to the conventional IRA. For one thing, singles making up to $110,000 a year (couples as high as

$166,000) are eligible to contribute as much as $4,000 a year. And that's the case no matter if they're taking part in a retirement plan where they work or not. Like traditional IRAs, Roths also let people over 50 kick in as much as $5,000 every year.

Another advantage happens at the withdrawal stage. Although a Roth IRA provides for no tax deductions for any sort of contribution, from there on you're completely free of the taxman—the money grows tax-free and may also be withdrawn without any tax implications whatsoever. And, unlike conventional IRAs, you can continue to make contributions regardless of your age. Nor are you required at any point to make withdrawals, making Roths a suitable choice if you want to build up an inheritance to pass along to someone else.

Like conventional IRAs, Roths establish a 10 percent penalty on any withdrawals made before age 59½. You also have to have a Roth in place for at least five years before you can begin withdrawing even one penny without any sort of penalty. But, an interesting provision allows Roth investors to withdraw any contributions they make at any time, without penalty.

Here's an example. Say you have been investing in a Roth for seven years, making the maximum $4,000 contribution each year. At the end of that seven-year period, the account has done fairly well—it's now worth some $50,000. You can withdraw as much as $28,000 (seven times $4,000) without any penalty—only if you touch the money that's construed as a return on your investment do you open yourself up to the 10 percent early withdrawal penalty.

A Roth is also advantageous if the owner of the account passes away. Similar to the withdrawal advantages under conventional circumstances, whoever inherits a Roth IRA gets the money tax-free. By comparison, a conventional IRA that's passed along to an heir is taxed. In either case, however, the early withdrawal penalty is waived for the beneficiary.

Golden Years Gaffes

No matter which IRA appeals to you, be wary about too much of a good thing. Should you ever exceed the specified contribution limit for either a traditional or Roth IRA, you'll be slapped with a 6 percent excise tax.

Retire Right

What about a scenario where you're already older than the 59½-year threshold but the Roth IRA hasn't been in place for the mandatory five years? In this case, you have to wait until the five years is up before you can begin to make withdrawals penalty-free.

But Roths and traditional IRAs also share many common features. Both provide tax-free growth for whatever money you invest in them (remember, the difference only crops up once you begin to make withdrawals). Both allow complete freedom for you to choose the investment that actually makes up your IRA account. That can be stocks, bonds, mutual funds—whatever you like and whatever best serves your investment goals. You are also free to adjust your investment mix to reflect any changes in your risk tolerance or objectives.

Retire Right _____

One possibility worth considering for an IRA is mutual funds that are automatically adjusted by the brokerage firm or other business from whom you buy them. Rather than you having to do it yourself, these mutual funds adjust your investment mix—usually from more aggressive to more conservative—as you get older.

How to Choose

Now that you're inundated with information about both kinds of IRAs, which one should you choose if you have no IRA at all at this point?

Like so many things to do with planning for retirement (that old caveat yet again), there's really no hard-and-fast answer, as both choices offer advantages and potential drawbacks. But, here's something of a laundry list of issues that may make the quandary a bit easier to tackle:

 ◆ If, by chance, you're eligible to take the tax deduction afforded by the traditional IRA, the question becomes a bit problematic. On the one hand, no one would blame you for grabbing the up-front tax break. Nor, given its prior record of "consistency," would it be entirely foolish to take the tax deduction rather than leaving yourself at Congress's mercy (and its propensity for tinkering with things, such as the tax-free withdrawal provision of a Roth).

 ◆ On the other hand, if your income now is too high to take the traditional IRA deduction, you're better off opting for the Roth. If nothing else, a tax break at the end of the retirement cycle is better than no tax break at all.

 ◆ The Roth may also be a solid choice for younger people getting started with their retirement program. If, by chance, you expect to be able to accumulate a sizable cache to fund your retirement, better to have that money available without a spank from the tax paddle.

◆ Roths are also a solid choice due to their greater flexibility come retirement. As we pointed out earlier, there is no mandatory withdrawal provision—great for people planning on living a long time who want to have the greatest amount of leeway with their savings. And, as also noted, the Roth is a great way to pass money on to others—unlike traditional IRAs, which are not particularly inheritance-friendly.

◆ Roths also offer tax advantages other than the ones we've covered. In some instances, a great deal of taxable income after retirement—such as that from conventional IRAs—can cause your Social Security benefits to be taxed as well. The tax-free withdrawal provisions of the Roth mitigate this concern.

◆ Finally, if you open an IRA and expect to access the money within five years or less, go with the traditional IRA. Roths' five-year withdrawal penalty window will only force you to take a needless hit.

Retire Right _____

Whichever IRA makes the most sense for you, it's always best to fund it to the max— and to do it as early in the year as you possibly can. Although the usual deadline is the tax filing date of April 15—later if you get an extension—a few extra months in every year can mean a difference of tens of thousands of dollars or more when you retire.

To Convert or Not?

Perhaps you have a traditional IRA in place—maybe you've had it for years and funded it to the max religiously. Now, you've heard about all the wonderful benefits and advantages afforded by the Roth—things that may not have been around when you first started funding your good ole IRA.

Should you take the plunge and convert your old IRA to a Roth? On the surface, the prospect seems a no-brainer. In effect, you're opting out of a taxed program (withdrawals from a traditional IRA) for an alternative where every penny you withdraw after you retire is tax-free.

But, once again, there are hurdles. If you choose to roll over a traditional IRA into a Roth, you will have to pay taxes on whatever you move to the new account—more specifically, on any contributions and earnings that were either tax-deductible or tax-deferred. In a way, it's understandable—if you got a deduction on everything you put into a conventional IRA and want to move it into a Roth to gain tax-free access after retirement, it's something of a double dip.

Theoretically, that can translate to a substantial sum. Consider this scenario—when you were young and in a low enough tax bracket to take a complete deduction in a conventional IRA, you may have accumulated a substantial amount of money over time—money that, if you are now in a higher bracket, would be taxed at that higher rate if you moved it into a Roth.

There are also income limitations. Currently, if your adjusted gross income is greater than $100,000 in the year you want to convert, you're not allowed to change from a conventional IRA to a Roth.

However, there are scenarios where a Roth conversion makes sense. If you anticipate being in a higher tax bracket after retiring, take the tax hit now and convert—better a tax slap now than a tax wallop later. Also, it's a good choice if you have a nondeductible IRA that hasn't grown that much in value—perhaps one you started a couple of years ago and that has pretty much languished where it is. If that's the case, your taxes will likely be light and, from there, you can enjoy all the pluses of a Roth.

> **Golden Years Gaffes**
>
> If, by chance, you do have to pay some taxes on a conversion, try to use money other than funds from the IRA itself. Not only does that move more money into the Roth—and, hence, that much more to grow in value—you'll be subject to the 10 percent early withdrawal penalty if you're younger than 59½.

Some Caveats

By this point, the charms of an IRA—be it a traditional or Roth—should have you completely won over. Small wonder—with their flexibility and varied advantages, it's hard to see how an IRA might not become an integral element of your retirement planning.

But we have covered some potential landmines and drawbacks. Here are a few more for you to bear in mind to make certain that your IRA is an unqualified blessing rather than part curse.

Moving IRA Funds Around

When you first open an IRA, you may assume that you've made a lifelong friend. And, in a sense, you have—your IRA will be with you throughout your working life and, from there, doing its financial bit to help underwrite your retirement.

But that's not to say that where you keep an IRA is always going to remain the same. If, for instance, you were working with a financial planner or broker who has moved on to another firm, you may wish to follow him or her. Likewise, you may be disappointed with your IRA's performance and would like to shift over to something with greater potential.

There are two ways to do this safely:

- **Rollovers.** Here, you let the *custodian* of your IRA account know that you plan to close out the account and that you want a check for the entire amount.

> # def•i•ni•tion
> A **custodian** is the institution that holds your IRA. It can be a bank, brokerage house, or similar place.

The key here is to let your custodian know that you intend to take the proceeds and, rather than just pocketing them, put them into another IRA account. In that fashion, you're letting your custodian know not to withhold any taxes.

The other key is the federally mandated time frame. You have 60 days to put the money into a new IRA account. Fail to do that, and you can be touched up for a 20 percent penalty.

Also pay attention to rollover limitations. The IRS only allows you one rollover per account every 12 months. Even if you roll over only a portion of assets within a particular IRA account, the remaining funds can't be touched for 12 calendar months.

> **Golden Years Gaffes**
> Take note—limitations on rollovers apply to 12 calendar months, not once every year.

- **Transfers.** This is often the easiest and safest means of moving IRA funds. Simply instruct your current IRA custodian to transfer the funds directly to another custodian. In this fashion, you never take possession of the money in any way, which eliminates concern over the 60-day limit with rollovers. This also eliminates the 12-month rollover limitation, so, theoretically at least, you can execute transfers as often as your little heart desires.

The downside, however, is speed. With rollovers, the whole process can be completed in a matter of a few hours. Transfers, on the other hand, often take up to several weeks.

> **Retire Right** _____
>
> It's not unheard of to have more than one IRA—many people have several. If you have more than one, if at all possible keep them with one custodian. They'll be simpler to track and custodial fees may be less expensive than if you spread them around among several custodians.

How to Invest Your IRA Assets

One of the beauties of IRAs is their inherent flexibility with regard to where you put the money you invest in them. Unlike other retirement vehicles, IRAs are just about wide open to most any sort of retirement choice. You can choose individual stocks, mutual funds, bonds, certificates of deposit, even something as rock-solid conservative as a traditional savings account.

> **Retirement Reality**
>
> There are two major prohibitions with regard to IRAs. One is collectibles, including art, stamps, antiques, and other like items. You may also not invest in real estate you own, such as your own home or rental property.

Believe it or not, that range of choice can actually set up another boondoggle with regard to your IRA—specifically, where you should put your money and, as a result, just how aggressive you should be.

Some people may opt for a more conservative route, choosing stable investments such as CDs or money market funds. Their thinking is that an IRA can be a stable backstop to an overall retirement plan. Best to keep it in as safe a position as possible.

Others disagree, arguing that IRAs are an ideal choice for more aggressive options, such as stocks or mutual funds. With a possible long-term time frame facing them before they expect to access funds for retirement, their feeling is that an IRA is the best place to roll the dice a bit.

There's no right or wrong in this argument. But it does illustrate the range of choice you have with your IRA—and, in turn, how critical it is to gauge the right investment approach for you.

Topics to consider include:

◆ **Your age.** The longer you have until retirement, the more risk you can comfortably take on. Studies show that time mitigates the ups and downs of potentially more profitable investment options, such as those tied to the stock market.

◆ **Your risk tolerance.** You may be the youngest holder of an IRA on record, but that doesn't make an aggressive investment approach a no-brainer. Get to know the level of risk with which you're comfortable and go with it. Going against your comfort zone may not only cost you sleepless nights, ultimately it may simply be counterproductive. For instance, if you invest too aggressively, you may constantly be shifting your investment choices (within IRA limitations, of course) from one option to the next. Jumping from one investment to another makes little sense. (More on this topic in Chapter 13.)

◆ **Where your other holdings are.** Taking the first two factors into consideration, the most effective way to determine the right investment for an IRA is to consider it as a part of a whole. See how your other retirement options are positioned. If, for instance, your 401(k) is sunk into potentially volatile company stock, that would argue for a fairly conservative approach with your IRA. By the same token, if you have a Keogh or SEP that's fairly conservative, that may suggest a more aggressive posture with your IRA. The bottom line: don't treat your IRA as though it were in a vacuum. Make it a part of your overall plan and balance it accordingly.

> **Golden Years Gaffes**
>
> One option you should avoid with your IRA are tax-advantaged options such as municipal bonds, which are free of federal and, often, state and local taxes. Your IRA is already tax-deferred—it doesn't make sense to place a tax-exempt vehicle in an IRA. Moreover, they're taxable when you start to withdraw funds.

The Least You Need to Know

◆ IRAs—be they traditional or Roths—are a powerful addition to your retirement funding plan.

◆ The major difference between the two is taxes—contributions to a traditional IRA may be tax-free, while proceeds from Roths can be withdrawn without any tax impact.

◆ It makes sense to choose a traditional IRA if you can take the up-front deduction.

◆ If you can't take the deduction, choose the Roth. You'll be able to receive your money in retirement without any tax implications.

◆ If you anticipate being in a higher tax bracket come retirement, consider converting a traditional IRA into a Roth—again, the advantage of tax-free withdrawals.

◆ Move IRA funds carefully. Either roll them over yourself (bearing in mind how quickly you need to complete this) or arrange a direct transfer.

The Basics of Investing, Part One: Mutual Funds

In This Chapter

- ◆ Pluses and hurdles
- ◆ The primary types of funds
- ◆ Selecting a fund
- ◆ Buying a fund
- ◆ How to track a fund
- ◆ Thoughts on portfolio balance for retirement

Up until now, we've talked a great deal about the importance of finding the right vehicle in which to invest your retirement dollars—be that your company's 401(k), a Simplified Employee Pension, or an Individual Retirement Account.

If one of those choices is the vehicle, then it's time to turn your attention to the fuel that will make it perform the way you wish it to.

Choosing the right sort of investment—or, more likely, investments—for your retirement plan isn't necessarily simple. Nor should it be taken lightly—the consequences of selecting just the right investment can have far-reaching implications.

But it isn't impossible by any means. In this chapter, we'll introduce you to what, for many investors, is the bedrock of their retirement plan—mutual funds. We'll also offer some ideas and strategies to help you craft just the right mix for your retirement plan.

Mutual Funds—an Overview

Lots of investment choices are rather limited or singular—a stock, for instance, represents an investment in one particular company, as do bonds that are frequently issued by companies looking for necessary cash.

Not so with mutual funds. In its essence, a mutual fund is an investment company that pools funds from many investors and, in turn, invests it in a broad array of stocks, bonds, and other types of securities.

How They Work

The workings of a mutual fund are simple in their essence. When you buy shares in a fund, you are joining other investors who have also bought into the fund. A professional fund manager then handles those funds, buying and selling various investments in hopes of producing the best performance possible for the overall portfolio.

> **Retirement Reality**
>
> Mutual funds are by no means brand new. The first fund, known as the Massachusetts Investors Trust, was set up in 1924.

def•i•ni•tion

> **Shares outstanding** refers to the total number of shares owned by investors.

As you probably know, the price of individual stocks can change constantly throughout a day of trading. Mutual funds are different. They receive only one price per day—at the end of each day's trading, based on what the securities in the portfolio are worth. The price per share, also known as the net asset value (NAV), of a mutual fund is the current market value of the fund's net assets divided by the number of *shares outstanding*. In most cases, that is the price that any investor pays to buy into the fund during the next day of trading.

Advantages and Drawbacks

The thousands of mutual funds currently available to investors offer a wide variety of advantages, including:

♦ **Diversification.** This may be as significant a plus as mutual funds may offer any sort of investor. Investing on our own—with the often limited funds available to us—makes sufficient diversification difficult. By their very function, through the pooling of your investment dollars alongside those of other investors, mutual funds can offer virtually instant diversification across a wide variety of investments, including stocks, bonds, and cash.

♦ **Lower investment risk.** Diversification is a key element that reduces investor risk. By spreading holdings over a number of investments—some aggressive, others more conservative—investment risk can be reduced. And mutual funds provide that very type of diversification.

♦ **Professional money management.** Few of us are genuinely adept at picking winning investments—at least, on a consistent basis. When you invest in a mutual fund, your money is being overseen by a team of financial professionals. Moreover, they're on the job all the time. Unless you have free time to constantly monitor an investment portfolio, that's a level of attention that's hard to match.

♦ **Expense management.** Buying and selling stocks on a regular basis can add up in commission costs, even if you use a *deep discount broker*. By comparison, many mutual funds operate very efficiently, resulting in reasonable costs for investors (although this is not always the case—we'll get into this later in the chapter).

def•i•ni•tion _____

A **deep discount broker** is an investment house that sells stocks and funds very inexpensively. The downside: you often get little, if any, guidance.

♦ **A fund to meet your needs.** Since there are so many funds from which to choose, it's not difficult to find one to match any sort of investment style or goal.

Of course, the world of mutual funds is not a perfect one. Downsides include:

♦ **Performance.** There are great-performing mutual funds. There are also ones whose performance is abysmal. It's essential to know what to look for to separate the champs from the also-rans.

◆ **Cost.** Like performance, the cost of operating a mutual fund can range from dirt cheap to outlandish. And again, that's a shopping consideration we'll cover in some detail later in this chapter.

◆ **Responsibility.** Investing in a mutual fund means doing your homework and then giving the money to someone else to handle. If you're a hands-on sort of person, that lack of involvement may be unnerving. And, as we'll discuss below, some funds invest in companies that you might not wish to support.

◆ **Image versus reality.** This may seem hard to believe, but not every fund outlines a particular investment approach and then follows that to the letter. We'll also cover this in detail later, but know for now that not every fund on the block does just what it says it's going to.

Overview of Major Fund Types

With an overview of mutual funds' basic performance features and other information as to how they work, we can start becoming acquainted with the various types of available funds. We'll cover each fund's major features and the advantages and drawbacks to each, particularly for investors looking for a suitable vehicle to save for retirement.

Aggressive Growth Funds

These funds take a forceful approach, investing in companies that, while they may be relatively small now, have the greatest potential for success—and, hence, appreciation of stock value. These are suited to people with a long-term investment horizon—say, someone in their 20s and 30s who have a sufficiently long time frame and can ride out market volatility. On the other hand, these are not suited for people nearing retirement, as they may not have enough time to rebound from unexpected drops in the market.

Growth Funds

These are similar to aggressive growth funds, but a bit more toned down. They also look for companies whose stock has real potential for growth, but with less potential volatility. These funds are suited to investors with a shorter time frame before retirement—someone in their 30s or early 40s. They're also suited to anyone interested in growth but not the ups and downs that aggressive growth funds can experience.

Growth and Income Funds

These funds are a blend. In one respect, they invest in growth companies, so they're aggressive. On the other hand, they try to balance that with more conservative holdings, such as large companies whose stocks yield high *dividends*.

These funds can be suited to someone on the verge of retiring—10 or so years off—who wants to play it safe but doesn't want to sacrifice all potential for growth. By the same token, unless you're extremely jittery about any sort of risk, growth and income funds may be unnecessarily safe for young investors with a long time horizon.

Index Funds

These popular funds have been the subject of some controversy. Index funds try to match the rate of return of stock indices, such as *The Dow Jones Industrials*.

Put another way, if the Dow Jones Industrial Average has earned 12 percent in a particular year, index funds geared to that index will try to match that rate of return. There are also other index funds that are set up to mirror other indices.

If you'd be happy just matching the returns of a broad range of the market, these funds are a solid choice. Since they tend to buy and hold stocks rather than engage in extensive trading and selling, they can also be more cost-effective to own than more active funds.

def•i•ni•tion

Dividends are payments to shareholders authorized by a company's board of directors. They can be in cash or additional shares of the company's stock.

The Dow Jones Industrials is made up of 30 of the largest publicly held companies traded on the New York Stock Exchange.

On the other hand, these funds would be frustrating to an investor who would like to better market averages. Moreover, an index fund can be something of a lemming—if the market as a whole is going down, so likely will the fund (unlike a more actively managed fund which can shift gears and perhaps hold its own better).

Small-Cap, Mid-Cap, and Large-Cap Funds

These funds invest in stocks based on the size of the company. Small-caps are the most aggressive, usually targeting companies valued less than $1 billion. Mid-caps, which tend to invest in companies ranging in value of $2 billion to $10 billion, are a bit more conservative. Large-caps look for stability and income; as a result, they target only large, very well-established firms.

International Funds

As the name implies, these funds invest in companies located outside the United States. Some look to capitalize on areas of the world just beginning to develop economically (these are often referred to as "emerging growth" areas) while others target countries and regions that are more developed and stable.

Sector Funds

While many funds take in companies from a broad range of industries, sector funds concentrate on specific economic sectors. These can include areas such as health care, energy, or specific forms of technology. These can be among the most aggressive (and potentially volatile) funds from which to choose. Since by design they avoid the sort of diversity that can stabilize other sorts of funds, they can rise if an industry performs particularly well and fall just as easily if it doesn't.

Socially Responsible Funds

These are also often referred to as "green" funds. These are funds that limit their portfolios to companies that have good environmental records, good labor practices, or other attributes the fund would see as socially valuable. As such, these funds don't just look at a company's performance and financials—they also want to know how the company got to where it is.

Real Estate Investment Trusts (REITs)

These are funds that invest in property, including shopping centers, apartment buildings, and similar commercial operations.

 Golden Years Gaffes _____

Believe it or not, there are funds—known as "bear funds"—that only do well when the market is doing poorly. Avoid them. These are not suited to any sort of long-term strategy.

Factors to Consider When Choosing a Fund

Now that we've gone over some of the features of mutual funds and the varied forms they can take, let's have a look at some of the issues you should consider when choosing a fund.

Performance

Not surprisingly, this is of paramount importance—and rightly so. Every investor wants to put his or her money in a fund that does well.

But there's more to it than just that. First of all, check out long-term performance. A lot of funds toot their horns when they have an above and beyond year. That's great unto itself, but be sure to check performance over a longer period of time—5 to 10 years and even longer, if the fund has been around that long. Examination of long-term performance lets you see how a fund has been managed as part of a long-range approach—not just one year when luck might have been on its side.

Moreover, don't limit performance to the fund itself. Have a look to see how the fund has done against funds with similar portfolio make-ups. Again, a fund's numbers that, unto themselves, seem like world beaters may look shabby if other funds in its class are performing at a much higher level.

Risk

Risk, in its own way, is just as important as performance. Although any fund has to take on a certain amount of risk to produce returns, the amount of risk can differ substantially from one fund to the next. And that makes it a critical consideration in your thinking.

The first thing to do is to familiarize yourself with the fund's holdings. See how heavy the portfolio is with stocks and, from there, see what sorts of stocks the fund owns. Not only are stocks inherently more risky than other sorts of investments—bonds and cash, for instance—but the type of stock also matters a great deal. For instance, a fund that owns large, established companies is going to be a good deal less volatile than another that owns smaller, more developing companies.

Another way to evaluate risk is to know a fund's standard deviation. This statistic refers to a fund's performance from one year to the next. A fund that swings wildly from very good years to very poor years has a large amount of standard deviation and, as a result, is riskier than a fund that doesn't vary as much.

Expenses

No fund operates purely for free—to enjoy a fund's rewards, you have to pay something. That something comes in the form of fees and expenses. And they can vary a great deal from one fund to another.

More specifically, expenses relate to the cost of operating a fund. They can include trading costs, administrative expenses, salaries for fund managers and other employees, and a host of other costs. And every one of those costs is ultimately subtracted from the return paid out to a fund's investors.

Don't assume those costs are small and meaningless. Some funds levy fees that amount to several percentage points. These are known as *expense ratios*.

def•i•ni•tion

An **expense ratio** takes in all expenses incurred by a fund's operations and expresses them in terms of percentages. An active fund carries an expense ratio of roughly 1.5 percent, although some funds can go as high as 3.0.

From there, apply a fund's expense ratio to see how much it might cost you to own that fund. In the case of a 1.5 percent expense ratio, that means that, for every $100 invested in that fund, $1.50 is subtracted from any return.

That may not seem like a lot but, multiplied by the size of your investment and added up year after year, a fund's expenses can really eat into your return. That makes it important to take expenses into account—the smaller they are, the greater your ultimate return.

 Retire Right

Index funds have exceedingly low expense ratios, since they tend to buy and hold stocks rather than engage in active trading. That's worth taking into account.

Portfolio Turnover

Portfolio turnover means how often a particular fund buys and sells its holdings. Like an expense ratio, it is usually expressed in percentages. For instance, a fund with 100 percent turnover has changed its holdings completely.

Portfolio turnover can cut both ways. On the one hand, a high turnover rate may suggest a fund that's trying to be as aggressive as possible in pursuing the best returns. On the other, turnover adds to a fund's expenses—and, as index funds illustrate, turnover is often unnecessary to obtain good results.

Loads

Yet another form of potential expense is a load. A load is the cost to invest in a fund—a commission paid to a broker, financial planner, investment firm, or anyone else from whom you buy a fund. Loads can be levied at several points—some funds charge loads when you purchase shares (a front-end load) while others levy loads when you sell shares (back-end loads). And, they can be substantial—upwards of 7 to 8 percent of the money you're investing.

Although there are any number of load funds with long-term winning records, there's no evidence to suggest that load funds are better than those that don't charge loads. So, as a rule, stick with no loads and pocket the savings.

 Golden Years Gaffes

Another red flag having to do with load funds is the commission. Often, if a planner or broker is pushing a load fund, it's because of the commission they'll earn—not because the fund is right for you.

Taxes

This has nothing to do with the taxes you might pay when taking proceeds from a fund. Rather, it addresses the taxes that the fund itself has to pay as a result of profits—expenses that are deducted from a fund's return to its investors.

To gauge this, look for a fund's tax-adjusted return. This lays out just how much a fund earns after taxes. Another gauge is a fund's tax efficiency ratio. This ratio is figured by dividing after-tax returns by pretax returns. The scale generally runs from 100, which represents the greatest tax efficiency, on down. A solid tax efficiency benchmark is 90 percent.

Closed-End vs. Open-End Funds

Open-end funds sell an unlimited number of shares and buy back investors' shares when they sell them. Closed-end funds, on the other hand, have a limited number of shares. When an investor sells shares, other investors buy them on an exchange.

A closed-end fund can have a subtle effect on the value of the shares you own. Since they are traded on an exchange rather than the fund itself buying them, the actual price you pay may differ slightly from the actual value. If, for instance, a closed-end fund is doing well, you may pay a bit more to buy shares; if it's underperforming, you may be able to buy them at a discount.

Fund Size

While not as critical as other considerations, fund size is an aspect you should be aware of. For one thing, too large a fund may be unwieldy to operate, which can increase cost to investors. That's one of the reasons some funds often shut off sales to new investors—the extra influx of cash only makes them more difficult to operate.

Management

Like most any other form of endeavor, there are stars in the world of mutual funds—fund managers who have made a name for themselves by racking up year after year of spectacular returns.

That said, does a fund's manager really matter all that much? It can, but only up to a certain extent. Granted, if you do your homework and find a fund with a star manager, it never is a bad idea to go with a winner. But bear in mind that managers—like star baseball and football players—move on to other funds if a better offer comes their way. If that happens, you can be left out in the cold. And funds are often run by teams of managers, so who's to say what can happen if one of them bolts to another fund?

Although particular managers can play a role in a fund's success, it's better to examine a fund's philosophy and approach. If that's implemented consistently, the issue of who's calling the shots becomes considerably less important.

Where to Find All This Information

Finding all these details may seem a Sisyphean task, but it's not as hard as it looks. Here are some places to investigate.

The Prospectus

One of the most central places to find out the particulars of a fund is through its prospectus. By law, every fund must provide prospective investors with a prospectus, which is a comprehensive document that outlines the fund's performance, management, statistics, and other issues.

Financial Publications

There are also a variety of financial magazines and publications that offer comprehensive overviews of the particulars of funds, including highlights of top performers.

Retire Right _____

Online, one central repository for mutual fund information is Morningstar (www. morningstar.com). The site offers extensive news, analysis, and rankings of every major type of mutual fund available to investors.

Fund Screens

In days gone by, the argument could genuinely be made that analysts, brokers, and others in the financial community had greater access to financial information than the average investor.

The Internet has pretty much sent that notion down the drain. Now, there are any number of websites where you can get up-to-the-minute, comprehensive investment news and analysis. Some sites are run by brokerage houses, others by news organizations, still others by private parties.

In fact, many of them have taken the chore of fund selection and automated it through the use of fund screens. How this function works differs from one site to another, but their basic function allows you to input certain parameters and financial objectives. From there, the system returns with recommended funds that match those guidelines.

Fund screens can be a terrific tool. They take much of the legwork out of finding the right funds for your portfolio. Moreover, they can be exhaustively specific in letting you narrow the kind of fund you're interested in to highly specialized parameters. Finally, they're completely objective. There's no salesperson with any sort of hidden agenda.

Buying a Mutual Fund

You can buy a mutual fund from a brokerage house or from the fund itself, and you may or may not be faced with a minimum initial investment. Another shopping option is known as a fund supermarket. This is a brokerage firm that lets investors select funds from a number of different fund families.

Brokerage Houses

These come in a variety of forms, from full-service houses that provide advice and guidance to deep discount brokerages. The downside to using a broker is that you'll generally pay a commission (particularly steep if you opt for the full-service brokerage house).

From the Funds Themselves

This is the most direct—and cost-effective—way to buy shares in a mutual fund. All you need to do is contact the *fund family* and tell them you're interested in a particular fund.

def•i•ni•tion

A **fund family** is a company that maintains several different mutual funds. These are usually set up for different financial objectives.

You can contact a fund family by mail, telephone, or via the company's website. From there, they'll send you an application or a prospectus (many fund families let you download prospectuses online). Read the prospectus, then fill out the application and return it along with a check for your initial investment. That's it.

Investment Minimums

You may find that a company requires a minimum initial investment. How much this comes to varies—some funds have no minimums at all, while others require several thousand dollars up front to get started. Check to see if any fund you're interested in has a minimum investment.

Another option is an automatic investment program. Here, instead of having to pony up a substantial sum all at once, a fund lets you set up an automatic system where money is regularly withdrawn from an account, such as savings or checking.

> **Retirement Reality**
>
> Investigate automatic-investment programs carefully. While some invest the money in the fund of your choice, others put the money into an account and let it sit there until you've saved enough to reach their minimum investment level.

How to Track Your Fund

Once you buy a fund, you'll naturally want to keep a close eye on it to see how it's performing. One way to do that is through a newspaper. Here, you can get information on daily price movements, annual rates of return, declaration of dividends, and other information.

Perhaps the easiest way to track your fund's progress is online. Many news sites let you look up your fund's activity for the day (and other pertinent information) using the fund's ticker symbol. A ticker symbol is a letter or series of letters that represent a stock or mutual fund.

Retire Right _____

Many newspapers, particularly smaller ones, have limited fund listings. If you can't find yours, look in one of the major financial dailies, such as *The Wall Street Journal.*

If you operate a financial software program on your computer, the job becomes all the easier—and more comprehensive. Programs generally let you download quotes directly onto your computer. Over time, you can accumulate long-range data and statistics to analyze how your fund is doing.

Golden Years Gaffes _____

Although it's an easy trap to fall into, try not to pay undue attention to your fund's price movement every day. You're in this for the long haul, so watch long-term performance, not daily ups and downs.

Some Ideas on Portfolios for Retirement

We'll get into the topic of investment strategies—along with where you happen to be in your progress toward retirement—in substantial detail starting with Chapter 13. But now, having just addressed the topic of mutual funds, it's helpful to raise the issue of portfolios—specifically, what sorts of funds you should own given your age and your goals for retirement.

If you're limited to certain choices, such as a 401(k) with only a few fund options, this may not be quite so important to you. But, with IRAs and other retirement vehicles, the mix of portfolio is completely up to you—and it's an important choice.

As we said earlier, it's important to take your tolerance for risk into considering when tackling this question. No matter your situation, owning a fund that's too aggressive for your comfort level simply isn't worth it.

How many years you have to retirement is a key factor to consider in making portfolio decisions. For example:

◆ **Twenty or more years to retirement.** As a rule, this is when you can afford to be most aggressive. That means funds heavily weighted with stocks; go with the more aggressive stock funds we mentioned earlier in this chapter. You have the time to ride out corrections and open yourself up to significant long-term growth potential. At the least, consider a fund—or mix of funds—that's at least 80 percent stock heavy.

♦ **Ten to 20 years to go.** Here, you should be a bit less aggressive. Look for a mix of roughly 65 percent stocks, with the remaining 35 percent divvied between bonds and cash (say, 25 percent bonds, 10 percent cash). The thinking here is that you still want to be somewhat aggressive in terms of growth, but not so aggressive as a longer time frame might comfortably afford.

Retire Right _____

These sample portfolios assume you're on track with your retirement savings. If you're playing catch-up, you might wish to be a bit more aggressive.

♦ **Less than 10 years to go.** Here, preservation of what you've accumulated is more important than growth. Look for 40 percent stocks, 40 percent bonds, and 20 percent cash.

The Least You Need to Know

♦ Mutual funds are a great choice for retirement investing. They offer diversification, professional management, and cost-effective investing.

♦ When choosing a fund, look at long-term performance, not just one stellar year or two.

♦ Be sure to consider costs, portfolio turnover, tax efficiency, and other issues when choosing a fund.

♦ As a rule, stick with no-load funds. A load is an unnecessary expense.

♦ It's easiest—and most cost-effective—to buy a fund directly from a fund family. This can be done by mail, via phone, or online.

♦ The longer your investment time frame, the more aggressive you can afford to be with your choice of funds. Opt for more conservative choices the closer you get to your retirement date.

The Basics of Investing, Part Two: Stocks

In This Chapter

- ◆ Stocks—what they are
- ◆ Understanding the various types of stock
- ◆ The basics of stock selection
- ◆ How to buy stock
- ◆ Some stock strategies for retirement

Mutual funds are a great choice for many people mapping out a retirement funding program. As we discussed in Chapter 10, they're easy to buy, offer a variety of choices, diversify your investments, and provide professional financial management.

But some of us prefer a more hands-on approach, one where we're calling the shots—not some fund manager you've never even met. And that's where investments such as stocks can fit the bill.

In this chapter, we'll introduce you to the universe of stocks. We'll examine features, pluses, drawbacks, and strategies as to how they can fit into your overall retirement funding strategy.

Stocks—What They Are

Companies usually issue stock to the public to raise funds for any number of activities. When you buy shares of stock, you're in effect buying your own slice of company ownership.

You can buy stock for a variety of reasons, but it boils down to a simple truth: you have faith in the company, you believe it is going to perform well in the future, and, as a result, you expect the value of the stock to increase as the company prospers. Simple as that.

Stocks come in two basic forms. The first, and by far the more common (hence the name) is common stock. This is the type of stock that the public generally buys. Common stock represents a share of ownership in the company and also makes you eligible for any dividends the company may generate. Additionally, should the company fail financially, common stock entitles you to some form of payback—albeit often a small one—after creditors and others to whom the company owes money have been paid off.

Preferred stock has a bit more muscle than common stock. For one thing, dividends are guaranteed—they're often larger than common dividends. And, should the company collapse, preferred stock holders are ahead of common stock owners when it comes to getting what proceeds remain.

Types of Stock

Stocks come in a variety of forms, each reflecting the particular characteristics and financial makeup of the company they underwrite.

Some common categories of stock include:

- **Growth stocks.** These stocks are issued by companies that are growing both in operations and in income—ideally, the price of the stock is following suit. Since they tend to reinvest much of what they earn, it's rare that growth stocks pay any sort of dividend to investors. Not surprisingly, these can be among the riskiest of stocks to buy. If all goes well and the company flourishes, you can be in on the payoff. If the company falters—or even if the industry in which the company operates takes a hit—growth stocks can take a beating, often never to recover.

- **Value stocks.** Value stocks are something of the diamond in the rough in investing. They're similar to growth stocks in that investors want them to go up in value. The difference here is that the price of value stocks is out of whack—investors have yet to recognize their real value and, as a result, value stocks are undervalued and available at a discount. Like growth stocks, however, if the company doesn't shine as expected, that depressed stock price may stay right where it is.

◆ **Income stocks.** Rather than growth, income stocks are designed to produce reliable income through high dividends. These tend to be large, very well-established companies—far more predictable than growth or value stocks.

◆ **Blue chip stocks.** These include some of the biggest, most recognizable companies around, including General Electric, Coca-Cola, and others. These pay substantial, reliable dividends and can offer some growth as well. The downside is they can be among the most expensive stocks to buy.

◆ **International stocks.** These stocks are issued by companies outside the United States. In fact, under the umbrella of international, they can take in all sorts of other stocks, including growth, value, and income. While some of these companies are exceedingly well established and stable, others are more developing. International stocks can often serve as a complement to domestic stocks, as they often don't react in step with the American markets.

> **Golden Years Gaffes**
>
> Two types of stock to avoid with your retirement are an initial public offering (IPO) and penny stocks. The first is a company's first stock offering and, as such, is exceedingly risky. Ditto for pennies, which are issued by small, risky companies.

Stock Exchanges: Where Stocks Are Traded

There are three primary stock exchanges in the United States. These are where investors of all sorts come together to buy and sell stock—sometimes selling for profit, occasionally at a loss, but always with an eye for profit potential.

The best known is the New York Stock Exchange. This is the largest market in terms of dollar trading activity and the second largest in terms of the number of companies it lists (roughly 3,000). Its list of companies reads as something of a who's who of the American business community.

By contrast, the American Stock Exchange is smaller—listing only some 800 companies—and the companies included are generally too small to qualify for listing on the New York exchange.

The third market is the largest. The NASDAQ (National Association of Securities Dealers Automated Quotations system) takes in more than 4,000 companies. It is a purely electronic trading network and it is the busiest of the three in terms of the number of shares traded daily.

Selecting Stock

Choosing the right stock—or mix of stocks—for your portfolio can be a challenge—particularly so for something as important as your retirement. Many people devote their entire lives to this field of study. We'll start with some basic ideas and strategies to get you started.

Some Basic Steps

For all the complexity and involved goings-on in choosing winning stocks, there are some overriding basics that need to be taken into consideration. You should always …

- **Look at the company's annual report.** This is an essential first step in getting to know a company's stock. An annual report offers a detailed view of a company's varied makeup and activities, including precisely what the company does, its management, its history, types of revenue, and other critical information. Without this basic knowledge, all the subsequent analysis in the world may be useless.

- **Look at long-term trends.** When we discussed mutual funds in Chapter 10, we emphasized the importance of examining the fund's long-range history, not merely a snapshot taking in a year or two. Do the same with individual stocks. See which way the company is headed. Are its sales and income increasing? Are they expanding into new markets? And, just as important, are they doing all the right things with a reliable degree of consistency?

- **Compare it with similar companies.** Again, as with mutual funds, a stock in a vacuum may appear as rosy as can be. That glowing picture can blur if you discover that others in the same business are doing far better. When getting to know a company, compare it with its competitors and others in its field. Match up sales, profits, and overall growth to see if those numbers shine when compared with others trying to achieve the same sort of objectives.

- **Look at the numbers.** A company may be selling widgets at $5 apiece. But what happens if it's costing $6 a pop to make them? Those sorts of numbers and statistics are essential to separate genuinely successful companies from others that, once you peel away the outer layers, are actually struggling. Look at a company's spending patterns, debt, assets, and other numbers to see if everything to do with a company's financials is solid—not just one or two glowing numbers.

Where to Find the Numbers—The Balance Sheet

A company's annual report is, on the whole, framed to put the company in the best light possible. After all, it goes to investors—existing and prospective—so it's job one to keep them happy and confident.

But there's one part of the annual report where that spin isn't quite so viable. The income statement and balance sheet are about as empirical a look as you'll get at a company—the numbers, statistics, and other data that can reveal a variety of information about a company's current status as well as its prospects. That means it's important that you know what to look for in conducting your *fundamental analysis*.

def•i•ni•tion

Examining a company's operating statistics and numbers is, in a broad sense, referred to as **fundamental analysis**.

Major components of an income and balance sheet—grouped so you get an idea of what to compare with what—include:

◆ **Current assets.** This is the amount of assets that the company has on hand that can be turned into cash within the space of one year.

◆ **Current liabilities.** The other side of the coin—this is debt that the company has to meet within one year. Compare this with assets to make sure the company has sufficient funds at the ready to meet its short-term obligations.

◆ **Total liabilities and equity.** Between debt and stock owned by others outside the company, this figure represents every part of the company that is effectively owned by someone else. This has to match up with total assets.

◆ **Total revenue.** This is the overall amount of sales before taxes are deducted.

◆ **Cost of sales.** This is how much all that wonderful revenue is costing the company. If this exceeds revenues, that's a major red flag—sales are coming with too heavy a price tag.

◆ **Pretax income.** As the name implies, how much the company earns prior to the bite of taxes. It's not unheard of for some companies to earn a profit, only to shell out more in taxes. Keep an eye out for that.

◆ **Income tax.** Getting a refund isn't the best thing for a company. If you do badly enough, chances are good you'll get a refund. In the investing world, it's better to pay some tax—it's a sign you're making enough money to warrant it.

◆ **Net income.** This is a particularly important statistic. This is the amount of money a company earns after taxes—as reliable a bellwether of a company's strength as you can find. Always look for this.

◆ **Earnings per share (EPS).** This statistic shows the amount of earnings per share of company stock—another critical statistic.

Putting This All Together—Ratios for Analysis

Numbers and statistics can offer great insight into a company's operations and its prospects for success. The downside is there can be an awful lot of numbers, not to mention the challenges of piecing them all together to form a coherent picture.

Fortunately, there are a number of stock analysis calculations that do that very thing for investors. Known as ratios, you'll often see these cited by investment analysts and other financial professionals as they discuss stock selection.

That may suggest unduly complicated mathematics, but it's really not so heavy as all that. Here are several ratios, how they work, and what they can tell you about a particular stock.

Price-Earnings Ratio (P/E)

This is perhaps the most popular ratio used to analyze stock. In its essence, it illustrates how much an investor would be willing to spend in return for $1 in company earnings. In that respect, the formula involves dividing the stock price by the earnings per share.

The telling point of a P/E ratio can indicate several things. For instance, a high P/E means that investors are willing to pay more for a stock than its current earnings might warrant. That can be a sign of a company that's expected to do great things. One example of a high P/E was Google, which topped 100 a few years back (the average P/E range is 15 to 25 or so).

But a high P/E can also be a sign of risk. If nothing else, the price of the company's stock is out of whack with what it is earning. That can suggest a stock that the market has simply valued inappropriately.

One way to use a P/E is to compare a particular company with others in its industry. That way, you can see if the industry as a whole is fairly valued or if, by chance, one company's value has yet to be noticed by investors.

Price/Book Ratio (P/B)

This ratio compares a company's stock price against its net worth. It's calculated by dividing current stock price by a firm's *book value*.

The price/book ratio compares a stock's price to what a company is worth, rather than what it may be earning at a particular time. In that sense, the lower the P/B, the greater the chance of a good buy, as that indicates investors as a group have yet to recognize the genuine worth of a company. A P/B of 1 or less is considered low—the average P/B for Standard and Poor's 500 stocks is a bit less than 3.

def•i•ni•tion

Book value reflects the real value of a company. It's calculated by totaling all assets and subtracting debt and liabilities.

Many investors prefer price/book value to other ratios. Their thinking is that a company's value is hard to disguise or somehow make more appealing, which is always possible with earnings.

Price/Sales Ratio (P/S)

As the name suggests, this involves the price of a company stock alongside sales figures. This is calculated by dividing a current stock price by a company's earnings per share. Like other ratios, the lower the P/S, the greater the possibility that a company has plenty of upside potential. The average P/S ratio for the Standard and Poor's 500 is 2.3. By contrast, a high P/S can top 16, while a low P/S can be below 1.

Dividend Yield

This is something of a shift away from ratios involving the pure financials of a company's activity. This pits the dividend a company pays versus the price of its stock.

On one hand, looking just at dividends can be a telling sign—healthy companies consistently pay healthy dividends. But the picture becomes more involved when those dividends are divided by the current price of the company's stock. For instance, if the dividend yield is high, that can suggest a stock price that's undervalued. By the same token, a company may seem to be more established and less growth oriented with a

Retire Right _____

One caveat about dividend yield—it's of no use in judging the value of smaller, growth companies, which reinvest dividends rather than paying them out to stockholders.

lower yield. That means investors are willing to pay more for whatever dividend the company offers. A high dividend yield can better 10, while average for all Dow Jones Industrial Average stocks is a bit better than 2.

The best way to use ratios is to take advantage of every element that each one offers. If possible, employ more than one in breaking down a company's financials. That way, you stand the best chance of getting the more comprehensive and telling financial picture you can of a stock.

Technical Analysis

Up to now, we've pretty much concentrated on the numbers side of things—those numbers that show what a company does and how well it does it, particularly when compared with its competitors.

But many investors don't put much stock in that method. Rather, they argue, the whole point is to buy a stock at a low point and sell it later for a profit when it rises. And that, in turn, can best be determined by watching how a stock trades—not its operational numbers.

This is referred to as *technical analysis*. It actually breaks down into two salient components—price and volume. So far as price is concerned, analysts look at long-term trading patterns—those points that historically mark a low point in a stock's value (often known as a stock's support level) and a high point that a stock often encounters difficulty moving past (referred to as its resistance level).

def•i•ni•tion _____

Technical analysis has to do with charting a company's trading patterns.

Using these patterns, analysts try to predict at which point a stock has hit a low and, by the same token, when it appears to have topped off. Additionally, they study volume, or the amount of trading that occurs in a particular stock. This, they say, is indicative of investor interest in a stock—yet another factor that can push its value up or down.

The upside—for some, at least—to technical analysis is that it tosses aside reams of corporate data, earnings, and other information, focusing instead simply on long-term price movement. The negative aspect is that many well-known stock authorities argue—with some merit—that a stock's movement is driven by its fundamentals, such as profit and low debt. That's what effectively establishes those price movement patterns that technical analysts sweat over.

Retire Right _____

One way to hedge your bet is to use both technical and fundamental analysis when looking at a stock. It never hurts to know some company numbers as well as how the stock has performed.

Analysts

Brokerage houses and other financial institutions are overflowing with stock analysts—let alone other sources, including newspapers, magazines, and websites. As their name implies, their 24/7 job is to watch the stock market, pick out potential winners, and dissect them to determine if, in fact, they have genuine potential for investors. Not only do they suggest particular stocks, they also track them in detail, offering tips on when to buy additional shares or when it's time to sell completely.

On the one hand, using an analyst's recommendations to buy stocks is akin to a mutual fund. You're effectively deferring judgment—although not as complete as with a mutual fund—to a financial professional. And, since they are professionals, in theory at least, they should be able to devote more time and access more resources than the average investor on the street might be able to.

But it's not quite so simple as that. For one thing, like every other type of work, there are good analysts and those who are not so good (although, if they're genuinely horrible, odds are they won't stick around for too long). On top of that, depending on which analyst you're talking about and how you access their thinking, you may have to pay for the privilege.

Finally, although this isn't absolutely cut and dried, relying on an analyst somewhat runs against the whole idea of building your own stock portfolio in lieu of buying a mutual fund. The idea is to do it on your own—or at least somewhat on your own—and craft something that's suited to you and no one else. Defer completely to an analyst, and you're running counter to that.

One compromise point is to read a variety of analysts and take their varying opinions into account. From there, simply make your own call—treating their input as just another source of information from which you build your own judgment.

Stock Screens

Like mutual funds, stock screens can also be an exceedingly useful and time-saving tool in choosing the right stocks. Again, how this function works differs from one site to another, but they let you specify just what kind of stock you're interested in and, from there, the system returns with recommended stocks that match those guidelines.

One solid example is Morningstar's stock screener (http://screen.morningstar.com/ StockSelector.html?ssection=StockScreener). There, you can specify any number of characteristics, including type of stock, a certain level of financial performance, company size, and other criteria. From there, the system kicks back companies that match all of the specifics you've requested.

But be wary about paying for the privilege. These days, it isn't hard to find a stock screen that's available for free. Following is just a sample listing of sites to get you started:

- Morningstar (www.morningstar.com)
- MSN Money Stock Screener (http://moneycentral.msn.com/investor/finder/customstocksdl.asp)
- Yahoo! Finance (http://screen.yahoo.com/stocks.html)
- CNBC Stock Screener (www.cnbc.com/id/15839076)

How to Buy Stock

Like other sorts of investments, there are any number of ways to buy stock to fund your retirement. Here's a rundown of the choices available to you, along with their varied advantages and drawbacks.

Traditional Full-Service Brokerage House

For years, this was the sole option for anyone interested in buying stocks. The methodology is simple. You open an account at a brokerage house and you start working with a broker. From there, you buy stocks and craft a portfolio, just as you would with any other means of buying stocks.

The difference is in service—and the expense you pay for that service. A broker charges a commission every time he or she executes a trade on your behalf. While that varies from one brokerage house to the next, the cost can often be substantial.

In return for that expense, a good broker should work closely with you to develop a portfolio that's suited to your needs. Not only should this involve a fair amount of interaction between the two of you so your broker gets to know you, your investment style, and your needs, a solid broker should also be proactive. That means he or she will call with ideas that they think jibe with your situation.

Retire Right _____

Think any broker selling stock is fully on the up and up? Don't. Get a report on any broker with whom you're thinking of working from the National Association of Securities Dealers at 1-800-289-9999.

Going with a full-service broker has its advantages and drawbacks. There are investors who swear by their broker, citing their guidance and oversight. Others value the resources that many full-service brokers can provide, from research to programs designed to better educate investors.

But there is the cost—often substantial. And some argue that since full-service brokers are paid on a commission basis, their advice can often be driven—even in part—by a looming paycheck rather than your best financial interests.

Discount Brokers

These charge less than full-service brokers to execute trades. To illustrate: one discount firm chosen at random charges $17.95 for a phone trade involving up to $1,000 shares ($12.95 if you trade online and $37.95 if the trade involves an in-house broker). On average, discounters charge anywhere from one third to one fourth what full-service fees might levy in commission.

The tradeoff is there's a good deal less hand-holding with discounters. For the most part, it's up to you to do the research behind your investment decisions (which isn't as intimidating as it might seem at first, as many discounters have substantial research capability, particularly online).

Deep Discount

These are the cheapest of the cheap. Another example chosen at random: one online firm charges a flat $9.99 for all Internet-based trades, no matter the number of shares involved. Again, like other houses, the fee jumps substantially once you stray off the Internet—$34.99 over the phone and $44.99 if a living, breathing broker is involved.

> **Retirement Reality**
>
> Recently, the line between full-service and discount firms has blurred. Full-service brokers now offer less-expensive Internet-based services, while discounters are providing more traditional services.

Some Stock Strategies

Unto itself, the idea of buying stock is simple—you choose one that looks good and hope it goes up in value.

But there are several strategies that augment that basic function to better your chances for success. Here are four that may prove particularly helpful.

Dollar-Cost Averaging

Here, you invest a set amount of money on a regular basis, regardless of whether the stock is going up or down. The thinking is, if the stock has gone down in price, you're able to buy more shares. And, if the stock has gone up in price—who's complaining? This can help you amass a greater holding for your retirement in a cost-effective manner. But note: because of commissions, dollar-cost averaging is more suitable for mutual funds than individual stocks.

Value Averaging

This is a variant on dollar-cost averaging that takes into account stock price movement. For instance, say you wish to invest $300 every month. If, by the end of that first month, the stock has gone down to $280 in value, you next invest $320 to bring the overall amount for the two months up to $600 as planned. By the same token, if the stock goes up to $330, you only have to invest $270 to reach the $600 target level.

Limit Orders

This is a system that lets you establish prices at which you wish to buy or sell. Here, you specify where you want to get involved with a stock—say one you like is at $45 and you want to buy at $40. You then instruct your broker (or the online system) to buy it when it drops to that level. If it goes lower, the sell order kicks in at the lower price.

The same works for selling. If you order a sale at $50, that's when the sale occurs. If the price goes higher, you automatically sell at the higher price. This helps lock in gains for your retirement.

The potential drawback to this system is the capriciousness of the market. If, say, you put in an order for $40 and a stock only drops to $40.50, you can lose out on a great investment due to a mere 50 cents.

Stop Loss Orders

This is specifically designed to limit your losses and protect whatever profit you may have earned from a stock. To illustrate: you buy a stock at $10 and it moves to $30. You then set up a stop loss at $20—if the stock moves to that level, the stock is automatically sold, protecting a $10 per share profit.

One particular bit of advice: don't set up a stop loss too close to a stock's current price—say, $28 on a stock currently valued at $30. You may protect your profit, but you may also be selling yourself short if the drop is only a short-term bump after which the stock soars.

The Least You Need to Know

- If you have a retirement plan that allows them—such as an IRA—stocks can provide great long-term growth potential. But, like other investments, be sure to diversify.

- Stocks represent a share of ownership in a company and come in varied types.

- When choosing a stock, use the company's annual report to get to know the company inside and out. Know how profitable it is, how much debt it carries, and other issues. This is known as fundamental analysis.

- Some investors prefer to track the trading patterns of a stock. This is known as technical analysis.

- Investigate various types of brokerage operations carefully. Don't necessarily sacrifice service for cost.

- Strategies such as dollar-cost averaging and stop loss orders can also be effective tools in developing a winning stock portfolio.

The Basics of Investing, Part Three: Bonds and GICs

In This Chapter

- ◆ Types of bonds
- ◆ How bonds earn money
- ◆ The risks of bonds
- ◆ How to buy bonds
- ◆ Bond mutual funds and GICs
- ◆ The role of bonds in your retirement

In this third and final chapter that addresses various ways to invest your money for retirement, we take something of a different turn off the road we've been following. As you know, mutual funds and stocks represent a form of ownership in a company. You buy shares in hopes that, as the company prospers, so will your share of the pie.

Bonds and guaranteed investment contracts hold a different role in the investment world. Not to say they're necessarily a better or worse choice than a form of equity investment but, rather, an alternative—a form of balance that can lend stability and strength to a retirement funding portfolio.

Bonds—What They Are

Bonds serve a different function when it comes to providing a company—and other entities—with the financial means to grow. As we said earlier, a stock is a form of ownership. Not so with bonds. A bond is a form of loan—in buying a bond, you're effectively entering into a contract with the issuer of that bond to pay whatever money you put up, plus interest.

Each bond generally specifies just how often it will pay interest to investors—usually twice a year. On top of that, how much each payment comes to is also usually pre-arranged.

Bonds also have a specified lifetime, which is also known as the "term." Once a bond reaches its term, investors have received the last of their interest payments and, at that point, also receive the *face value* of the bond.

def•i•ni•tion

Face value refers to the principal, the amount of money you invested when you bought the bond. It's also known as par value.

Bonds generally fall into one of three categories when it comes to varying length of terms:

- A short-term bond is usually anything less than 3 years.

- Intermediate bonds can run from 4 years up to 12.

- Long-term bonds' terms last for 12 years and even longer.

In general, the longer the term of the bond, the greater the interest that bond will pay its investors. The downside, of course, is that the longer the term of the bond, the longer you have to wait to get your initial investment back.

Types of Bonds

As is the case with most any other sort of investment, bonds come in a variety of forms, each of which can serve to address a particular investment need or financial goal.

Corporate Bonds

Corporate bonds are issued by firms looking to raise money for any number of activities, from corporate expansion to underwriting development of a new product line.

Many firms, in fact, prefer to raise cash via bonds in lieu of other options, such as issuing stock or seeking out a bank loan.

Corporate bonds take in two distinct subsets. The first is known as an investment grade bond. These, simply put, are the cream of the crop of the bond world. They are generally issued by large companies with impeccable financial credentials. As a result, these can be among the safest and most reliable bonds an investor can purchase.

The other end of the bond spectrum takes in junk bonds. In a way, that name is something of a misnomer. Rather than being worthless, junk bonds are issued by companies without the financial means to deal in investment-grade issues.

That classification cuts both ways. On the positive side for investors, given that junk bonds are seen as riskier than investment grade, their *yield* is often greater than that of investment grade. But, with junk bonds, since the firms issuing them lack the financial stability of investment-grade issuers, there's a chance that the companies will fail to pay off investors as the bonds specify.

Just how can you tell the difference between industrial-class bonds and those with a greater degree of risk? Well, for one thing, the company issuing them should tell you something—a member of the Dow Jones 30 isn't as likely to put out bonds with a risk of default; a company with only a few years of operating history stands a better chance of doing that.

def•i•ni•tion

Yield is the effective rate of interest that a bond pays to investors.

But there's a more empirical way to do it. Bonds are rated by ratings agencies such as Moody's and Standard and Poor's. Each attaches a letter (or series of letters) which, at a glance, encapsulates the safety and credit solvency of the company issuing the bond.

For instance, the system at Moody's is as follows:

- Aaa—Exceptional financial security.

- Aa—Excellent financial security

- A—Good financial security.

- Baa—Adequate financial security.

- Ba—Questionable financial security.

- B—Poor financial security.

- Caa—Very poor financial security.

- Ca—Extremely poor financial security.

- C—The worst of the worst. These are usually already in default.

Retire Right _____

For additional information behind what ratings mean, go to www.moodys.com or www.standardandpoors.com.

When it comes to finding suitable investments for your retirement, these ratings can prove a critical safety measure. Unless you are operating from an extremely long time horizon with decades before you plan to retire, it's generally prudent to stick with higher-rated bonds with a greater certainty of safety.

Know, too, that a bond's rating can change. For instance, Moody's or Standard and Poor's can drop a rating if a company suffers through a particularly harsh financial period. That, in turn, may suggest a bond that isn't quite so solid as you once believed.

Golden Years Gaffes _____

Generally, a rating of Baa or better is "investment grade." Below that is "junk"—bonds that offer higher potential returns but also the greatest amount of risk. As a rule, it's best to avoid junk bonds for your retirement portfolio.

Treasury Bonds

These are issued and backed by the federal government. They come in various forms, including securities, notes, savings bonds, and other formats. They include:

- **Treasury bills.** These are government securities that can mature in a few days up to several weeks.

- **Treasury notes.** These are also government securities but with long maturation—as long as 10 years.

- **Treasury bonds.** These earn interest every six months.

- **I Savings Bonds.** These are tied to inflation. If inflation goes up—eroding the purchasing power of money—so does the amount an I Bond pays, protecting the value of the bond from inflation.

- **E and EE Savings Bonds.** These pay interest based on current market rates. They can mature in as long as 30 years.

One of the biggest advantages to treasuries in their varied forms is their security—backed in full by the federal government. They are also exceedingly convenient to buy and levy no commission or sales charges. The downside is that returns can be rather modest—you may do just as well or even better with money markets and CDs. And, like CDs, cash them in prior to their maturity date and penalties can accrue. For instance, you have to hold an I Bond for at least a year. If you redeem it before holding it five years, you forfeit three months' interest.

For more information on treasury programs of all sorts, check out TreasuryDirect at www.savingsbonds.gov.

Zero Coupon Bonds

These offer an interesting twist so far as payback is concerned. They pay interest, but in a lump sum when the bond matures. The advantage to that is you can buy these bonds at a deep discount—50 to 80 percent of their face value, depending on how long a maturity date the bonds carry.

These can be particularly handy for funding your retirement. For instance, if you know a particular zero coupon bond will pay $10,000 when it matures in 20 years, you can plan on having that amount of money at that time. That makes zero coupons an effective retirement funding tool, since you know precisely what you can expect at a particular time. Moreover, you can buy several zero coupons with different maturity dates, thereby providing a structured, predictable flow of funds.

Municipal Bonds

These are bonds issued by local and state governments. They help pay for all sorts of municipal projects, including schools, highways, hospitals, housing, sewer systems, and other important public programs. One of the particular lures of municipal bonds to investors is that their return is exempt from federal taxes and, in many cases, state and local taxes as well.

"Munis" (as they are known) actually come in two distinct forms:

♦ General obligations bonds are backed by the credit rating of the particular branch of the government that sells them to the public. These are generally considered very safe.

♦ Revenue bonds. These are generally sold for a specific project, such as building a highway or bridge. These are a bit less predictable because payback to investors depends on the project itself ultimately producing sufficient revenue to pay back those investors.

That raises a question: how should you choose between tax-free muni bonds and other sorts of bonds that may pay a higher rate of return? That depends on the bond's yield as well as your tax bracket. There's a simple formula that lets you make this calculation. Take the yield of a tax-free bond and divide it by one minus your tax rate. For example, a 4 percent municipal bond for someone in the 25 percent tax bracket would produce the taxable equivalent of 5.3 percent. Translated: go with any bond you may be considering that pays 5.3 percent or better. Anything less than that, and you're better off with the tax-free alternative.

International Bonds

These are bonds issued by companies based outside the United States. Like stocks, they can occasionally offer higher yields than domestic bonds. The downside is—depending on the area of the world involved—greater political or economic instability. Additionally, there's the risk of the American dollar increasing in value versus foreign currencies. If that occurs, foreign bonds drop in value.

A particularly large percentage of the foreign bond market is government bonds, as many countries do not have corporate bond markets developed to the extent that the United States does.

How Bonds Make Money

As noted earlier, bonds provide investors a return through a series of regular fixed payments. In that respect, they can be an ideal choice for retirement planning, providing a stream of reliable, predictable income.

Retirement Reality
Bonds may be predictable, but over time, they don't compare favorably with stocks. Since the 1920s, long-term government bonds have returned an average slightly in excess of 5 percent. Stocks have topped 10 percent.

But it isn't quite so cut and dried as that. Bonds can also generate income as a result of interest rate changes.

As a rule, bonds have an inverse relationship with interest rates. If interest rates go down, existing bonds can become more valuable. The reason is that newer bonds will be issued at a lower interest rate, making the older bond's higher rate that much more valuable.

Here's an example of what can happen if you try to sell a bond before it reaches its maturity and interest rates are changing. Say you buy a 10-year corporate bond with a 6 percent yield. You pay $1,000. On the most simple level, that means you'll earn $60 every year you continue to own the bond.

A year after you bought the bond, interest rates fall to 5 percent. At that level, you could probably sell your bond for about $1,100. That makes sense, since your 6 percent bond is worth more than the new ones coming out at 5 percent. Put that profit together with the $60 you earned in interest for one year, and that's a total profit of about 16 percent.

The longer the term of the bond, the greater the impact of interest rates. That, too, figures—if you're holding a 7 percent bond for a long period of time, that offers a lot of opportunity for interest to slide considerably. And the lower interest rates go, the more valuable your bond becomes.

The Risks of Bonds

For all their conservative nature when compared with stocks, bonds do carry some risks. And, in designing a retirement portfolio, it's essential to know those potential pitfalls.

- **Interest rates.** This can be very destructive, particularly with long-term bonds in a period of rising interest rates. The higher rates go, the less your bond is worth. One way to build a portfolio that's less vulnerable to interest rate movement is called laddering. This is a strategy in which you buy bonds that mature in a certain order—one matures one year, another in two or three years, and so on. The thinking is, if interest rates climb, you will shortly have funds to invest at higher rates once some of your bonds mature. And, if interest rates go down, longer-term bonds will still provide relatively high returns.

- **Credit risk.** We also covered this earlier, but it bears a brief reminder. The lower the credit rating, the higher the risk of default.

- **Liquidity.** This refers to your ability to sell a bond you own. This may not matter if you plan to hold a bond until maturity, but it can be a problem if you wish to sell, say, a bond whose credit rating has dropped. This is considerably less of a problem with federally backed treasuries and other bonds issued by the government.

◆ **Call provisions.** This isn't so much of a problem as it is a consideration. Many companies "call" their bonds early, meaning they pay them off prior to the pre-arranged maturity. This can happen during periods of dropping interest rates, as companies can reissue new bonds and pay less in interest. The biggest headache for you is the decision of how to invest the money that's suddenly back in your lap—at a time when bonds are likely paying less than they did before. Check the bond's prospectus before you buy. That will tell you whether the bond can be called and, if so, the earliest that can happen.

◆ **Inflation.** This can develop slowly but, over time, can prove a significant drawback to bonds. As you know, inflation is the effect of rising prices on the purchasing power of money. That same effect can occur with bonds, particularly ones that are held for a long period of time. Even with a very modest 2 percent inflation, a bond yielding 6 percent is actually only returning 4 percent.

> **Retirement Reality**
>
> When it comes to offsetting the effects of inflation, stocks have historically enjoyed more success than bonds.

How to Shop for Bonds

Like other sorts of investments, there are a variety of ways you can buy bonds.

Full-Service Brokerage Houses

Just as is the case with stocks, you can patronize any number of well-known, full-service brokers to buy bonds. But, like stocks, you're likely to pay more in commissions than you would with other options.

Discount Brokerage Houses

This is one less costly alternative to conventional full-service operations. The tradeoff is less guidance and hand-holding from a broker—the burden of research is on you.

Direct Purchase Plans

This is the most straightforward way to buy bonds offered by the federal government. A program known as Treasury Direct establishes a regular schedule of auctions at which time bonds are sold to the public.

When buying bonds, be sure to do a bit of shopping. Prices can vary from one broker to the next. And, as we suggested with regard to laddering bonds, don't buy bonds in a vacuum. Try to diversify your holdings with regard to term, type of bond, and other characteristics.

Retire Right

For more information about TreasuryDirect, go to www. savingsbonds.gov.

Speaking of Diversity—Bond Mutual Funds

If the idea of researching and shopping for individual bonds seems too time-consuming or intimidating, there is an alternative. Like stocks, bonds are also sold in the form of mutual funds.

Their basic function is also similar to stock-based funds. Bond mutual funds let you pool your money with other investors'. The funds, under professional management, are then invested in a portfolio of bonds.

Since interest rates affect bonds directly, the price and return of bond funds differs from stock funds. The overall return of a bond fund comes, in part, from the total interest payments the fund's various bonds earn. Additionally, the fund's price is also affected by interest rate movement—positively if interest rates fall and decreasing if interest rates rise.

Like stock funds, bond funds have a net asset value (NAV)—a dollar value for one share of the fund.

Bond funds also offer many of the same advantages as stock funds. For one thing, you're able to enjoy instant diversification or, at the very least, greater diversification than you might be able to have buying individual bonds on your own. That lowers overall risk, particularly with respect to bonds being called and defaulting outright.

Bond funds are also more liquid than many individual bonds, as it's generally simple and straightforward to buy and sell shares. And, like stock funds, you also enjoy the advantages of professional, experienced management.

Funds are available that emphasize all sorts of bonds, including treasury bonds and other federal bonds, tax-free municipal bonds, and corporate bond funds. Additionally, there are zero coupon bond funds, international bond funds, and convertible bond funds (these are bonds that may be converted into stock). There are also funds that cut across several different sorts of bonds, thereby furthering overall diversity.

What to Look for in Bond Funds

When shopping for a suitable bond fund, one significant difference between stock funds and bond funds is interest rate sensitivity. As we've discussed, bond prices react to interest rate fluctuations—that makes it important to gain a sense of how a given fund may respond to interest rate shifts.

To do that, read the fund's prospectus and look for the fund's bond duration. This is the average maturity of all the bonds the fund owns. In fact, bond funds are grouped according to duration: short term (1–3 years); intermediate (4–12 years); and long term (12 years and longer)—just the same as individual bonds.

And the relationship between interest rates and a fund's duration is the same as exists with individual bonds. Short-term funds are the least volatile when it comes to interest rate shifts but also offer the lowest return. By the same token, longer-term funds trade off higher paybacks with a greater degree of interest rate volatility.

In addition, consider the following issues when shopping for bond funds:

♦ **Like stock funds, stick with no-loads.** There's really no need to take on the added expense of a load.

♦ **Pay attention to expenses.** As is the case with stock funds, some bond funds operate more efficiently than others. The lower the expenses, the less subtracted from returns paid out to investors.

Retire Right _____

Like mutual funds and stocks, a number of financial websites provide screening services to help you select a bond fund based on performance, safety, and other factors.

♦ **Check the credit rating of bonds in the fund.** Like individual bonds, an overload of poorly rated bonds in a fund may increase the return— but it certainly increases the risk of default.

♦ **Watch for minimum starting investments.** Some funds are rather modest; others mandate substantial sums to open an account.

How to Follow a Bond

Bond prices, like stocks, are listed in some of the more financially complete newspapers. To track your bond, here are some terms you should get to know:

♦ Bonds are presented in a left to right column format. The first item on the left is the issuer—the company or other entity who issued the bond.

- Next is the bond's coupon rate. This is the interest rate the bond paid at the time of its issue.

- The next figure is a two-digit number—this is the year when the bond is scheduled to mature.

- The next two numbers are the bond's yield and volume, which represents the amount of trading that occurred in the prior trading day.

- From there, you see the close (the price at which the bond concluded trading). The last column is net change, which shows how much the bond gained or lost in value as a result of the trading day.

Guaranteed Investment Contracts (GICs)

One final retirement funding option that is something of a variant on bonds is known as a Guaranteed Investment Contract, or GIC. These are issued by insurance companies or banks and are marketed to companies with defined contribution plans, such as 401(k)s. In fact, GICs have become a mainstay choice in a host of 401(k) plans.

Like a bond, a GIC involves a promise that, having invested your money, you will receive a certain return within a specified period of time. Contracts can run up to five years and, like a bond, the interest rate is fixed. (As of this writing, five-year GICs were paying in the vicinity of 4.3 percent annually.)

The upside to GICs is, as the name implies, your rate of return is guaranteed. The downside is your principal is not guaranteed, as it is with lesser paying options such as federal Treasury notes.

Where Bonds and GICs Fit in Your Retirement Program

Having covered bonds, bond mutual funds, and GICs in some detail, it begs the question: What is the best way to use them when putting together a retirement funding program?

For many reading this book, the question may be moot, at least up to a point. For instance, if you're taking part in a 401(k) plan where you work, bonds may not be an option available to you. By the same token, as we just saw, GICs may be a different story, as they are rather popular 401(k) options.

But you may have an IRA, a Simplified Employee Pension, or a retirement program you've set up on your own where you have complete freedom of choice. Bonds and GICs are very much a choice for you, if indeed they fit.

That, in turn, raises a number of issues. First is the amount of time you have until retirement. As we will see in some detail in Chapter 13, a long time frame is the optimal spot to be in. Not only do you have the most amount of time to save, you also have sufficient time to be reasonably aggressive with your investments. Since you have adequate time, you can ride out volatility and enjoy the growth potential that an aggressive position can achieve.

That puts a strong case against a significant portion of your portfolio going into bonds and GICs. As we've discussed, stocks and mutual funds have it all over bonds—historically speaking—when it comes to growth. That's a precedent you want to take full advantage of.

But notice we said "significant." For one thing, never lose sight of your tolerance for risk. If the thought of being 100 percent invested in stocks gives you the willies, it simply isn't worth going against your nature in hopes of scoring slightly higher returns. That argues for bonds and GICs in the mix to offset that aggressiveness (we'll discuss specific breakdowns in the next chapter).

Know, too, that bonds and GICs should likely play a greater role in your portfolio the closer you get to retirement. As you near 10 to 15 years until your retirement, you don't want to be as exposed to volatility as you might have been able to handle in early years. Safety and capital preservation become more important—that, too, makes the case for stocks and GICs.

Finally, once you're retired, bonds and GICs can prove integral elements of your portfolio. Here, rather than growth, safety and income are paramount. And, as we've seen, those are bonds' and GICs' stock-in-trade.

Should bonds and GICs characterize your retirement portfolio? Not necessarily. But nor should you ignore them outright. Now that you've come to know them a bit, we can move on to discuss how they and other investments can come together—no matter where you happen to be on the retirement funding continuum.

The Least You Need to Know

- Bonds are issued by companies, the federal government, and other local government agencies to fund all sorts of activities.

- Bonds are rated according to their safety. The lower the ranking, the greater the potential payback, but the risk is greater as well.

- Bonds are also affected by interest rates. If rates go down, existing bonds go up in value because they pay more than bonds issued when rates are lower.

- Bonds are also available in mutual fund form. Like stock funds, they offer diversity and professional management.

- GICs (Guaranteed Investment Contracts) are also a form of guaranteed payback. They are popular in 401(k) plans.

- Bonds don't offer the growth potential of stocks, but they can be useful for diversification and to balance the risks of stocks.

Timing Is Everything

The first two parts of the book were largely topic-focused. Part 3, by comparison, takes more of a chronological look at the retirement funding continuum, showing how strategies covered in prior sections of the book fit best in your progress toward retirement. We'll start with what you can do at a young age to begin planning your retirement. Next, we'll examine the importance of monitoring your progress as you get close to retirement. This part wraps up with a variety of strategies and ideas to help your retirement savings last as long as you need them to.

Chapter 13

If You're Young

In This Chapter

- ◆ The importance of risk tolerance
- ◆ How aggressive should you be?
- ◆ Max out to the max
- ◆ Going on autopilot
- ◆ Job shopping? Check your retirement
- ◆ Don't overlook IRAs

You're young. You may be fresh out of school, hard at work at your first job (or hard at work trying to find that first job). Your life—personal as well as professional—stretches ahead of you in a seemingly endless continuum.

With that sort of preamble, talking about the importance of planning for the day some 40-plus years down the line when you hang up your working shoes may seem—well, to put it politely, a bit premature.

Not at all. When you're young is the absolute optimal time to start thinking about—and acting on—your retirement. As we will see, not only does an early jump on the process afford you that much more freedom of choice, you also provide yourself with the best opportunity possible to amass the largest retirement nest egg you possibly can. And that's a pleasant outcome that's never too early to start thinking about.

Time Equals Opportunity

We have touched on this briefly in prior chapters, but it bears a bit of repetition—and greater detail—here. Simply put: if you're young and you're thinking about your retirement, time is one of the most powerful weapons in your retirement planning arsenal.

We've touched on why. Not only does time tend to smooth out short-term volatility in what you have your retirement nest egg in—such as the stock market—the power of compounding affords you the greatest opportunity possible to amass a significant sum of money by the time you're retired.

A few financial scenarios can really bring this concept home:

A 22-year-old is planning to retire at age 65. He is able to save $100 in a tax-deferred 401(k) every month. The 401(k) account averages a 7 percent annual return. By retirement time, the retirement nest egg has grown to more than $328,000.

Now, let's up the stakes a little. Our 22-year-old can still put aside $100 every month, but now he's a bit more comfortable with a more aggressive investment position. The ride is a bit rough but, over the same 43-year period, his portfolio now averages a 10 percent return every year. End result: $857,000, more than double the amount earned with a mere 3 percent less in annual return.

Retire Right

If you're interested in working out a few scenarios of your own, point your browser to the savings calculator at www.bankrate.com/brm/cgi-bin/savings.asp.

What really brings the importance of a lengthy timeline to the forefront is even the most modest reduction in time. Let's take the same scenario as in the first example—a target age of 65, $100 monthly savings, and a 7 percent annual return. However, our subject starts saving 10 years later, at age 32. At the other end of the equation—$154,406, some 48 percent of what would have accrued had things gotten started a mere 10 years sooner. You would have to roughly double your monthly savings to catch up to the amount that 10 years more would afford with $100.

Just to fill things out, the same scenario with a 10 percent return comes out even more dire—$309,000. You would have to save about $200 every month to match the returns that $100 with an extra 10 years can produce.

Are we trying to scare you? Not really. What we are doing is offering graphic illustration of a few salient truths when it comes to funding your retirement. They are:

- **The sooner, the better.** Getting started with your retirement can only be more fulfilling and rewarding the sooner you start.

- **Even small delays can have significant consequences.** The calculations we've offered paint a bleak picture of what can happen if you put off retirement savings for even as little as 10 years.

- **The earlier you start, the less the pressure that's on you.** The scenarios we worked out resulted in substantial payoffs with a mere $100 every month. The sooner you start, the less the mandate that you save to the absolute max (of course, as we'll discuss later, maxing out your retirement savings is never, ever a bad idea).

- **The longer you wait, the greater the pressure.** By the same token, the shorter your timeline to retirement, the more you're obligated to save to make up for lost time.

Risk Tolerance—There's the Rub

That circles back to a topic we've addressed briefly before but which now commands more complete attention—*risk tolerance*.

Needless to say, risk tolerance can mean different things to different investors. For example, some investors may not bat an eye if their retirement savings drop 10 percent with a downturn in the markets. That same 10 percent slide may send others careening to the phone, demanding that their broker liquidate every last share.

def•i•ni•tion

Risk tolerance refers to the amount of uncertainty and volatility with which an investor feels comfortable.

Personal discomfort aside, risk tolerance can also have some very practical aftereffects. For one thing, if you're conservative by nature and your retirement savings has somehow found its way into aggressive investments, you may be tempted to pull the plug at the first sign of any sort of volatility.

That's a problem in two ways. First off, if you do change your holdings, there may be costs involved—commissions, taxes owed, and the like. Moreover, it's a self-defeating proposition; if you're in over your head from a risk-tolerance standpoint, you're likely to bail at a low price point—the most costly for you. If you can't stand the ride, you won't be able to sit through drops that ultimately lead to rebounds—and the kind of profit that an aggressive posture can offer you.

All that said, it can be very advantageous when you're young to determine your risk tolerance—and, from there, to craft a retirement portfolio that matches that tolerance rather than conflicting with it.

Risk Tolerance—A Quick Quiz

We know that risk tolerance is an important element in finding the right investment mix—particularly at a young age. Although your needs and goals may change over time, who you are and how you feel about investing may not change all that much.

Fortunately, there are ways to decipher your risk tolerance. Mark J. Snyder Financial Services of Medford, New York, has devised a questionnaire to help you figure out just what your risk tolerance might be.

That said, take a few minutes to consider the following questions. (These questions are part of a more comprehensive investors' quiz which you can find in Appendix B.)

Primary Objective

Think about your investment goals. How would you generally categorize your primary objective?

- ◆ **Capital Preservation.** This is emphasis on safety and stability. Future growth of income and principal are of minor importance. You have a low tolerance for large fluctuations. Give yourself 1 point.

- ◆ **Current income.** You want a high level of current income. Future growth of income and principal are secondary objectives. 2 points.

- ◆ **Balanced.** Roughly equal emphasis on current income and potential for future appreciation and income growth. 3 points.

- ◆ **Long-Term Growth.** Emphasis on future appreciation. Year-to-year principal stability is not important. 4 points.

Investment Returns

Over the past 70 years, the following investment vehicles returned the following average yearly gains:

- ◆ Stocks: 11 percent

◆ Bonds: 5.2 percent

◆ Cash (treasury bills) 3.7 percent

At the same time, inflation has averaged 3.7 percent.

Knowing this, what would you consider a reasonable average annual return for your portfolio?

◆ Less than 5 percent: 1 point

◆ 5 to 8 percent: 2 points

◆ 9 to 12 percent: 3 points

◆ 13 percent or greater: 4 points

The following bullets summarize how much the stock market has fallen in any given year since 1900:

◆ Routine decline (5 percent or more): About three times a year

◆ Moderate correction (10 percent or more): About once a year

◆ Severe correction (15 percent or more): About once every 2 years

◆ Bear market (20 percent or more): About every 3 years

Assume that you have $100,000 invested. That sum represents your entire savings. Given the information you know about the possibility of a down stock market, what is the maximum level of decline you would comfortably accept with your $100,000 investment?

◆ $95,000: 1 point

◆ $90,000: 2 points

◆ $85,000: 3 points

◆ $78,000: 4 points

Now tally up your three point totals. Score them according to the following guidelines:

◆ 3 to 5 points: Very conservative, uncomfortable with any or very little risk.

◆ 6 to 8 points: Conservative to balanced, somewhat comfortable with a small amount of risk.

- 9 to 10 points: Aggressive. Comfortable with risk.

- 11 to 12 points: Very aggressive. Equally comfortable with significant risk.

This is not intended to be an exact indicator, but it can prove an effective barometer in giving yourself a view of just how much risk you may be willing to take on.

Finding the Long-Term Mix That's Right for You

Now that you have a sense of what your risk tolerance is, we can begin to devise some sample portfolios that take that as well as your relatively young age into consideration.

First, let's start with what many investment authorities consider the "classic" balanced portfolio. That's made up of 60 percent stocks, 30 percent fixed income (such as bonds or GICs), and 10 percent cash. In fact, if you look at many balanced mutual funds, that's just the sort of mix you're likely to find.

But notice that we kept that rather generic—a sort of middle-of-the-road compromise. If you're young and you're saving for your retirement, that means you can afford to crank that up some on the side of additional aggressiveness—maybe as high as 80 percent stock and 20 percent fixed income.

But bear in mind some caveats when approaching that sort of formulaic approach. For one thing, don't lose sight of your risk tolerance. We won't repeat things unnecessarily, but it simply doesn't work to gut out an approach to investing that just doesn't fit you.

But, by the same token, don't let your fears get the best of you—particularly if you're young. It's normal—perhaps even healthy—to be wary about the risks of aggressive investing. But don't let it lead to inertia—or, at the very least, a portfolio that's inadequately positioned with stocks to allow for the best possible long-term results.

Golden Years Gaffes

A recent Employee Benefit Research Institute study found that some 16 percent of 401(k) participants had no equity exposure at all in their 401(k)s. That, say investment authorities, is simply too timid to reach retirement goals.

Here's another exercise that may make you feel better about taking on some risk in your portfolio, particularly if you're young. Statistics suggest that, in any given year, stock mutual funds have a one-third to one-fourth chance of losing money. Over the course of five years, those odds plummet to a meager 4 percent. From there, the likelihood becomes steadily lower and lower.

That's as effective an argument as you can make for working toward a comfort level with an aggressive investment approach when you're young. The longer you stay with something, the more risk is mitigated by time.

Another Way to Tackle Risk Tolerance

Another way to approach the conundrum of risk tolerance is to do a bit of reverse math. First, figure out how much you expect you will need in assets when you retire and when you expect you'll want to retire (flip back to Chapter 4 for a walkthrough on this topic). Then, determine how much you think you'll be able to save on a monthly basis. From there, all you need to do is bring those two numbers together by figuring out what sort of return you'll need to average to achieve your long-term retirement goal with your monthly benchmark.

Here's a sample scenario: say you've calculated that you want a $500,000 nest egg by the time you retire at age 65. You're 25 years old now and you expect that you can set aside $200 a month on average toward retirement. To reach that goal, all you would need to average is 7 percent a year (more specifically, a 7 percent return over the course of 40 years totals $509,868).

That's the good news. The not-so-hot news—at least if your risk tolerance is rather slim—is that stocks in some capacity offer the best possible opportunity to hit that 7 percent average. It's not an astronomic level—one that doesn't mandate stocks with a high degree of volatility—but fixed-income choices simply aren't likely to make a 7 percent return over time.

That means you don't have to go over the edge risk-wise to find an investment vehicle that meets that goal. For instance, according to Morningstar, domestic mid-cap value funds—a very solid, not overly aggressive choice—have averaged nearly 11 percent over the past five years—more than adequate for the returns required by the example we've laid out. While not as stellar, domestic large-value funds have returned roughly 7.5 percent over the same time frame.

If you use this formula to determine what sorts of investments meet your needs, the Internet affords any number of ways to streamline your search. Sites such as Morningstar.com provide comprehensive search engines to help you pinpoint stocks and mutual funds that not only meet your necessary return requirements but that also fit within your risk tolerance.

Golden Years Gaffes

By comparison, one of the few fixed-income choices that meet the 7 percent average we needed in our example are high-yield bond funds (9.34 percent)—highly volatile junk bonds.

As a rule, if you're young and just starting out on a retirement funding program, chances are good that your available funds may be somewhat limited, at least at the outset. If that's the case, it's a good idea to stick to mutual funds as opposed to individual stocks. As we've already discussed, funds let you enjoy diversification and professional management, even if your financial means are relatively modest.

Max Out to the Max

There is yet another way to approach the risk tolerance challenge. This puts the onus on you—rather than opting for a risk level that may exceed your comfort zone, compensate by setting aside more to invest.

Let's go back to the scenario we worked up in the prior section. With a $500,000 retirement goal over a 40-year time frame, we figured you'd need to earn 7 percent on monthly savings of $200 to reach that target.

But what if, having examined your investment options, you find that none of the available choices jibe with your comfort level? Maybe you saw a few promising mutual funds, only to pick out a year or several years when they all suffered through subpar returns?

The answer: up your investment ante. To illustrate: if you find that a 5 percent annual return is, in fact, within your comfort zone (something that, as of this writing, you can just about get with certain Certificates of Deposit), you would have to increase your monthly savings to roughly $325 to compensate for the lower returns.

That may be doable for some and out of reach for others. But, no matter your risk comfort level or long-term investment goals, it does illustrate an important point, particularly if you're young—if at all possible, save the maximum amount that you can toward your retirement.

We've touched on this before, but its importance is particularly critical to young people with a long time to go before retirement. First, as we just discussed, saving to the absolute maximum is one effective way to counterbalance any skittishness you may have about certain investments. It's a simple maxim—the more you save, the less chance you have to take. Moreover, it's also an effective weapon to offset the effects of inflation.

Another point about maxing out is that it doesn't have to involve massive sums of money. Even if your max is only slightly greater than what you're saving now, the long-range benefits can prove substantial.

To illustrate: saving $200 a month for 30 years produces more than $241,000 at an average annual return of 7 percent. Add a mere $50 to that monthly amount and the eventual payout jumps to more than $301,000. Up it by a full $100 to $300 a month and the result over 30 years comes to $361,000. The longer the time frame and the greater the regular amount of savings, the bigger the payback.

The import of maxing out your savings becomes all the more vivid if you happen to take part in a 401(k) plan where your employer provides a match. Depending on where you work and the plan in which you participate, your employer may provide rather generous matches—up to $1 for every dollar you yourself contribute (up to a certain limit).

Retire Right

Need ways to free up additional savings for retirement? Flip back to Chapter 6 for some suggestions.

Here's another tip to help you max out a 401(k) plan. Rather than setting a particular dollar amount for your contributions, specify a percentage of your salary. That way, as you get raises and other boosts to your at-work income, your 401(k) contributions increase automatically, keeping you at the maximum contribution level.

Retirement Reality

Here's a helpful way to look at a match. Say your employer kicks in 50 cents for every dollar you put in. That's a 50 percent return right off the bat.

But, even if you aren't in a 401(k) or other sort of plan that kicks in a match, maxing out your retirement savings is a solid long-term investment—in yourself and your retirement.

Hit the Autopilot

One of the beauties of 401(k) plans—and a boon to maxing out your retirement savings—is that it all happens automatically. Once you can participate in a plan, you tell your plan administrator how much you wish to set aside from every paycheck and it all happens without your having to lift a finger.

That's a powerful strategy—one that you would do well to implement if, by chance, you're saving for your retirement in something other than a 401(k).

The easiest and most direct way of doing that is to set up an automatic withdrawal program. Most mutual funds allow you to do this without cost. All you have to do upon opening an investment account is to specify another account—such as a savings or checking account—that the fund may access for contributions. Specify an amount and how often you wish to make deposits and, from there, the fund withdraws that amount and invests it according to your directions.

Although the thought of some outside entity dipping into your bank account on a regular basis may be unnerving to some, the idea makes a world of sense. First off, you put your retirement investment program on autopilot. Like a 401(k), your investment strategy moves forward without your having to do a single thing.

That makes for systematic investing—a key element in building up a substantial retirement nest egg. The more you put into your retirement plan—and the longer you do it—the greater the sum you'll be able to enjoy at the other end. Automatic withdrawal programs make that happen.

Moreover, an automatic withdrawal program takes the "decision" of whether to invest or not somewhat out of your hands. We've all been there—we know it's important to save for our retirement, but there's a car payment that needs to be made or a high-definition television that we simply can't go another day without, and on and on. Those may or may not be worthy places to put your money, but an automatic withdrawal program makes sure that your retirement savings aren't sacrificed at the altar of some other financial necessity—or, worse, whim.

Job Shopping? Ask About Retirement

If you're still on the hunt for a job—and for many young people, it's a common situation to be in—you're naturally focused on salary, commute times, health insurance, and other elements relating to the position.

Don't overlook your company's retirement plan. As you probably surmise by now, it can prove every bit as important an element of your employment package as any other issue.

Those in the position of hiring employees know it, too. A recent small business retirement survey by the Transamerica Insurance and Annuity Co. found, among other things:

◆ A large majority of employers (74 percent) believe that employee-funded retirement plans are important in attracting workers. Roughly the same amount (75 percent) also believe that a solid retirement program is essential to keep good workers once they've been hired.

- Workers and employers agreed that an employee-funded 401(k) program with a company match was preferable to a plan funded exclusively by the company (65 percent versus 28 percent).

- The survey also found that employee-funded retirement programs were considered just about as important to workers as health and disability insurance.

- Lastly, more than two thirds (68 percent) of companies taking part in the survey said they offered their employees a match in their 401(k) programs.

The bottom line: retirement benefits matter, and both companies and the people whom they hire are aware of it. That said, when looking for a job, place a solid retirement plan up among the top items on your shopping list. Years down the line, you'll be thanking yourself.

Don't Turn a Blind Eye to IRA

You may have the best retirement program possible where you work. You're young and you're funding your retirement to the max. Both the years ahead and your current tax bill are smiling.

But, your work toward a solid retirement may not necessarily be done. If you have the means to do so, consider opening an Individual Retirement Account (IRA) to augment what you're doing on the job.

We covered IRAs in great detail in Chapter 9, but a brief reminder—no matter whether you have a retirement plan at work, IRAs are a great place to stash extra cash toward your retirement.

Here's why: anything you put into an IRA grows on a tax-deferred basis until you start to withdraw it beginning at age $59\frac{1}{2}$. And that can make a big difference over time, particularly when you compare it with saving in something that's open to taxes.

Where to find the extra cash to fund an IRA if you're already funding a 401(k) where you work? Look at it this way—calculate how much you're saving in taxes through your 401(k)'s pretax savings provision. Consider that found money, and stash it into an IRA.

Another plus—if you're young and are in a position to open an IRA for the first

Retire Right _____

The importance of an IRA is magnified if, by chance, you don't have a retirement plan where you work. Open an IRA and fund it to the hilt.

time, go with the Roth (and, through that, access its tax-free withdrawal privileges). Consider yourself lucky in that you don't have to jump through the hoops—and possible expenses—of converting a conventional IRA to a Roth.

The Least You Need to Know

- Start saving for your retirement as soon as possible. The earlier you start, the better your results.

- Don't exceed your comfort level with risk. If need be, increase the size of your contributions to offset a more conservative, lower rate of return.

- Try to save the maximum amount possible toward your retirement. You'll end up with more and, along the way, take some of the pressure off yourself.

- Consider an automatic withdrawal program to fund your retirement investments. It takes the decision out of your hands and makes your savings systematic.

- Consider the quality and scope of the retirement program when job shopping.

- If you can, open and fund an IRA. It can add extra muscle to any retirement program you have at work.

Midway to Retirement

In This Chapter

◆ Calculating where you are

◆ Are you better off than you thought?

◆ Adjustments when needed

◆ Balancing retirement with other needs

You've reached something of the halfway point in your retirement journey. That term is somewhat mercurial—for some, halfway may mean as few as 15 years or so; for others, you still have upwards of 25 years before retirement actually takes place. It all depends on where you are on the continuum and your particular retirement goals.

No matter the specifics of your situation, it's an opportune time to take stock of where you are—just how much progress you have made toward your retirement goals, what has changed along the way and, every bit as important, certain things that you might do to adjust your plan to help ensure that all happens as it should.

That midcourse evaluation is the meat of this particular chapter. Here, we'll help you determine just how well you've done so far, what changes—if any—you might need to make, and how to balance all these issues with other elements of your financial life. Consider this something of a checkup—one designed to identify all that's working properly and pinpoint those elements that still can be corrected without undue harm.

How Do You Stack Up?

One way to find where you stand with regard to saving for retirement is to compare yourself with others in similar situations.

The Employee Benefit and Research Institute has done just that. Through its 2006 Retirement Confidence Survey, the Institute has compiled a variety of telling facts and numbers pertaining to how good a job Americans are doing to prepare financially for retirement.

One portion of the report has to do with various age groups and how much each group has saved toward retirement. The table below summarizes a portion of that particular finding:

Reported Total Savings and Investments for Retirement (not including value of primary residence or defined benefit plans)

	All Workers	Ages 25–34	Ages 35–44	Ages 45–54
Less Than $25,000	53%	73%	49%	43%
$25,000–$49,000	12	11	14	14
$50,000–$99,000	12	7	16	12
$100,000–$249,999	11	4	12	14
$250,000 or more	12	5	9	16

Source: Employee Benefit Research Institute and Matthew Greenwald & Associates, Inc., 2006 Retirement Confidence Survey.

Those numbers paint a sobering picture. While the younger participants have time to make up the financial chasm that many of them face, the statistics for the older groups are particularly discouraging.

Given the topic of this chapter—people roughly halfway to retirement or so—snippets of detail from the findings are downright distressing. For instance, nearly half of participants as old as 44 have yet to save more than $25,000 for retirement. Perhaps even more stark—more than 4 out of 10 participants age 45 to 54 have yet to break through that same $25,000 savings threshold.

If, by chance, your situation is akin to one of these groups, it's a bona fide wake-up call to assess where you are in your retirement funding program and, if need be, really kick start it into action. With only 20 years or so to until your last paycheck, you haven't any time to lose.

> **Retirement Reality**
>
> By the way, the age 55 and older group is somewhat split—a rather gruesome 43 percent say they have $25,000 or less. Happily, 26 percent say they've stashed at least $250,000.

Gauging Where You Are

Now, let's turn to your situation. Having reached the approximate halfway point toward your retirement, just where are you in your progress in meeting your financial goals?

There are a number of ways to figure this. One simple way is to compare where you are with regard to your stated financial goal. Here's a brief breakdown of how that might go:

◆ Let's say you determined that you'll need $500,000 to retire.

◆ You began saving $5,000 a year at age 25, split between a tax-deferred 401(k) and an IRA. That portfolio has averaged a 9 percent average annual return.

◆ You have been saving for 20 years and you hope to retire at age 65.

◆ Result: good news. Your retirement nest egg is now worth some $276,000. Given that you're roughly at the halfway point on your retirement continuum, you're on track to reach your $500,000 goal.

But don't get locked into the simple formula of "halfway there equals half the amount I'll need." Remember, since you're starting your calculations from here on with a substantial sum—in this case $276,000—you're likely going to end up with a good deal more than just double that amount when it's time to retire. In fact, thanks to compounding and other factors, starting with $276,000 and staying with $5,000 a year in retirement savings at 9 percent annual return gets you to $1.9 million by age 65.

> Note: All these calculations specify an annual contribution, but calculations are figured on a prorated monthly basis (for instance, for the $5,000 a year example, the calculation is based on roughly $416 a month being deposited into a retirement account).

But our example also contains a number of caveats and other issues that you would do well to bear in mind. First is the substantial difference that can occur with reduced savings. For instance, if you had only managed to save $2,000 a year—$3,000 less than the figure we used—you would only have some $110,000 by the time you hit age 45. By the same token, if your investments hadn't matched the 9 percent annual return we used, that, too, could short-circuit your progress. The same thing can also occur if you start saving later or completely skip saving anything at all in some years.

Know, too, that your return now may not be a suitable target as you get closer to retirement. As we've discussed earlier, the closer you get to retirement, the more you may want to dial down your portfolio and emphasize safety over return. That, in turn, raises the imperative of shooting for the best returns possible while you're in a position to ride out any volatility.

That suggests a more thorough examination of your situation rather than just a sense of where you are on the road from point A to point B. Here's a checklist that can prove helpful:

- First, sit down with recent statements from all your investments. See how they are performing individually. Compare that with comparable investments to see if they're keeping pace.

- Break down the particulars of your investments. How has recent performance compared with long-range performance? Have there been developments—a change in a mutual fund's investment approach or the departure of a key fund manager—that may have affected performance?

- Examine your investment pattern. As we've covered, a smaller, more systematic pattern of investing produces better returns than one large deposit dumped in only once a year.

- Are you putting away the absolute maximum you can toward your retirement? Are other possible drains—such as credit card debt—impeding your ability to fund your retirement to the greatest amount possible? Is your mortgage payment too high and might you free up additional funds through refinancing?

- How do you see the years ahead? Do you expect salary increases or, by the same token, other expenses you don't have to handle at the present time? How will they affect your ability to save for your retirement?

- If your spouse is also contributing to retirement, how well is he or she doing? Is it possible for them to save more?

◆ Have your retirement goals remained the same? Do you expect to retire earlier or later than you initially planned? Has your financial goal changed in any way?

These sorts of questions add both substance and context to the relatively simple measure of where you happen to be financially. And, as a result, they can help steer you toward future decisions—what, if anything, needs to be adjusted to meet your retirement goals, and how best to go about implementing them.

So sit down with your brokerage statements, your W-2s or 1099s, bank statements, and any other element that has a hand in your retirement funding portfolio. Using the questions we outlined previously, get a sense not only of where you are in your retirement progress as expressed in a single sum—the amount you've saved to date—but also how you got there and what you need to do in the future to keep moving forward.

Moreover, make this a yearly habit from now on. Monitoring your progress and the appropriate strategy for your retirement is always important. It becomes all the more so the closer you get to actually retiring.

Golden Years Gaffes

Many people include the value of their homes in their retirement analysis. This is okay, within reason, as home prices can fluctuate considerably. Focus primarily on your investments

What If You're Ahead of the Curve?

Now, let's tackle a rather happy outcome. Let's say you've crunched the numbers and done all your homework and you find that, in fact, you're ahead of schedule—perhaps by a substantial amount.

First off, kudos. Give yourself a major-league pat on the back. Given the various challenges that can confront a successful retirement funding program—not to mention the horror stories we saw with the statistics presented earlier in this chapter—you have every right to feel proud. Bask in it for a minute.

But, however positive that news is, it's also just cause for some careful thought. Being ahead of the curve may be terrific, but it does pose a couple of questions.

Should I Cut Back on the Amount I'm Saving?

Human nature being what it is, finding out you're ahead of where you have to be can lead you to relax some. Maybe there's a vacation you've been putting off for years that now seems a good deal more viable. No matter the temptation, you may now feel well positioned to enjoy yourself more now and worry a tad less about the future.

In three words: stay the course. There are many reasons not to give in to whatever temptation may be luring you away toward other financial needs and wants, including …

♦ **Your investments hold no guarantees.** There's an old catchphrase in the investment world that you've likely heard: "Past performance is no guarantee of future results." The reason you're probably familiar with that maxim is because it's true. For instance, a mutual fund that has returned an average of 10 percent for the past 20 years always stands a chance of underperforming. Nothing is a given. Never assume that what you've been able to achieve to this point ensures the same level of performance in the future.

♦ **Nor, for that matter, is your own future guaranteed.** You may be healthy and happily employed today. Sad to say, but all that can change—very quickly. You may be laid off or become ill and unable to work. A family member who falls ill may require care on your part. Those and other incidents can severely affect your ability to earn a living—and, as a result, fund your retirement to the level to which you may have become accustomed. Hedge your bets by keeping on track now when you have the full means to do so.

♦ **Stay the course and you could retire earlier.** Let's go back to the example we worked with earlier: you're the 45-year-old with a $276,000 nest egg. We showed how much you would have after 20 years, but we didn't say how much you would have well before that. Well, here's the good news: having amassed $276,000 by age 45 and staying the course, you would reach your $500,000 goal at age 51 (you would have $504,000, to be exact). Theoretically, by staying with your retirement program from beginning to end, you could retire some 14 years earlier than you initially planned.

Don't take this exercise as gospel, of course. For one thing, it assumes a solid 9 percent annual return for a 26-year period. And, for your retirement funding needs, it takes other sources such as Social Security out of the equation completely. Not only would you not be eligible for benefits for 11 years (and at a reduced rate then, at that) you would also effectively cut back on your eventual benefits by working less and earning less at the same time. And, finally, the thought of stopping work at the relatively young age of 51 may simply be unappealing.

But it does illustrate that staying the course no matter how well you have done to date can raise some possibilities in areas you may not have considered. For instance, 51 may seem much too early to retire; on the other hand, 58 or so seems a good deal more attractive. Well, now the news gets even better—provided all our factors hold true, you'd be able to retire with a substantial $935,000—some $435,000 more than your initial goal and seven years earlier to boot.

Retire Right

Here's as good a reason to keep working as might ever exist. Remember, if the worker in our example stays on the job until age 65 and the investment results stay the same—the nest egg becomes $1.8 million.

What's Wrong with Having a Bit More?

This is not an argument on behalf of out and out greed. That being said, if you're ahead of where you expect to be, where's the harm in staying the course and, in the end, possibly come out with a good deal more than you expected? Again, all that does is open up a whole new realm of possibilities— a more active or engrossing lifestyle, more travel, or simply a greater gift of financial strength to pass along to your heirs.

Golden Years Gaffes

Be wary of reaching a retirement goal, only to set a new one, and so on. It's great to save all you can, but make that saving a goal for your retirement, not an end in itself.

Making Adjustments

Now, let's tackle the other end of the spectrum—one where your progress to date is not sufficient to meet your goals.

A reminder—although it seems easy to say "I'm midway to retirement so I should have one third of my nest egg in place," it doesn't work that way—luckily. Remember, the more you've been able to save, the more the effects of compounding take hold, increasing your overall return in future years.

Let's look at another example—one where someone manages to save $1,000 a year with a 9 percent annual return. The goal is $300,000. By the time our worker reaches age 45—20 years into the program—his total comes to $55,600—seemingly well off track from that $300,000 benchmark.

But compounding, time, and the amount he has saved to date save the day. By staying the $1,000-a-year course and earning 9 percent a year, our worker at age 65 will be able to retire with $390,0000—well more than the initial $300,000 goal. Again—an argument for an early start and discipline to stick with the program over time.

But what if the reverse is true—what if you're one of the many people with 20 or so years to go until retirement who isn't on track to get to where you want to financially?

Let's take something of a worst-case scenario from the Employee Benefit and Research Institute study cited earlier in the chapter: a worker age 45, with some $25,000 saved for retirement. Using the same 9 percent return cited above, if she didn't add a single penny to that amount, her cache at retirement at age 65 would be $140,000—an ample sum unto itself, but grossly inadequate to fund most sorts of retirement.

Now, let's step up a notch—the same 45-year-old but with savings of $50,000. Using the same dynamics we've used to this point, that amount would grow to $280,000. That's a bit more in most people's ballpark, but still rather limiting.

Why? Think back to Chapter 4 when we worked through some scenarios about how much you might need to live a lifestyle comparable to the one you have now. Although things will differ from one person to the next, we determined that 80 percent of current income was a reasonable estimate.

Now, let's apply those to those folks with little or no retirement savings to date. For instance, let's say a worker retires at an annual salary of $40,000. Eighty percent of that is $32,000.

Applying that to the two modest retirement savings we just worked out illustrates how limiting they can be. In the first scenario—a $140,000 nest egg—the money would run out in a little more than five years. Even the larger sum—$280,000—only lasts for some nine years. Moreover, the higher your income—and the closer you want to live to that level—the faster the drain on what you've been able to save.

That illustrates the importance of catching up if you determine that what you've been able to save to date will prove inadequate come retirement. Moreover, it's by no means a hopeless cause. Here are some strategies to consider.

Save More

A bit obvious, but with good reason. Investment returns may come and go, but the one element of control that you have over the process is the amount of funds you can save toward your retirement.

Nor does it necessarily have to be massive amounts. Let's go back once more to the 45-year-old with a mere $25,000 saved. Even if she were able to put aside just $100 a month at 9 percent for the 20 years leading up to retirement, the overall nest egg grows to $217,000. Up that to $200 a month, and the total rises even further to $284,000.

The news is even more encouraging the greater the savings you already have in place. For the person with $50,000 set aside at age 45, the same $100 a month at 9 percent comes to $367,000; $200 a month boosts that to $434,000.

Retire Right _____

Shoot back to Chapter 6 for ideas on how to free up funds for additional savings.

Look to Boost Your Returns

The problem may not be an inadequate amount of savings on your part. In fact, you may be saving to the absolute upper limit of what you can afford.

Instead, your retirement plan is being short-circuited by inadequate investment return. Perhaps you've chosen investments that have performed poorly, or have too much money in investments that are too conservative to produce adequate returns.

That makes an adjustment in your portfolio something seriously worth considering. Again, sit down with your investment statements and crunch some numbers. See how individual investments have done, as well as your overall portfolio. That will suggest what might need to be changed—and how drastic a change may be required.

If you've been saving for some time and even if your portfolio has only returned a modest amount, the amount of adjustment may not have to be all that extreme. Here's one scenario to illustrate that principle:

You've been saving $2,000 a year for 20 years in an IRA that, on average, has returned 5 percent (you've stuck pretty much with certificates of deposit and conservative bond funds). At this point, you've accumulated some $68,000. Trouble is, you retire in 20 years and you're hoping to pocket some $400,000 by that point.

Good news. Keeping with your $2,000 annual IRA contribution, all you need to do is shift your portfolio slightly to ramp up your annual return to 8 percent—a modest 3 percent increase. Not only are there a host of solid investment choices capable of doing that on a consistent basis (for instance, check back to the mutual fund screens mentioned in Chapter 10 and you're sure to find a variety of suitable funds), that relatively modest shift gets you to your goal—$435,000 by age 65. Time and the value of compounding on what you've already saved come to the rescue once more.

Of course, just how great a shift may be needed depends on where you are. If you're just a bit off pace, even a modest tweak in returns can do the job. But, if you're in serious catch-up mode, you may have to look to boost your returns significantly to have a reasonable chance to reach your retirement goal. (We'll cover this in greater detail in Chapter 15.)

Split the Difference

Perhaps the idea of having to up your investment return—and, concomitantly, your investment risk—is unnerving to you. By the same token, you simply don't have scads of unused money lying around to take up the additional slack by itself.

The solution: take the middle course by upping your contributions and your investment aggressiveness at the same time.

That choice proves ideal for a number of investors, particularly those averse to risk, because it doesn't force you to take on an investment position you're completely uncomfortable with. But it does require some discipline—and a larger financial commitment.

Let's take the example we just used and balance to account for increased investment return as well as greater savings. We already determined that upping the annual return to 8 percent gets us to the $400,000 target goal by retirement.

Now, let's assume that you're at the same point at age 45—$2,000 a year saved at 5 percent interest, resulting in some $68,000 with 20 more years until retirement. If you merely increased your annual return to 6 percent and stayed at your $2,000 contribution level, your ultimate take would be roughly $300,000—some $100,000 shy of your goal.

What to do? Rather than aiming for a higher rate of return, up your contribution levels. Sticking with a 6 percent rate of return, and at the same time upping your annual contributions to a bit more than $4,000 a year, gets you reasonably close to the target of $400,000 at retirement—$380,000, to be exact.

Retire Right

If you break the extra amount down every month, consider investing it every month, maybe through an automatic withdrawal program. It's automatic and boosts your overall return.

As we said, there's a good deal of financial discipline involved—in this case, double the amount you're saving every year. One way to approach that is to break it down into smaller chunks. In this instance, an additional $2,000 a year is only an additional $166 a month—in many places, the cost of a very nice dinner or two out. Approach it in that fashion, and the additional amount to be saved is a good deal less intimidating.

Choose: Your Retirement or Other Goals (Like a College Education)

Throughout this book, our emphasis on the importance of adequately funding your retirement has been consistent. There's no doubt about it: when it comes to financial priorities, your retirement should be very much toward the top of that list.

But it's likely that it's not the only consideration, particularly if you're in the position addressed in this chapter—in your 40s or thereabouts, about halfway through the retirement funding process.

Other priorities can come in any number of forms—maybe a new house, a new car, perhaps a vacation that you've dreamed of taking. But those are relative small fries when compared to the prospect of saving to pay for a college education.

There's a very good reason that college can prove the primary rival to your retirement plans. Simply put, college is an expensive proposition, and becoming all the more so all the time. As of this writing, the average cost at private universities topped $33,000 a year. For public schools, the average was less but still a hefty $16,400.

Tough call—your postwork comfort or Junior's future? Actually, say most financial authorities, not really so difficult at all. Rule of thumb: fund your retirement to the max and use whatever may be left over to help underwrite college costs.

 Retire Right

If college is on the horizon for your son or daughter, get the latest in costs at the Princeton Review (www.review.com).

That may seem a bit simplistic—not to mention cold—but there are several solid reasons behind it. First, you're the only one responsible for funding your retirement—you and whatever Social Security you can count on. That's it.

The cost of a college education, on the other hand, can be approached from a variety of angles. There's savings, of course, but that's only the beginning. There are scholarships, grants, loans, work-study programs, and a host of other ways to help meet what is undeniably a substantial expense. And, as we've mentioned in prior chapters, should push come to shove, you can also access funds in your retirement savings should they prove imperative to meeting college costs.

So, you may be like many in facing the cost of retirement and higher education at roughly the same time. Tackle the former first, then go after the latter as best you can. Switch that around, and you may only doom your kids to having to help you financially once you're retired and your savings have gone dry.

The Least You Need to Know

♦ It's important to gauge where you are in your retirement savings plan to see if any adjustments are needed.

♦ Be sure to take what you have saved into account when projecting how much you may need. It's not a simple matter of "halfway there, I should have half the money I need." Compounding works to your favor here.

♦ If you're ahead of schedule, consider staying the course to offset any unforeseen bumps in the road.

♦ If you're behind schedule, consider adjusting your portfolio to become more aggressive.

♦ Other options are to increase the amount you're saving or split the difference—saving more and tweaking your return only slightly higher.

♦ If you're trying to save for retirement and college at the same time, emphasize retirement savings first.

Ready to Retire!

In This Chapter

- ◆ Figuring out where you are
- ◆ Putting the pieces together
- ◆ Following the 4 percent rule
- ◆ Adjusting when necessary
- ◆ How to access your savings
- ◆ Finding help

After years of careful thought, planning, and execution, you're at retirement's doorstep. However terrific that may be, that doesn't mean all your retirement planning can now come to a happy close. Anything but. Although much of what you wanted to achieve may be in place, you still have some decisions to make.

With this chapter and the next, we tackle the issues of knowing precisely where you are and, in turn, how to access your assets so that you use them in the most intelligent and efficient manner possible. That way, you position yourself to live the retirement you planned for, with an adequate financial base as a bedrock of support.

Gauging Where You Are

Some years back, you may have calculated some sort of lump sum that you figured would be adequate for your retirement. Put that all together and you figured you'd be in clover.

Now that you're actually there, however, it's important to do a more thorough analysis, taking in not only how much you may have saved but also other income sources. And not just that—you'll need to gauge how much you may expect to spend over the course of your retirement, how much you'll need to access on a regular basis, and what you might have to do to make sure everything lasts.

Let's take a simplistic example to illustrate just how important this can be. Let's say you have saved $600,000 for your retirement. You're at age 62 when you hang up your working shoes. Moreover, you've estimated that, based on your lifestyle prior to retirement, you expect to spend $50,000 a year to enjoy your golden years in the way you choose.

On the surface, it sounds great. Trouble is, at $50,000 a year, that $600,000 nest egg is cracked and cooked in a mere 12 years. Granted, you'll likely have invested in it to generate additional income—not to mention the additional help from Social Security—but the fact remains that the long-term security of your retirement is rather dicey under this particular scenario.

This shows the importance of taking a comprehensive look at your situation, examining your assets and other income sources as well as your expected expenditures. That, in turn, can point you toward money management strategies and investment ideas that offer you the best possible chance for success.

First, Add It All Up

Step one in the process is tallying up everything you have in terms of assets and potential sources of income. These—which will naturally include issues and elements we have covered in prior chapters—should include …

- Company pensions.
- IRAs and other tax-advantaged individual savings accounts.
- Social Security.
- Other assets, including taxed accounts.

Next, offset that by listing your expected expenditures. This will likely be a good deal longer list than your income sources. Include housing, food, health care (a major wild card), transportation, and a host of other costs.

If this seems daunting, the federal government can provide some assistance—or, if nothing else, some perspective. Every year, the U.S. Census Bureau does what it calls a Consumer Expenditure Survey. The study takes in a variety of income and spending patterns for a number of Americans.

Of particular use to us here is a chart that summarizes income and spending by Americans according to their age group. The chart breaks down spending in rather exhaustive categories, covering everything from major benchmarks such as housing and health care to seemingly picayune categories like housekeeping supplies and tobacco and smoking supplies. (The complete summary chart is included in Appendix B.)

> **Retirement Reality**
>
> Want to see how we as Americans spend our money? You can download the entire 2005 Consumer Expenditure Survey at www.bls.gov/cex.

For our purpose of getting a handle on expected spending in retirement, however, a few major findings are of particular interest. For instance, the survey found that average annual expenditures rose between the ages of 25 to 54, starting at some $45,000 and topping off at $55,584. From there on, however, spending dropped—between 55 and 64, average spending checked in at $49,592; 65 to 74, $38,573; and 75 and older, $27,018.

There's some implicit good news here—the older we get, the less we spend overall. According to the study, the cost of housing drops significantly—between the ages 35 and 44, the average annual housing expenditure is $18,482, versus only $12,474 between 65 and 74. Likewise for food, transportation, and entertainment.

But it's not an exclusively one-way slide toward frugality. Not surprisingly, health care costs rise as we get older. While annual average spending for health care between 35 and 44 checks in at $2,272, that figure nearly doubles by the time we reach 65 and older.

Nor are they mutually positive. Although what we actually spend may decrease during retirement, the percentage of that spending versus actual income jumps enormously. For instance, when you're 30 or 40 years old or so, your spending might represent some three quarters of what you take in income-wise (less if you're frugal and a saver). By the time you're retired, however, that percentage jumps to above 90 (in fact, it's almost certain to hit 100 percent sometime after you retire).

How are these numbers useful to you? For one thing, since the next step in knowing where you stand as you approach retirement is to tally your expenses, it can be helpful to see where you stack up with regard to national averages (that, in turn, can earmark potential targets for savings, something we'll hit on in Chapter 16).

Additionally, though, these numbers may give you a sense of something that can be genuinely hard to get a handle on—how much you're going to spend in your retirement. Granted, take national averages with a grain of salt (I've been looking all my life for that 2.5 average children per household the feds have been talking about). Moreover, know that your past spending patterns can also offer insight into how you're actually going to spend come retirement.

The best bet: take both into account when working up estimates of your post-retirement spending requirements. Use your own experience as a basis, but take into account data that shows, in many areas, that we simply don't spend as much after we retire compared to the way we may have tossed money around before.

Putting It Together

Okay, now you've got a comprehensive list of all your assets and income sources along with a reasonable summation of how much you expect to spend in retirement. Now we need to calculate just how long you're likely going to be around to enjoy it all.

Predicting life expectancy is something of an educated crapshoot, but it is important to gain at least a likely sense of how long you may live come retirement. We talked in earlier chapters about the likelihood of expanded longevity—now it's time to see how that applies to you and, if so, how much.

Not surprisingly, the Internet has a host of interactive calculators that let you input all sorts of information to obtain an estimate of how long your life may turn out to be.

Sample a few. Here are a few worth trying:

- www.livingto100.com

- www.moneycentral.msn.com/investor/calcs/n_expect/main.asp

- http://gosset.wharton.upenn.edu/mortality/perl/CalcForm.html

- www.fastfa.com/life.jsp

> **Retirement Reality**
>
> Some calculators offer more than just an estimated life span. Many offer tips to improve your lifestyle and, as a result, better your odds of living longer.

One way to leverage the number of life expectancy calculators is to use several, then average out the results. That way, differing methodologies and factors can be taken into account to give you at least a rough idea of how long you might expect to live.

Withdrawing Money (While Continuing to Invest What Stays Behind)

At this point, you have seemingly all the factors in place to determine where you are and, in turn, how long you can expect your assets to last you in retirement.

But, unlike other sorts of financial planning scenarios we have addressed, once you've retired the dynamics become a bit different. On the one hand, you're tapping into your assets to fund your retirement. At the same time, you need to have your retirement assets generating some sort of return. In effect, it's a two-way flow—money going out, while those funds that remain continue to grow to pay for future years.

That means how much you can reasonably afford to take from your retirement holdings on an annual basis isn't simply a matter of taking what you have and dividing by how many years you'll live in retirement. It also depends on how well your remaining funds are working for you, effectively slowing the drawdown on your assets.

That means it's imperative to take all these somewhat offsetting factors into account when working to gain a sense of just what is feasible for your retirement funding on a yearly basis.

The 4 Percent Withdrawal Rule

To begin to get a sense of what sort of strategy might work best for you, it's actually helpful (unlike other circumstances) to begin with a bit of conventional wisdom. This is known as the 4 percent withdrawal rule.

Simply put: a number of researchers have determined that most people should withdraw no more than 4 percent of their retirement assets in any given year. Translated: if you have $1 million in retirement savings, you should take out a maximum of $40,000 annually. And, factoring this out rather simplistically, that means your savings would last some 25 years.

If you're wondering why such a relatively low amount—particularly when you recall that the historical rate of return for stocks is considerably higher—one reason is volatility. The market can rise and fall in any given year, often sharply. Where your money happens to be—and where it might fall on the continuum of stock market movement—can greatly affect how much money you can access.

The other wild card is inflation, which, as we have seen, erodes the value of your money on an ongoing basis. To illustrate: assuming an annual inflation rate of 3 percent, what you can now buy with $10,000 will cost you nearly $13,439 in some 10 years' time.

Retire Right

There's a nice inflation calculator that shows both drop in purchase power and necessary additional savings at www.hellodollar.com/archives/2005/10/inflation_calcu.html.

That said, one recent update is to use the 4 percent withdrawal rule as a benchmark for only your first year of retirement. Every year thereafter, you would adjust the amount to compensate for that year's inflation. For instance, assuming the same 3 percent inflation rate, an initial annual withdrawal of $30,000 would ideally increase to $30,900 the following year to account for the drop in spending power.

Making Adjustments

On the one hand, 4 percent may seem like a pittance to live on. And, too, no matter how much 4 percent comes to, it may prove inadequate to fund your retirement in the fashion that you had once hoped to achieve.

For one thing, it's essential to bear in mind that 4 percent annual withdrawals is really something of the bottom-of-the-barrel scenario. Put another way: 4 percent very much errs on the side of caution as a hedge against unforeseen snafus that can affect the overall value of your savings. That can make it a valuable planning and budgeting benchmark.

Moreover, there's something you can do as well to further hedge your bets—and, as a result, perhaps safely boost the amount of money you can withdraw annually to underwrite the retirement you truly want.

Investing After You've Retired

In prior chapters, we covered the topic of investments extensively, discussing a variety of ways to build up your retirement nest egg in the most effective and reliable means possible. Now, we turn to the topic of how all that money you've accumulated should be invested once you've retired. It's important because, taken in conjunction with the initial target withdrawal of 4 percent annually, how your money performs for you will lend a hand in determining how long it will last—and how much you may be able to actually access in any given year.

As a rule, we covered the concept of being more aggressive with a long time frame and scaling that back somewhat the shorter the time frame becomes. For instance, with some 20 to 30 years to go until retirement, we discussed the importance of a portfolio heavy in equities, which offer the greatest opportunity for growth.

Now that you're actually ready to retire, you may assume that preservation of what you've put together should be of primary importance. It's certainly not to be ignored—after all, you don't want to lose what you have by making needlessly aggressive investment choices.

But, let's revisit the concept of time frame once more. In a sense, you're now looking at a brand-new time frame, but one that may be every bit as long as the one you had in your run-up to retirement. Put simply: if you saved some 30 years to get to retirement, you may well be looking at 25 years or more to maintain that nest egg during your retirement.

That means your money simply can't sit there. For most of us, we have to think carefully about how our retirement funds should be invested to make certain that we don't outlive them.

Let's start by going back to the amount of money you've determined you'll need annually. To get the discussion rolling, let's say you figure on $40,000 a year. With Social Security tossing in $10,000 a year, that brings that down to $30,000 a year. To fund this, you've saved $500,000.

On a simple basis, that $500,000 would only last a bit more than 16 years. For many people, that won't even come close to lasting long enough. Moreover, it doesn't take the effects of inflation into account. So you need to do something with that nest egg to offset the drawdown for your retirement. What to do?

Try to Beat Your Withdrawal Rate

One rule of thumb is to try to consistently beat the rate of withdrawal you've decided on—in this case 4 percent. For instance, if you place your retirement funds in a portfolio returning 6 percent a year on average and inflation is running at 3 percent a year, that $30,000 a year payout suddenly lasts 22 years. Average 8 percent, and you're up to 30 years. On the other hand, merely matching the 4 percent withdrawal rate only makes your assets last 18 years.

Not only can your portfolio's rate of return dictate how long your retirement nest egg will last, it can also influence how much money you can withdraw from one year to the next. To illustrate: if you take our initial $500,000 amount and place it in a portfolio earning 6 percent a year, that effectively allows you to withdraw $32,628 over the course of 20 years—some $2,000 more per year than you had initially budgeted for. An 8 percent annual return ups that to more than $38,000 a year over the same 20-year time frame.

However appealing this may be, keep a few cautious thoughts in mind. First, as we pointed out earlier, it's best to be as conservative as possible in your initial retirement account withdrawals. That's the best sort of hedge against unexpected expenses in the future. Even better, if your retirement assets remain reasonably solid as your retirement progresses, you can always consider upping your withdrawals in the future.

Moreover, as we've stressed throughout this book, it's important to craft a retirement strategy that takes your risk tolerance into account. For many folks, a few extra thousand dollars a year may simply not be worth the added stress and anxiety of an overly aggressive investment approach.

And, finally, while we've seen that some portfolio return is essential to make your nest egg last, your retirement is no time to be taking needless chances. Craft the portfolio that fits your funding needs, not one that's needlessly volatile.

What Rate of Return Do You Need?

What sort of investments are necessary depend on the rate of return you need. Many stock market studies have found that a simple mix of 60 percent stock (generally stable holdings such as index funds) and 40 percent fixed-income vehicles such as investment-grade bonds was adequate for most needs.

Again, the Internet can also provide a wellspring of assistance. The brokerage house T. Rowe Price provides an online calculator (www3.troweprice.com/ric/RIC) that lets you play with various scenarios to figure what sort of portfolio mix provides the returns you'll need. It's even detailed enough to offer a likely success rate for whatever breakdown you select.

Remember, too, that many fund companies have mutual funds geared specifically to the growth and funding needs specific to retirement. For instance, Vanguard's Target Retirement 2010 Fund blends a mix of index funds and bond funds—the breakdown works out to roughly 55 percent stocks and 45 percent bonds, not too far removed from the basic 60–40 mix we discussed earlier. Additionally, the fund automatically adjusts to a greater proportion of bonds as you get further into your retirement.

If these sorts of funds appeal to you, shop carefully, as the portfolio mix can vary considerably from one fund to another. In contrast to the Vanguard Retirement Fund, the Fidelity Freedom Fund 2025 has upwards of 71 percent of its holdings in stocks.

Additionally, as we covered in Chapter 10, keep a particular eye on fees and other expenses. The lower the costs associated with owning a fund, the greater your returns (and, hence, the greater the likelihood that your retirement portfolio will hold up over a long period of time). To illustrate: the Vanguard and Fidelity funds we just mentioned have expense ratios of .21 percent and .72 percent, well below the average of 1.5 percent for domestic stock funds.

How to Withdraw Funds

Now that we've tackled some fairly significant issues regarding how much you'll need in your retirement from one year to the next as well as how to structure your holdings to make them last, a fairly simple question pops up: just what is the best way to actually access the money?

Just how critical this issue is depends on your situation. For instance, if much of your retirement is in an annuity, the choice is out of your hands, as annuities mandate a schedule of fixed monthly payments.

But you may have a variety of holdings where it's up to you to decide how to access the money. Keeping in mind the percentage parameters we discussed earlier, here are a few strategies worth considering:

- As a rule, take money from taxable savings accounts first, including any dividends and interest you may receive. Try to keep any tax advantages for as long as possible.

- If possible, move assets from an employer-sponsored plan into a conventional IRA. If you have a 401(k) from your job, it may have limitations as to how often you can access the money (not to mention that the investment choices are invariably more limited than an IRA). That said, moving the assets directly into an IRA offers greater flexibility.

- Consistent with the notion of taking money from taxed sources first, it's generally a good idea to leave your Roth alone for as long as you can. Since those assets can be withdrawn tax-free, that's a plus you want to save until later in your retirement, when you may not be as well positioned financially to pay any taxes.

 Golden Years Gaffes

There is one scenario that argues against moving a 401(k)'s assets into an IRA. Depending on the rules for specific 401(k)s, if you're between the ages of 55 and 59½, you can withdraw funds from a 401(k) without incurring any penalty. With an IRA, you have to wait until you reach 59½.

◆ Monitor performance. When taking withdrawals, keep an eye on the investments they're coming from. If, for instance, one particular mutual fund is performing better than another, target the lesser performer for withdrawals. That way, you keep your money where it's doing the most good for a longer period of time.

If Need Be, Get Some Help

It never hurts to consult with a financial professional to get whatever help you may need. And, in many cases, a financial planner is your best bet.

Planners come in all shapes and sizes. Some work on an ongoing basis with clients, while you can hook up with others every so often to discuss ideas and strategies. Some provide a complete array of services, including such products as insurance, while others stick pretty much to investing.

Whatever the specific type, a solid planner can prove invaluable in helping you map out a retirement portfolio that matches both your goals and your comfort level.

If a planner seems like an appealing idea, here's a checklist of issues to consider:

❑ Ask friends and co-workers for recommendations. If someone's satisfied with his planner, ask how he works with the planner—does he just invest, or is he involved in other activities such as estate planning or tax issues?

❑ If possible, try to work up a list of several candidates and interview them. Ask about their experience, training, and other elements of their professional background. Ask if they've ever been disciplined for any reason. If they have, don't be shy about asking about the particulars.

❑ Ask the planners if they work with anyone with a situation similar to yours. Have them detail precisely what they do and how they arrived at those financial choices. Ask them for a sample of their work to gauge the depth of their financial advice and whether it's suited to your needs.

❑ Ask for referrals to clients with whom the planner has worked. This is something that most planners should find more than reasonable. Planners on the up and up should be more than happy to substantiate their successes by letting you talk with other clients.

❑ Finally, be clear as to how they're compensated. Some planners work on a fee-only basis, while others are paid a commission for the products they sell (many people are wary of commission-based planners, suggesting that the motivation for commissions may prompt them to push products that are not necessarily in their clients' best interests).

To find a planner, you can contact the National Association of Personal Financial Advisors at 1-800-366-2732 (www.napfa.org) or the Financial Planning Association (900-322-4237; www.fpanet.org). They can provide you with referrals to planners in your area.

The Least You Need to Know

◆ If you're on the verge of retiring, gauge where you are by adding up all your assets as well as expected expenses.

◆ Know that you're likely to spend less in retirement than you did before that. But know, too, that the percentage of your income that you will spend on expenses in retirement will jump considerably.

◆ Many experts recommend withdrawing no more than 4 percent of your assets every year during retirement. Adjust that amount for inflation every year.

◆ Calculate how much your portfolio needs to continue to earn in retirement to ensure your nest egg lasts as long as you do.

◆ When withdrawing funds, start with taxable assets first. Leave tax-advantaged vehicles such as Roth IRAs untouched for as long as possible.

◆ If you could use some help mapping out your retirement funding (or any other part of your retirement planning), a financial planner may be a valuable ally.

Chapter 16

Making Sure It Lasts Long Enough

In This Chapter

- ◆ Review, then review some more
- ◆ Adjusting your portfolio
- ◆ Fine-tuning your budget
- ◆ Inexpensive travel
- ◆ Handling debt
- ◆ Additional steps
- ◆ Watch out for scams

Once you've retired, you've perhaps found that you're drawing down more from your retirement savings than you thought you would. On the other hand, maybe everything is going according to plan and you want to have some strategies close at hand in case something misfires in the future.

In this chapter, we'll offer ideas and strategies that you can use to augment a solid withdrawal and portfolio investment strategy—steps that can help hedge your bets to make certain that your retirement savings stay around as long as you do.

Review Your Position Regularly

One way to make certain that your retirement savings last as long as they're needed is to set up and follow a comprehensive review schedule. Plan on carrying out the review at least annually and perhaps even more often should you be concerned about how your savings are holding up.

Your review should include:

◆ Analysis of investment performance. In Chapter 15, we showed how important a certain rate of return can be in keeping your retirement assets reasonably intact as you withdraw funds. Track to see if your investments are performing as they should, both individually and as a group. Software programs such as Quicken make this easy and automatic. You can also update investment performance on many of the websites we've already mentioned.

◆ See if your withdrawals from your savings are proving adequate for your needs. Chapter 15 suggested the rule of thumb of withdrawing no more than 4 percent of your overall retirement assets, at least in the initial few years of your retirement. Gauge that against your actual expenses. Is it enough to meet your actual financial obligations?

◆ See how your expenses are tracking. Chapter 6 emphasized the importance of setting up and following a budget as you prepared for retirement. It's no less valid now that you've reached retirement. In determining just how much you would need to withdraw in retirement, you worked up estimates on how much you might spend on particular items and expenses. Now's the time to see how close you came.

◆ In particular, have any unexpected expenses—both one-time and ongoing— cropped up that have thrown off your plan? Do you expect them to continue or is it more likely a short-term aberration that doesn't warrant any sort of adjustment on your part?

Once you've had a chance to review money coming in as well as funds headed out, you can pinpoint where your overall plan may be coming up short. From there, you can make necessary adjustments to get you back on track.

Adjust Your Portfolio

In Chapter 15, we suggested that one common mistake among retirees is inattention to the importance of continuing to invest what they've already saved toward their retirement. Looked at another way—if you're taking money out on a regular basis, what money remains behind needs to generate some income to help make it last as long as possible.

That's not merely a matter of investing or not investing—it's also an issue of investing appropriately. If the returns on investment for your retirement savings are inadequate, you may not run out of money as soon as if you did nothing, but you're doing little more than forestalling the inevitable.

With those ideas in mind, one possible problem is inadequate return on your investments. Sit down with your investments and see how they've performed so far. Then, calculate how soon you would exhaust your savings if they continue to perform at that level and you maintain your current level of withdrawals.

Let's work through an illustration. You saved $600,000 and, in the first two years of retirement, you withdrew $40,000 each year. During that same time, your portfolio returned 6 percent. If that were to continue with all those factors intact, your savings would be exhausted in 38 years.

Retire Right _____

A simple calculator that lets you do this quickly and easily can be found at http://hffo. cuna.org/annuityb.html.

That's great, but the better news is, if you need to increase that (say you retire very young), it doesn't take much of an adjustment to better your situation. For instance, upping the average annual return of the $600,000 portfolio cited above by a single percentage point adds nearly 4 years to the life expectancy of your retirement savings. Up it to an average of 8 percent a year and your savings will last some 26 years.

This simple formula also works in favor of greater cash flow, if necessary. Say, for instance, that the life span of your savings is of less concern (perhaps you retired at an older age and the likely amount of time you need to fund is less than other retirees). Instead, you find your cash requirements to be more than you anticipated. Again, tweaking your portfolio to increase your returns by even a modest amount can provide the answer.

To illustrate with our $600,000 savings: increasing annual rate of return from 6 to 7 percent produces roughly an additional $2,500 per year over an expected savings time span of 20 years. If you boost that to 8 percent, you're looking at an extra $4,500 a year over 20 years.

Two notes of caution, though. As we have emphasized before, it's best to be as conservative as reasonable in your savings withdrawals, particularly in the earlier years of your retirement. Better to play things close to the vest at the beginning and, if things hold up as you plan, to increase your withdrawal amounts further into your retirement.

Also, be wary of overreacting, particularly with investments tied to the stock market. A mutual find that underperforms its historic average by 1 percentage point in a given year is no cause for panic.

Rather than shifting to another investment, investigate the cause for the slight dip in performance. See if your investment reflected the market as a whole. Check to see how similar investments performed. From there, monitor future performance closely. If your holdings continue to provide returns inadequate for your needs, you may be justified in making changes to your portfolio.

Budget Adjustments

To a certain extent, the investment performance of your retirement portfolio is out of your hands. You can choose the best investments possible and manage them closely, but there's always an element of uncertainty when it comes to investing.

That really doesn't hold true with your budget. As a rule, you can control your spending to a far greater degree than you can the performance of your investments.

That makes drawing up and following a budget an important element to help ensure that your retirement nest egg stays around for as long as possible. Not only does a budget offer you a solid view of where your money is going, it also pinpoints potential areas for savings.

Start by going back and reviewing your list of expected expenses and bills that we covered in Chapter 15. Then, reconcile that with your actual spending. Track your expenses for a month or two—see what matches up with your projections and what exceeds them.

Golden Years Gaffes

This isn't a trumpet call to live like a monk who eschews all worldly pleasures. You don't have to eliminate expenses—just bring them under better control.

If you identify points of overspending, determine if those are expenses that you can trim back. For instance, if you find you're making three or four trips to the grocery store per week, one less visit can save a potentially substantial sum over time. Ditto for meals out and others forms of discretionary spending.

Here are some other tips that can help massage your budget back into line:

- **Keep an eye on ATM activity.** Automatic teller machines can be an insidious budget buster—push a few buttons, grab the cash, and head on out, only to forget to record it. Try limiting trips to the ATM to once a week to get all the cash you'll need. If you do go more than once, record the withdrawal in your checkbook on the spot.

- **Avoid emotional buying decisions.** You worked hard all your life to save to enjoy your retirement—why the heck shouldn't you get that big honkin' plasma TV? It's understandably tempting. But budgets can be broken in half by spur-of-the-moment spending choices. Give it a day or two—if that TV still seems like a worthy purchase (and one that you determine you can genuinely afford), go for it.

- **Know the reason for buying something.** Some of the things we buy we genuinely need. Others we buy for other reasons—loneliness, depression, and other emotional causes among them. Think about why you want to spend money—it may be more of an emotion-based decision than a rational one.

- **Plan ahead for significant buys.** Rather than taking a knee-jerk reaction to spending—particularly for high-ticket items—work out a plan in advance to pay for it. For instance, if you and your spouse decide a trip to Europe is a dream come true, begin setting aside savings long before you step foot on the plane rather than just dumping it onto a credit card.

- **Don't forget about an emergency fund.** In Chapter 6 we discussed the importance of earmarking money for emergencies. That's every bit as true now that you're retired—perhaps even more so. Confronting a major, unexpected expense can decimate an otherwise solid budget, so be prepared with an emergency fund. The general rule of thumb is three to six months of living expenses. If that's not doable, at least try to set aside something.

Travel on the Cheap

Travel is undeniably one of the great joys of retirement. But it doesn't have to be one of retirement's greatest expenses.

One way to keep your retirement savings intact is to focus on getting the most for your travel dollar. Here, the Internet can offer a wealth of information and guidance designed to zero you in on travel discounts, specials, and other money-saving deals. Some websites to consider include the following:

- Expedia (www.expedia.com)

- Orbitz (www.orbitz.com)

- Bestfares (www.bestfares.com)

- Hotwire (www.hotwire.com)

- Travelocity (www.travelocity.com)

- Budget Travel Online (www.budgettravelonline.com)

These and other websites often provide information on travel deals specific to older travelers. Additionally, many offer an e-mail system that alerts you to particularly good deals—many of which may be offered for a relatively short amount of time.

One of the keys to obtaining the best travel deals possible is to remain flexible. For instance, if you stick to specific departure and return dates, you're likely to find relatively few options. On the other hand, being open to a variety of travel dates—for instance, traveling midweek as opposed to the weekend—can provide substantial savings.

That also applies to a willingness to travel on short notice. For instance, many cruise lines offer discounts of up to 50 percent if you can up and go quickly.

Additionally, take advantage of the variety of travel programs, perks, and services that are exclusive to older travelers. For instance, members of AARP can access discounts for car rentals, airline tickets, and other travel-related products and services.

Older travelers are eligible for these perks, among others:

Retire Right

To find out about travel deals and other elements of AARP membership, go to www. aarp.org.

- Golden Age Passport provides lifetime admission to all national parks and other federal sites. You have to be age 62 or older. Price: $10.

- United Airlines offers its Silver Wings program for travelers 55 and up. For $24 a month, members get $300 in annual travel credits, additional bonus miles, and special offers.

- Amtrak offers a 15 percent discount for all seniors for all of its domestic train routes. Likewise, most European railway systems offer senior discounts.

No matter what your travel interests, it pays to be proactive. That said, when shopping for tours, be sure to ask if any discounts are in place for older travelers. But, by the same token, don't necessarily assume that the "senior" discount is the best deal to be had. Check out all available specials to make sure you land the lowest possible price.

> **Retirement Reality**
>
> Travel-related services are hungry for older people's business. If you're comfortable doing so, don't be afraid to dicker to see if you can get a better deal than what's initially offered.

Manage Your Debt

According to the Employee Benefit Research Institute, from 1992 to 2004, the percentage of households with significant debt grew faster in the 55-plus age group than it did for the overall population. The older people get, the worse the problem becomes. The average debt load for households with someone age 75 and older grew to an average of $20,234 during the same time period—a horrific 160 percent jump.

The reasons behind those numbers vary. For some retirees, that once-in-a-lifetime dream trip can only come via a credit card. But, for others—particularly those on fixed incomes and little in the way of savings—credit is more than a means to luxury. It's a way to make ends meet, particularly with rising health care costs. Couple that with limited options to boost income to pay off debt, and the problem becomes all the more severe.

Here are some strategies to help you deal with significant debt in retirement and—even better—ways to head it off before it happens:

- **Again—set up an emergency fund.** As we pointed out earlier, unexpected expenses such as medical costs can devastate a budget—and, even worse, plunge any household into debt. Protect yourself with an emergency fund of available cash—ideally, three to six months of living expenses.

- **Shop aggressively for low-interest credit cards.** To get the best deal possible, make sure your credit score is solid (order a report from one of the main credit reporting bureaus and correct any inaccuracies that may be harmful to your credit rating).

- **If need be, consolidate your debt into one low-interest card.** If you carry balances on more than one card, look into transferring all the balances to a card with a temporary low interest rate (these, known as "teaser cards," were discussed in Chapter 6). From there, pay it down as aggressively as possible.

♦ **Consider paying off consumer debt with a home equity line of credit.** This—based on the amount of equity in your home—often offers very low interest rates, and is tax-deductible as well.

♦ **If you need help, seek it out.** Many retirees are reluctant to get help—a sense of pride, perhaps coupled with embarrassment at having to turn to someone else. If that's an issue with you, dump it and look for a qualified credit counselor. A credit counselor can do more than just offer advice and guidance on ways to trim debt. They also negotiate with credit card companies, banks, and other lenders to get you a lower interest rate and more favorable repayment terms.

Retire Right _____

For help with the issue of debt, have a look at Consumer Credit Counseling Services at www.cccsintl.org.

Other Steps to Help Your Nest Egg Last

Here are a few more strategies that may prove helpful (some of which we've covered or will address in greater detail in subsequent chapters):

♦ **Refinance your mortgage.** We hit on this in Chapter 6, but it bears a quick reminder. If you've had your mortgage for a while, check to see how your interest rate compares with current interest rates. Even a modest drop in your interest can save you a substantial amount of money, particularly over the long haul.

♦ **Scale down your home.** Now that you're retired, you may have more home than you need (particularly if your children have moved away). If so, give some thought to moving to a smaller, less expensive alternative. We'll cover this in Chapter 22.

♦ **Move to a less expensive part of the country.** If you don't feel particularly tied to where you are now—or would just welcome a change of scenery—there may be less pricey places to call home. Refer to the discussion on researching a cost-effective retirement spot in Chapter 24.

♦ **If you do relocate, be sure to rent first.** It's less costly, and allows you greater freedom to move again if things don't work out in your new location.

♦ **Look into alternative housing arrangements.** Again, check out Chapter 24. Whether it's shared housing, cohousing, or some other out-of-the-ordinary arrangement, it can often prove a good deal less expensive than the conventional single-family housing choice.

♦ **Consider a reverse mortgage.** This allows you to leverage equity you have in your home for cash flow. More about this in Chapter 22.

♦ **Consider a part-time job.** Not only can that help fill in some financial cracks, working after it's no longer a rock-solid financial necessity can be both rewarding and stimulating (see Chapter 23).

♦ **Reevaluate whether you still need life insurance.** As we cover in greater detail in Chapter 20, life insurance's primary role is income protection. If no one else depends on your income, you might not need life insurance coverage any more.

Golden Years Gaffes

Remember, life insurance can be used to cover the resulting tax burden after someone dies and proceeds pass to heirs. Similarly, life insurance can be useful to cover funeral expenses, attorney fees, and other costs. Before canceling your life insurance, add up every asset and source of income that would still be in place or continue to come in after you die. If, all told, that would be sufficient to maintain your family's style of life, life insurance may be something you can dump. If not, keep it in place.

♦ **Check for lower auto insurance premiums.** Most major auto insurers offer cut-rate premiums for older drivers with solid safety records. Shop around to see who offers the best deal.

♦ **Keep an eye peeled for unnecessary fees and charges.** For example, your bank may have a surreptitious array of charges and fees that, over time, can add up. Study your statements carefully. If you find something that seems unjustified, ask to have it removed. If they refuse, shop for another bank that's more amenable to what you want.

♦ **Shop aggressively for everything.** This same rule carries over to most any other purchase. Wait for sales for big-ticket items. If you use something often and you have sufficient storage space, shop bulk warehouses. If possible, look to buy items out of season when they're likely to be less expensive.

♦ **Go after your senior discount.** Travel services aren't the only ones who offer price breaks to people above a certain age. Restaurants, pharmacies, and other retail and services routinely provide discounts to retirees. If you don't see a posted notice to that effect, be sure to ask about it. Moreover, if you're not particularly shy, ask if a business is willing to offer you a break to keep your business.

Avoiding Scams

By some estimates, people age 60 and over account for some 30 percent of all types of fraud.

Why? For one thing, chances are good that you have a substantial nest egg in place—a con man's ideal target. Moreover, if a retiree is the victim of a scam, he often doesn't know to whom he should report it—or, even worse, is too embarrassed to take action.

Some common scams include:

- **"Rolling Lab" schemes.** Here fake or unnecessary tests are administered at retirement homes or health clubs.

- **Pyramid schemes.** This is a type of investment fraud in which the promoters recruit investors and then use them to recruit more investors on the promise of terrific returns. Eventually, the organizers run off with the cash. Pyramid schemes are often sold as "investment clubs" or "gifting circles," and can involve the sale of products or distributorships.

- **Charitable solicitations.** Some solicitations on behalf of police and firefighter organizations and other charities are made by dishonest professional fund-raising firms. They can be persistent and may imply that if you don't donate, your safety will be jeopardized.

- **Telemarketing fraud.** Here, overly aggressive telemarketers push scams involving prize money, vitamins, health care products, and other goods. They can pressure you by saying the offer is limited or that it's free, although you'll have to pay for shipping and handling charges.

- **Internet fraud.** This is relatively new but no less destructive. Internet users can be duped into passing along credit card information or ordering items that are never delivered.

Fortunately, there are commonsense methods to protect yourself. For one thing, never give in to high-pressure sales tactics. It may be uncomfortable, but don't be afraid to say no and simply hang up the phone. If someone claims to represent a charity or some other organization, do some research on them before you commit a single penny. Also, make sure you get any details involving investments or other financial transactions in writing.

Finally, don't feel embarrassed about overreacting. If you feel threatened in any way, contact the police immediately.

Here are some additional resources on fraud and ways retirees (and others, for that matter) can avoid becoming a victim:

- **Federal Trade Commission** (www.ftc.gov); 1-877-382-4357. The FTC provides free information to help you spot and prevent fraudulent, deceptive, and unfair business practices.

- **National Do Not Call Registry** (www.donotcall.gov); 1-888-382-1222. The National Do Not Call Registry allows you to block telemarketing calls. You can call or visit the website to add your landline and cell numbers. Your registration will be effective for five years.

- **National Fraud Information Center** (www.fraud.org); 1-800-876-7060. A project of the National Consumer League, the National Fraud Information Center has tips and articles to help you recognize fraud and an online form to file a complaint.

- **Better Business Bureau** (www.bbb.org). This lets you check out businesses and charities of all sorts.

The Least You Need to Know

- Once you've retired, review your financial position regularly to ensure you're not drawing down your assets too quickly.

- If need be, you can adjust your portfolio to increase your returns. Small changes can make a substantial difference.

- Take advantages of low-cost travel options for retirees whenever possible.

- Keep an eye on your debt. If you're carrying too much, take steps to reduce it.

- Lowering your insurance costs, watching out for hidden fees, and shopping aggressively can also help keep your retirement assets intact.

- Watch out for fraud and other scams.

Part 4

Key Financial Concerns

Even the best-laid retirement plan can encounter a few bumps and challenges along the way. Part 4 covers a variety of specific financial topics that can have a significant impact on the quality of your retirement. Issues include taxes, health and other forms of insurance, long-term care, and other elements that can be addressed in a variety of ways, both before and during retirement. The part winds up with an overview of estate planning and the role it plays in protecting your savings and other assets.

The Tax Man–Older but Still Around

In This Chapter

◆ Are taxes that important in retirement?

◆ What to do before you retire

◆ Taxes and your Social Security benefits

◆ Ways to cut taxes post-retirement

◆ Employed? Be careful

◆ Resources to help your tax situation

It's natural (and necessary) to focus much of your attention and effort on amassing sufficient retirement assets. But if you don't take taxes into account, your retirement nest egg may take financial hits that often can be avoided. And that can affect the overall quality of your retirement.

This chapter is designed to head off that headache before it happens. Here, we'll discuss the importance of taxes with regard to your retirement and outline some strategies and ideas to help you address them in the most constructive and money-saving fashion possible.

Is It That Important?

Are taxes all that critical in retirement planning?

The answer is an unqualified yes. For one thing, as we will get into greater detail later, your overall tax burden can vary considerably depending on where you live. State income taxes, property taxes, sales tax, and other forms of taxation can, depending on the individual state, add up quickly. And that only contributes to the overall tax burden on top of federal taxes.

Another potential tax element has to do with Social Security. It sounds ironic when discussing a program that, when instituted, was designed to counteract poverty among the elderly, but the fact remains that it's likely that you will have to pay some tax on your Social Security benefits. That adds yet another layer of taxation.

Lastly, retirement, in a large way, is all about endurance—in both a physical as well as a financial sense. Just as you want to remain healthy and active for as long as possible, so, too, do you hope that your available assets will not diminish at a rate faster than necessary.

Unfortunately, that can happen, with taxes a contributing factor. Just as unexpected expenses, unnecessary spending, and other elements draw down your retirement nest egg, burdensome taxes can only open the drain wider.

A simple scenario illustrates how damaging taxes can be. Let's say, taking federal, state, local, and all other forms of taxes into account, you pay $500 a year more in taxes than you would had you planned more carefully. Added up over the course of a 20-year retirement, that comes to $10,000.

But it doesn't end there. Not only are you drawing down your retirement assets to pay those taxes, that's also money that isn't producing any additional income for you.

In fact, even your best efforts toward saving enough money for retirement can end up working against you from a tax standpoint. If you've accumulated significant balances in vehicles such as a 401(k) and IRAs, the time will come when you'll have to deal with mandated withdrawal provisions. And, if all that comes together at once, your tax bracket may be shoved higher—costing you even more in taxes.

 Golden Years Gaffes

Another potential tax booster in retirement: you may no longer have a mortgage, losing a significant tax write-off.

Bottom line: taxes matter. And, just as important, there are a number of ideas and planning issues that you can use to take some of the sting out of the tax paddle.

What You Can Do Before Retirement

There are several steps you can take before you retire to put yourself—and your retirement—on the best tax footing possible.

Consult a Tax Professional

One of the challenges of taking on the topic of taxes is that they vary considerably from one person to the next. What may work in one person's situation may be completely off base for another.

That's why it's a wise idea to invest some time and money to consult with a tax professional about your retirement. A certified public account, an *enrolled agent*, or some other tax pro can review your situation and analyze your overall array of retirement holdings and other sources of income.

Your tax pro should review all aspects of your tax situation, including your current tax bracket as well as your expected financial needs in retirement. From there, he or she can make recommendations on moving certain funds and strategies for tax-effective withdrawal.

Nor is there necessarily any need to rush to set up an appointment. As a rule of thumb, it's best to schedule your meeting with a tax professional anywhere from six months or a year ahead of the time you plan to retire. Not only does that give you adequate time to review your plan and make any changes, it also offers your tax pro the most current picture of your financial situation.

> ## def•i•ni•tion
> An **enrolled agent** (FA) has technical expertise in the field of taxes. He or she may represent taxpayers in audits, collections, and appeals.

> ## Retire Right
> To find a certified public accountant near you, go to www.aicpa.org. For an enrolled agent, check out www.naea.org.

Convert a Conventional IRA to a Roth—or Open One

If you're looking to trim taxes in retirement and are considering opening an IRA, a Roth's tax pluses make the decision a rather easy one. Although you lose out on potential tax savings up front—you may be able to deduct contributions to a conventional IRA—you can withdraw from a Roth tax-free in retirement. (See Chapter 9 for more on Roths and conventional IRAs.)

The question of whether to convert a conventional IRA to a Roth becomes a balancing act between immediate tax ramifications and those after retirement. If you choose to roll over a traditional IRA into a Roth, you will have to pay taxes on whatever you move to the new account—more specifically, on any contributions and earnings that were either tax-deductible or tax-deferred.

Depending on how well the IRA has performed up to the point of conversion, that may come to a substantial amount. However, if you have funds available from sources other than the IRA itself, converting to a Roth can make a good deal of sense. Even if funds to pay taxes come from the IRA itself, conversion may make sense if there's sufficient time left before you expect to withdraw funds from the Roth. That can allow time to recoup money lost to taxes.

There is yet another wrinkle. Currently, your adjusted gross income must be less than $100,000—otherwise, conversion to a Roth is not allowed. However, this income limitation is slated to be pulled from the books in 2010, making all conversions legal regardless of income.

While it may seem simpler to wait a few years until the income restriction is eliminated, keep an eye on your annual income if your earnings vary greatly from one year to another. If you happen to have a year where your income dips below the $100,000 threshold, you can leverage that to convert a conventional IRA to a Roth.

Diversify

As a rule, tax-deferred and tax-free retirement vehicles are generally the way to go. That means an emphasis on things such as 401(k) plans where you work and, as we just discussed, Roth IRAs.

In fact, if at all possible, it's a good idea to have both tax-deferred as well as tax-free vehicles as part of your overall investment portfolio. Doing so affords you the greatest amount of flexibility in terms of accessing your money in the most tax-efficient manner possible.

Let's take one scenario. Say, in a given year in your retirement, you expect your financial needs will be relatively modest (for example, you're living particularly frugally to save money for an expensive vacation later on). In that case, you can emphasize withdrawals from a 401(k) or a conventional IRA. Although withdrawals are taxed, you're taking money out in a year when there's likely to be a relatively slight impact on your taxes.

By the same token, if one year in retirement your income proves greater than usual (you've done some consulting work and managed to land a high-paying project), turn to your Roth IRA for whatever additional funding needs may be necessary. In a potentially high-tax year, the tax-free status of Roth withdrawals can prove exceedingly timely.

So, if time and opportunity permit, don't overlook diversifying your holdings among both tax-free and tax-deferred positions. As we've just seen, that mix can afford you a good deal of flexibility to keep your tax bill at a minimum.

Taxes and Social Security

As we all know, Social Security was instituted to help offset rampant poverty among the older segment of the American population. And, to a large degree, it has done that. In fact, many Americans lean heavily on the Social Security benefits as the bed-rock of their financial position in retirement.

But that largesse doesn't come without qualifications. Depending on your situation, a good portion of your Social Security benefits may be subject to tax—something to be aware of as you begin to access your Social Security benefits.

Here's how it works. First begin with your adjusted gross income. Add to that one half of your Social Security benefits and any *unearned income* you got during the year.

If the total is greater than $25,000 for a single person or $32,000 for a married couple filing jointly, up to 50 percent of Social Security benefits are subject to tax.

With $34,000 for a single filer or $44,000 for couples filing jointly, as much as 85 percent of Social Security benefits are taxed.

Let's not get needlessly worked up about this, though. Estimates hold that about two thirds of Social Security beneficiaries are not affected by the taxation of benefits. Moreover, so the argument goes, retirees with more assets of their own are better positioned to pay the tax on Social Security benefits than lower-income folks who rely more on Social Security.

def•i•ni•tion

As the name implies, **unearned income** is income you don't earn. Common examples are pension and annuity payouts, dividends, and interest and proceeds from life insurance.

Retirement Reality

Taxes collected up to 50 percent of benefits are returned to Social Security's trust fund. (In 2004, they provided 2 percent of the funds' total income.) Fifty percent and above goes toward Medicare.

Ways to Trim Taxes After You Retire

There are several strategies that you can employ after you retire that can limit and, in some cases, even reduce your overall tax burden. Some are straightforward, while others mandate a bit more effort and time. Take the list as a whole and see what ideas and strategies might work best in your particular situation.

Schedule Another Meeting with a Tax Professional

Once you've had a year or so of implementing the withdrawal plan you've worked out (with a tax pro's help or not), it's a solid idea to review how well it worked. From there, you can make any adjustments that, over the long haul, may place you in a better tax position as you continue into retirement.

Take Minimum Distributions Whenever Possible

This may seem a simplistic idea, but only withdrawing what you need—and constantly monitoring that need from one year to the next—can help avoid pushing you into a higher tax bracket and, as a result, a larger tax obligation.

One way to accomplish this is to avoid using saved assets until mandated by law (for instance, age $70\frac{1}{2}$ for conventional IRAs). However, if you do need to take distributions, calculate them carefully. Work closely with your budget to determine just the correct amount of cash you'll need (plus whatever may be necessary to pay any resulting taxes).

This also has the added advantage of creating smaller required minimum distributions later in your retirement.

Monitor your tax situation from one year to the next to see how you may adjust your withdrawals. For instance, in a year when you plan to make a number of charitable contributions—and, as a result, take advantage of the resulting deductions—you can always adjust your withdrawals up, since they're offset by the deductions.

As a General Rule, Tap Your Roth IRA Last

Since withdrawals from a Roth carry no tax consequences, it's a solid strategy to leverage that later in your retirement, when assets to pay tax bills may be lower than they were earlier in your retirement.

If You Have Them, Cash in Taxable Assets First and Try to Spread Them Out

The idea here is to keep tax-advantaged accounts in place for as long as possible to allow them to grow in size. To minimize the tax bite, consider selling taxable assets over the course of a number of years, thereby minimizing the tax bite at any one time.

Handle Company Stock Carefully

Speaking of taxable assets, if you own company stock in a 401(k) that has gone up a great deal in value, how you handle it can minimize your taxes. The key is to leverage what's known as *net unrealized appreciation.*

Here's how to handle it. When you take your 401(k) in a lump sum distribution, move the stock into a taxable account— anything else in the 401(k) can be rolled over into an IRA. You pay income taxes based on what you paid for the stock, but any appreciation (the net unrealized appreciation) will only be taxed when you actually sell the stock and take the proceeds.

def•i•ni•tion

Net unrealized appreciation refers to the difference in value between the average cost you paid for stock and its current market value. The stock must be in a tax-deferred account, such as a 401(k).

Even better, it's likely you'll only have to pay long-term capital gains of 15 percent. Had you rolled it into an IRA along with anything else that was in your 401(k), any withdrawals would have been taxed at your top tax rate—likely higher than 15 percent. However, you must hold the stock for 12 months following distribution from the 401(k) to get the long-term gain rate.

Don't Itemize Your Tax Deductions

After you retire, you're entitled to a larger standard deduction so long as you don't itemize. If you itemize, you lose it.

Don't Overlook Medical Expenses

Unless you have exceedingly comprehensive health insurance, it's likely that your out-of-pocket medical costs will go up as you get older. Items such as prescription costs, premiums, and doctor's visits can be deducted up to 7.5 percent of your adjusted gross income.

If Warranted, Challenge Your Property Tax Assessment

Income taxes are by no means your sole concern in retirement. If you think your property tax bill is too high, consider challenging it. First, contact your community's assessor to find out what your home's official assessed value is. Then, compare that with the assessed value of other comparable homes in your area. Also, talk with real estate agents to get the fair market value of comparable homes. If your assessment seems out of line, you can file a protest. That may reduce the assessed value of your home which, in turn, cuts your property taxes.

Another option is to investigate property tax breaks available to retirees, which is covered in the next section.

Move to a Tax-Friendly State

Not every state treats retirees the same when it comes to taxes. If you don't mind the idea of relocating, here are some state-specific tax issues to consider:

- A number of states provide a variety of tax breaks for retirees. For instance, in Colorado, persons age 55 to 64 can exclude as much as $20,000 in pension and annuity income (the amount jumps to $24,000 if you're 65 and older). Additionally, 10 states—Alabama, Hawaii, Illinois, Kansas, Louisiana, Massachusetts, Michigan, Mississippi, New York, and Pennsylvania—do not tax federal, state, and local pension income.

- **State income taxes.** Seven states—Alaska, Florida, Nevada, South Dakota, Texas, Washington, and Wyoming—have no state tax on personal income. Two others—New Hampshire and Tennessee—only tax dividends and interest.

- **Watch sales taxes.** Currently, Alaska, Delaware, Montana, New Hampshire, and Oregon have no state sales tax. Of the remaining states, a number have a single statewide rate, with some allowing local add-ons.

Retire Right

For a chart listing all state sales tax rates with a partial breakdown by item, go to www.taxadmin.org/FTA/rate/sales.html.

- **Social Security tax.** As we've already covered, your income from Social Security may be subject to federal tax. On top of that, 15 states tax Social Security benefits in some manner. They are Colorado, Connecticut, Kansas, Kentucky, Minnesota, Missouri, Montana, Nebraska, New Mexico, North Dakota, Oregon, Rhode Island, Utah, Vermont, and Wisconsin.

◆ **Property tax breaks.** Most states provide homeowners over a certain age with some form of property tax relief (although you may have to be low income to qualify). Every state also provides other forms of property tax relief, such as programs that lock in the assessed value of the home once the owner hits a certain age.

The bottom line is that, if you're considering relocating to reduce your tax burden, it's critical to take every potential form of taxation into consideration—not merely the obvious ones, such as state income tax. Not only that, but consider other expenses besides taxes, including housing costs, transportation, food, and other essentials. We cover these in Chapter 24.

Retire Right _____

Interested in how the states stack up with regard to overall tax burden? Go to www.taxfoundation.org/research/topic/9.html.

Working and Taxes

Another factor to consider with regard to taxes is the issue of working after you retire—an increasingly popular option.

The first and most obvious consideration is the effect of working on income taxes. Although the popular conception is that most retirees' income is considerably less than what they earned before they retired, income from pensions, Social Security, and personal savings can be substantial. Add to that income from some form of employment and you run the risk of inching up into a higher tax bracket.

As of 2007, federal tax brackets were as follows:

Filing Single	Rate	Filing Joint	Rate
$0–$7,825	10%	$0–$15,650	10%
$7,825–$31,850	15%	$15,650–$63,700	15%
$31,85051–$77,100	25%	$63,700–$128,500	25%
$77,100–$160,850	28%	$128,500–$195,850	28%
$160,850–$349,700	33%	$195,850–$349,700	33%
$349,700 +	35%	$349,700 +	35%

That means it's important to monitor all sorts of income, including anything from a post-retirement job, to make sure you don't inadvertently push yourself into a higher bracket and, as a result, pay more taxes.

If you're going to work in some manner after retirement, one strategy to consider is postponing Social Security benefits. As we covered earlier in this chapter, if you work prior to reaching what's considered full retirement age, you can reduce the amount of benefits you receive from Social Security. Whether you postpone benefits, of course, depends on whether you need the additional income provided by Social Security.

However, there is a positive side. If you work during retirement, you may actually boost the overall amount you receive from Social Security once you start to collect benefits. Remember, benefits are calculated based on your 35 highest years of earnings—even a modest amount of earned income produced after you retire may work in your favor.

Tax Resources

Nobody's about to argue—taxes can be confusing, intimidating, and, occasionally, downright maddening. Not only that, but that bewildering mix is constantly subject to change as Congress and other lawmakers pass, revoke, and tinker with tax regulations of all sorts.

That means it never hurts to ask for help if you think you'll benefit from it. As we've already mentioned, hooking up with a tax pro to plan and implement a tax-savvy financial strategy can be of invaluable help—not only in trimming your tax bill but also in keeping a handle on changes and updates to tax laws.

There are also a number of other places to turn:

♦ AARP provides a program called Tax-Aide—the nation's largest volunteer-run tax preparation and assistance service. Taking in some 32,000 volunteers, Tax-Aide provides free preparation and assistance to millions of low- and middle-income taxpayers. The program places particular emphasis on persons age 60 and older. More information is available at www.aarp.org/money/taxaide.

♦ The Internal Revenue Service offers the Tax Counseling for the Elderly (TCE) Program. Like AARP's Tax-Aide, TCE offers free tax assistance to persons age 60 and up. For more information on TCE, call 1-800-829-1040. Additionally, the IRS provides a variety of publications geared specifically to the tax concerns of older Americans. A complete list is available at www.irs.gov/individuals/retirees/article/0,,id=120167,00.html.

The Internet also offers a number of solid tax-related websites. A few worth a look include:

◆ http://taxes.about.com. This is a straightforward, helpful tax site.

◆ www.taxmama.com. Comprehensive and witty tax advice and discussion.

◆ http://articles.moneycentral.msn.com/taxes/home.aspx. This is MSN Money's Tax center.

◆ www.irs.gov/individuals/article/0,,id=109959,00.html. An interactive glossary of tax terminology.

◆ www.el.com/elinks/taxes. A terrific one-stop destination that provides links to a host of tax sites.

The Least You Need to Know

◆ Taxes are an important consideration that can affect the quality and financial security of your retirement.

◆ A tax professional can help you develop and implement an asset withdrawal plan that limits your tax liability.

◆ Look into a Roth IRA. Its tax-free withdrawal provision can limit your tax burden in retirement.

◆ Diversify your retirement holdings so you can make withdrawals based on the tax situation of a particular year.

◆ A good rule of thumb is to take minimum distributions whenever possible in retirement. This simple strategy can limit tax liability.

◆ If you don't mind relocating, certain states impose smaller tax burdens on retirees than others.

Chapter 18

Health Insurance

In This Chapter

- Forms of health insurance
- Gauging your health insurance needs
- How to hold down health insurance costs
- Specific situations, helpful solutions
- When I'm 65 …
- All about supplemental insurance

Much of the planning that goes into retirement has to do with saving—setting aside money for investing and, ideally, stockpiling the most money you can to fund the sort of retirement you want.

The topic of health insurance, on the other hand, has to do with spending; more specifically, what you need to know and how to allocate sufficient financial resources to avoid the financial catastrophe that can happen when illness or accidents occur—and your insurance is inadequate to meet the cost.

Moreover, it's a two-step issue. There's health insurance while you're still working prior to retirement and health insurance after you retire. In both cases, planning and executing appropriate choices can save you considerable expense and headaches, not to mention help you enjoy your retirement years to their utmost.

Why It's So Important

Statistics released by the Census Bureau in 2006 found that 46.6 million people lacked health insurance—nearly 16 percent of the population. That's a 1 percent increase (or some 5.4 million) from 2001.

The primary reason for the steady rise in the number of uninsured people is that a growing number of employers are eliminating company-sponsored plans.

> **Retirement Reality**
>
> According to the Citizens Health Care Working group, costs for health care per person were estimated to be $6,300 in 2004. That is expected to leap to $12,300 by 2015.

The potential long-term effects of the shrinking number of people with health insurance is cataclysmic. As medical care costs continue to climb at the same time, the expense of any sort of illness or injury—particularly one involving long-term care or a hospital stay—can devastate a family's finances. And that includes money that might otherwise be earmarked for retirement.

Types of Insurance

All this boils down to a powerful truth—if your employer offers some sort of health insurance, be sure to take advantage of it. On top of the simple imperative of having health care coverage, at-work health insurance is inevitably a bargain when compared with individual policies you have to buy on your own.

If you're one of the growing number of employees who work at a company that offers no health insurance coverage, it's essential to get some. That starts with understanding the varied types of health insurance—an equally important consideration if your company offers health coverage.

Health insurance generally comes down to two basic types—fee-for-service and managed care.

Fee-for-Service

Fee-for-service is the more expensive of the two but offers greater flexibility. For one thing, you can go to any doctor you choose (which is terrific if, for instance, you like a physician you've been seeing for years and have no desire to switch). The same goes for other sorts of medical services, including hospitals and laboratory work.

Generally, the coverage pays 80 percent of any costs you accumulate (after you've met the deductible). You as the patient are obligated to pick up the remaining 20 percent (known as the copayment).

There are a few wrinkles. First, fee-for-service only covers illness and accidents—preventive care such as physicals, inoculations, and mental health care are out. Most fee-for-service plans establish limits on how much they will pay in a given year as well as how much the plan is obligated to pay overall.

In fact, the conventional 20 percent you have to pay may, in fact, turn out to be more than you bargained for. That depends on how expensive your health care provider is. The insurance will calculate its 80 percent share based on what it deems "usual and customary" costs for a particular service. If by chance the actual bill exceeds those limits, you're responsible for the leftover.

Managed Care

Managed care plans (which also go by the name of health maintenance organizations, or HMOs) are considerably less expensive than fee-for-service arrangements—for instance, a routine doctor visit may only cost you a few dollars out of pocket. Additionally, premiums are generally lower than fee-for-service, as are deductibles. On top of that, unlike fee-for-service, preventive care, drugs, and mental health treatment are usually covered.

The downside to managed care is a great deal less freedom of choice and flexibility. With managed care, you're provided with a list of physicians, hospitals, and other health services included in the plan. Use them and you're covered by the plan. Go outside the network and your costs are your responsibility. Moreover, access types of medical care not covered by the plan—say you go to a specialist without a referral from your primary care physician—and you're on your own as well.

In response to drawbacks to both managed care and fee-for-service, the insurance industry has tweaked some variations that are effectively hybrids of the two. One such option is point-of-service (POS), which, like managed care, maintains a list of hospitals, physicians, and other health care providers you may access. However, you can go outside of the plan's specified providers, provided you're willing to meet deductibles and copayments.

Evaluating Your Health Insurance Needs

Now that we have a handle on your at-work health insurance options, we can turn to the topic of evaluating your needs and, as a result, pinpoint the sort of coverage that works best for you—both as you approach retirement and after you retire. If nothing else, holding down costs leaves you that much more money for other retirement needs (and wants).

This may not pertain if you have insurance at work. Chances are still reasonable that your company offers a particular type of plan and that's the one you have to go with if you opt in.

On the other hand, you may have a choice as to what sort of health coverage might work best for you. On the surface, managed care would seem to be the hands-down winner, at least so far as out-of-pocket expenses are concerned. However, it's important to investigate whether a bit more money spent on a fee-for-service plan might not be worth it.

The first step is to take stock of your health care needs. Sit down and make a list of the sorts of health services you and your family access, including such things as prenatal care, pediatric services, physical therapy, and other services. For one thing, that can give you an accurate gauge of the sort of coverage you'll need from any heath plan.

From there, check both fee-for-service and managed care plans and cross reference their features with the health care needs you identify. See what's covered and what's not. See to what degree a particular service is covered and the upper limits of that coverage. Examine specific types of services, such as immunizations, prescription drug coverage, mental health counseling, and other types of care to see if they're covered and, if so, to what extent.

Retire Right

No matter which plan you choose, investigate the provider by calling your state department of insurance. They can provide information on networks and doctors who have provided poor patient care.

But don't stop with a simple list of coverage options. Ask people you know who have used a managed care service about the quality of coverage they've received. How long has it taken to get in to see a physician? Are referrals to specialists a hassle? Given their druthers, would they be more satisfied with a doctor or other provider they could choose without the constraint of a managed care plan's list of eligible providers?

By the same token, ask folks you know who are using a fee-for-service plan. Do they feel they're getting a good deal for the extra expense? Are they accessing necessary health services faster than managed care participants?

Holding Down Your Health Insurance Costs

The most direct means of trimming your health insurance costs might seem to be the plan that costs the least. Not necessarily—for one thing, cheap at the outset may prove more expensive in the long run. Moreover, there are other ways to hold down insurance costs regardless of the type of the plan you use.

First, if you're married and both you and your spouse have health insurance where you work, consider the necessity of accessing both plans. For one thing, it's simply more money out of pocket. For another, it's becoming increasingly rare for one policy to, in effect, pick up coverage where another leaves off.

But that doesn't necessarily mean dropping one policy and going with the other for all your insurance needs. For instance, examine the benefits and drawbacks of keeping both plans with each plan covering one spouse (you may end up saving out-of-pocket expenses over the long haul). The issue becomes a bit more complicated if children are in the picture. Here, examine both policies to see what sort of combination might work best for overall family coverage.

Another strategy to trim costs is to investigate what is known as "catastrophic" coverage. It's a type of policy that's aptly named. This is coverage with an exceedingly high deductible—often as high as several thousand dollars.

While you run the risk of significant out-of-pocket expenses if you need the coverage, that's offset by premiums that are significantly lower than they would be with lower deductibles. You're betting that, over time, you'll save enough in premiums so that it more than matches the deductible you may one day have to meet.

Retire Right _____

If you opt out of any insurance, know what you'll have to do to sign up again if something goes wrong with the coverage you choose.

If you opt for catastrophic coverage, take the money you save and put it in a money market account. That can help you meet the deductible if necessary.

In fact, it's important to consider varying levels of deductibles if your plan mandates them. If you opt for higher deductibles, your premiums will be less. On the other hand, you'll pay more up front should you need the insurance. Weigh both the risk and potential rewards to arrive at a deductible level that brings your premiums within the range of your budget, but not so high as to provide a crippling expense should you need the coverage.

Another alternative crops up if your employer happens to offer a flexible spending account plan. This program allows you to set aside money from your salary tax-free (much as you do with a 401(k) plan). These funds can then be used to help pay for medical expenses that are not covered by your employer's health plan, potentially saving you a substantial amount in out-of-pocket costs.

Still another option—particularly if your company doesn't provide health insurance—is group insurance provided by professional associations, alumni groups, and other organizations. Fraternal and religious organizations are another possibility.

Special Situations

Not everything to do with health insurance is particularly cut and dried (in fact, very little). However, above and beyond what you need to address in a conventional workplace setting, there are certain special situations and circumstances regarding health coverage that mandate some specific strategies.

If You're Self-Employed

Naturally, the necessity of buying health insurance on your own becomes all the more obvious—and essential—if you work on your own. Use the strategies we outlined in this chapter to help determine what sort of insurance you may need as well as the best sort of coverage to meet your insurance requirements.

Although this can be a substantial financial obligation, there are some advantages from a tax standpoint. Normally, medical expenses (and that includes premiums) are not tax-deductible until they meet or exceed 7.5 percent of your income. Not so when you're self-employed—you're eligible to deduct them no matter what they amount to. Another option is to write off the premiums as an adjustment to your income. (This option has limitations. First, your business needs to show a profit. Additionally, you can't do it if your spouse is covered by an employer-provided plan.)

If You Lose Your Job

Losing a job isn't limited to the loss of a paycheck. Gone, too, can be health insurance, which is particularly devastating if the coverage was comprehensive and affordable.

Fortunately, there is an option to keep your coverage in place. The Consolidated Omnibus Budget Reconciliation Act (known better by the acronym COBRA) requires companies with 20 or more employees to allow you to stay on your health plan for an additional 18 months after you leave your job.

The downside to this is that all premiums are your financial responsibility. Although they may be substantial, COBRA provides a viable alternative to keep your coverage in place while you look for a new job.

Retire Right

While you're looking for a new job, also shop for temporary insurance—it may be less expensive than the COBRA option.

If You Retire Early

If you're contemplating early retirement, you're naturally focused on accumulating sufficient assets to fund what will likely be a longer-than-normal retirement.

But an equally significant challenge is health care coverage. As we will cover later in this chapter, you're eligible for Medicare benefits when you reach age 65. Retire sooner than that, and you can face something of a no man's land when it comes to health insurance.

There are, however, some strategies that may make health insurance viable for early retirees:

Golden Years Gaffes

Lack of affordable health insurance—not a lack of savings—is often the reason that people put off early retirement.

❑ **If your company offers retiree health benefits, grab them.** Fewer companies are offering this these days, but if yours does, take advantage of it—it may be your most cost-effective option.

❑ **Obtain individual coverage.** Another choice, albeit a potentially costly one. One cost-effective option is the catastrophic form of coverage outlined earlier in this chapter. Again, though, the downside can be a hefty deductible should you ever have to use the insurance.

Retire Right _____

When shopping for individual coverage, Paul Zane Pilzer, author of *The New Health Insurance Solution*, recommends that you consider separate coverage for family members, particularly if your spouse is younger. The reason: health insurance for families is often based on the age of the oldest member.

With a family policy, Pilzer also suggests putting the policy in the name of the younger spouse. That way, that person still has coverage when the older spouse becomes Medicare-eligible.

❑ **Look into other health insurance options**. Don't overlook groups and organizations, such as alumni organizations and professional associations, for cost-effective health coverage options. If you run a business, your local chamber of commerce may be able to help as well.

❑ **Consider COBRA.** An admittedly expensive option, but available nevertheless, this might be most appropriate for someone who retires at, say, age 64 and has less than the upper 18-month limit before Medicare begins.

❑ **Start saving—now.** A study by the Employee Benefit Research Institute indicates that a 55-year-old retiring today will need some $83,000 to cover premiums and out-of-pocket medical expenses not covered by group insurance for the 10 years before Medicare kicks in. For individual coverage, the amount shoots up to an astonishing $256,000 for a person with an ongoing condition mandating prescription drugs.

The bottom line—if you're considering retiring early, be sure to take health care costs into account when calculating your financial needs. Moreover, if opportunity permits, start as early as you can. To illustrate: a 45-year-old planning to retire in 10 years would have to set aside nearly $700 a month to cover the $83,000 expense we just cited. However, drop that back to a 35-year-old planning the same course and the monthly savings obligation drops back to a more manageable $345.

Medicare

Your 65th birthday is just cause for celebration—at least from a health insurance coverage standpoint. It is at this point that you become eligible for Medicare.

In a nutshell, Medicare is the United States' health care program for persons age 65 and up. The program is financed by several sources, including payroll taxes paid by workers and their employers as well as monthly premiums that are deducted from Social Security checks. The overall program takes in some 770,000 health care professionals and more than 6,000 hospitals throughout the country.

Retirement Reality

Medicare was enacted in 1965 as one of President Lyndon B. Johnson's Great Society programs.

Medicare is subdivided into four parts:

♦ **Part A**—This is hospital insurance that helps pay for inpatient care in a hospital or skilled nursing facility. It also covers some home health and hospice care.

♦ **Part B**—This helps pay for physicians' services and other services and supplies not covered by hospital insurance.

♦ **Part C**—Known as Medicare Advantage, this provides people with Medicare Parts A and B with all of their health care services through certain provider organizations.

♦ **Part D**—This provides prescription drug coverage through independent insurance companies.

Each of these parts shake out in different ways. For instance, most people age 65 and older who are citizens or permanent residents are eligible for free hospital insurance under Part A. By contrast, anyone eligible for Part A benefits can enroll in Part B by paying a monthly premium (as of 2007, the average monthly premium for this portion of Medicare was $93.50 a month or $1,122 per year).

If you have Medicare Parts A and B, you also have the option of joining a Medicare Advantage Plan (Part C). The advantage to this option is that, unlike Parts A and B, Part C is more comprehensive, generally covering many of the services that are covered by supplemental insurance known as Medigap (which we will hit on later in this chapter).

Part D, which first took effect in 2006, is specific to prescription drug coverage. This portion of Medicare is completely voluntary and may be unnecessary should you have prescription drug coverage from other sources.

How to Enroll

If you are already receiving Social Security benefits in some manner, you will be contacted several months prior to your eligibility and provided with directions for enrollment. When you're eligible, you will automatically be enrolled in Parts A and B; since B carries premiums, you have the option of turning down that part of the coverage.

Note: if you decide not to enroll in Part B when initially signing up, you can do so later during an annual general enrollment period. However, your monthly premium goes up 10 percent for every year you wait.

If you are not already receiving benefits, contact Medicare roughly three months prior to your 65th birthday to obtain all necessary information and directions.

How to Choose What's Right for You

Given the range of options and choices offered under the Medicare umbrella, it's essential to consider your health coverage needs and, from there, choose those elements of Medicare that are right for you.

Obviously, each person and family's situation will dictate different choices. However, there are a few general guidelines that can help make the selection process a bit more straightforward.

One solid idea is to calculate your health care costs, including visits to doctors, hospital stays, medications, and other expenses. Then, compare that with any premiums you'll be obligated to pay under Parts B, C, and D. See if the added premiums make sense or if, by chance, you can handle some out-of-pocket expenses.

Take other insurance into account as well. For instance, if you have a private insurance plan, check to see how its coverage fits with Medicare medical insurance. Pay particular attention to any gaps in coverage. If your company offers retiree health benefits, compare those with premium-based Medicare services as well.

Retire Right _____

Medicare's website (www.medicare.gov) offers a variety of information and comparison tools that help you choose the right Medicare options.

Pay particular attention to the new Medicare drug coverage provision. Estimates hold that more than 40 million Americans have a drug benefit plan outside of Medicare. If that's the case, check to see if your plan is equivalent to the Medicare drug plan. If it isn't, you may wish to consider signing up for the Medicare plan at first opportunity—remember, the longer you wait, the higher your premiums become.

Supplemental Insurance

However comprehensive Medicare is in its varied forms, it's important to bear in mind that the program will not cover every one of your health care expenses. For instance, Medicare does not cover routine preventive care, including physical exams and preventive foot care. According to the Kaiser Family Foundation, a health care policy organization, Medicare pays only 56 percent of the cost of participants' overall health care costs.

That can make supplemental health insurance (also known as Medigap policies) a topic worthy of consideration. Indeed, according to the Kaiser Foundation, 87 percent of seniors buy supplemental insurance. These, as the "gap" portion of the name suggests, are designed to cover those treatments, services, and other expenses not covered by Medicare.

Even though supplemental insurance is offered by private insurance companies, there are 12 standardized plans. These are identified by the letters "A" through "L." The A plan offers the most rudimentary coverage, while L is the most comprehensive.

How do you choose which one is right for you? If it's within your budget, it's usually a good idea to go with the most comprehensive plan possible. That said, shop aggressively. The good news is that plans are identical from one company to the next—for instance, one company's D plan will be the same as another's—so comparisons are easy and straightforward.

Aggressive shopping is also critical due to the great disparity in premiums from one company to the next. How much you pay will also depend on other factors, such as your general state of health and what part of the country you live in. But Medigap coverage can prove pricey, often as high as several thousand dollars a year—yet another reason to begin saving for health care costs in retirement before you actually retire.

Know, too, that Medigap is not necessarily a panacea. For instance, like Medicare, Medigap does not cover long-term care needs, such as help at home or permanent nursing home stays. And, like other forms of coverage, premiums tend to rise as you get older.

Retire Right

Remember to compare Medigap plans with Medicare Advantage. This may prove a more cost-effective way to fill in coverage gaps. For additional help in choosing a Medigap plan, go to www. medicare.gov/Publications/ Pubs/pdf/02110.pdf.

The Least You Need to Know

♦ Health insurance is often as important a factor in retirement as savings, so be sure to factor it in when calculating your retirement needs.

♦ Fee-for-service health insurance is more expensive than managed care, but allows more flexibility. Managed care is less expensive but limits you to certain health care providers.

♦ If your employer offers health insurance, take advantage of it. If not, be sure to get the most comprehensive coverage you can afford.

♦ Hold down health insurance costs by raising deductibles or considering "catastrophic" coverage.

♦ Medicare is designed to pay some, but not all, of your health care needs after age 65.

♦ If you're concerned about holes in Medicare coverage, consider Medigap insurance, which adds additional health insurance protection.

19

Retirement Communities and Long-Term Care Insurance

In This Chapter

- ◆ Retirement communities—an introduction
- ◆ How to select a community
- ◆ When a nursing home may be needed
- ◆ All about long-term care insurance
- ◆ Is LTC really worth it?
- ◆ How to select and buy long-term care insurance

In an ideal world, we would all retire under the best circumstances possible. For some, that would mean staying in your own home, enjoying solid health that allows you to remain reasonably independent and active. Some may prefer retirement communities—facilities and planned neighborhoods for people who may need just a bit of assistance in their daily lives.

Unfortunately, sometimes a nursing home or other sort of comprehensive care facility may be required. And, given the expenses of such places, that naturally leads to a discussion of long-term care insurance—what it does, who should buy it, and why you may want to give it some thought.

Whether you're researching your own retirement needs, or acting on behalf of an aging parent or other relative, this chapter can provide important information about retirement communities and long-term care options and issues.

Retirement Communities—An Introduction

As you probably know, options for retirement communities abound. And that, in turn, can lead to some confusion as to what is actually available as well as the varied sorts of programs and services they provide.

However, it's really not as complicated as all that. In their essence, there are really six primary options for retirement communities:

- **Independent living arrangements.** These are designed for retirees who are healthy and able to look after themselves. These consist of individual homes or apartment complexes, usually with a security system to protect the entire community. Such facilities often offer a variety of social activities and other programs for its members.

- **Assisted living.** Here, retirees have some health issues but not of a severe enough nature to mandate a greater level of care. Assisted living provides housing with on-site services offering help with things such as bathing, dressing, and cooking meals.

- **Congregate housing.** This is a variant of assisted living, offering both a level of assisted care as well as private living space. Congregate housing generally provides group meals and other community-based social programs.

- **Board and care.** Like conventional assisted living, residents receive help with basic care. The primary difference between board and care and conventional assisted living is board and care generally offers group meals and other activities for residents who want to spend time with friends and neighbors.

- **Nursing homes.** These are skilled nursing facilities that provide comprehensive round-the-clock care for retirees with significant medical issues. They may also offer short-term programs for retirees needing some form of rehabilitation or physical therapy.

> **Retirement Reality**
>
> Communities aren't defined just by services and facilities. A growing number cater to specific groups, such as gays, members of particular religions, and others.

♦ **Continuing care retirement communities.** This is a hybrid of a variety of programs. This involves several sorts of housing and living arrangements, including independent living facilities, assisted living, and a nursing home. The idea is that retirees can remain in what is basically the same retirement community, with the option to change the level of care they receive as their individual needs mandate it.

How to Choose the One That Meets Your Needs

The decision of what sort of retirement community fits your needs can be rather intimidating. However, you can make the task easier by familiarizing yourself with the specific programs and services various sorts of communities provide.

Individual Services

Let's start with more individualized services. These are generally offered in assisted living facilities and not in independent living arrangements where residents can see to these responsibilities themselves. Depending on the facility, these can include …

♦ Bathing.

♦ Dressing.

♦ Cooking and cleaning.

♦ Use of the toilet.

♦ Help in getting around the house.

♦ Keeping up with prescription schedules and medications.

♦ Transportation around the community and outlying areas.

♦ Help in taking part in the community's social and recreational programs.

Group and Community-Based Programs and Services

While personal care and other like services may be important, don't overlook the broader sorts of group activities, programs, and facilities a community may offer its residents. These can include …

♦ Housekeeping.

♦ Laundry.

- Communal meals.

- Exercise facilities and opportunities, such as fitness programs, workout rooms, swimming pools, tennis courts, golf courses, and sauna and steam rooms.

- Nutritional counseling.

- Barber and beauty shops.

- Libraries.

- Activity facilities and other spaces for gatherings, meetings, and parties.

- Church, temple, and other religious facilities and services.

Questions to Ask

Choosing the retirement community that fits your needs and preferences isn't an exact science. There are many subjective factors to bear in mind, many of which may boil down to a gut reaction.

However, certain questions can help in the process. Here's a sampling of issues and ideas that may prove helpful:

- First, evaluate as honestly as possible what sort of community you might enjoy and, in turn, would provide the type of services and programs you would genuinely need. Are you reasonably independent and can you expect to remain that way for the immediate future, or would you benefit from assistance of some sort?

- Ask friends or relatives for referrals and suggestions. If someone you know genuinely enjoys their retirement community choice, find out what makes it such a good fit.

- Be sure to visit several sorts of communities. No two communities are exactly alike, so be certain to tour several to gain a sense of quality of care, cleanliness, friendliness and support of the staff, and other issues. Be sure to talk with both residents and employees to gain a sense of how satisfied both are (happy residents are generally a by-product of happy, satisfied employees).

- Is the move temporary or for the long term? For instance, some retirees may only need to stay in an assisted living facility to recover from surgery or some other sort of medical procedure. Others may be looking at a much longer time frame.

◆ Is privacy important? This can be a key consideration for many people, particularly those who have spent the vast majority of their lives in their own homes. Certain retirement community arrangements afford a fair degree of privacy; others less so. Will a degree of privacy have to be sacrificed due to a need for a certain level of ongoing care?

◆ Have they had any problems in the past? We've all heard the horror stories of retirement communities that have gone bad in all sorts of ways. If the facility is licensed by the state, ask if you can see the latest inspection report. If any issues or problems are identified, ask what they've done about them.

◆ Ask about any sort of age restrictions. Retirement communities naturally impose a minimum age for residents. However, rules vary when it comes to younger visitors. For instance, if your children and grandchildren visit, find out if they'll be able to stay with you. Ask, too, if there are any restrictions regarding pets.

◆ Compare costs. Like the services and programs each provides, costs can also vary considerably from one retirement community to the next. The general rule of thumb is, the more the services and amenities (golf courses, plush dining facilities, and the like), the greater the expense. Know just what you need and want and what you can happily do without. In addition, study cost structures carefully. For instance, in some communities services such as housekeeping and laundry may be wrapped in a comprehensive fee, while others may treat them as an add-on. Know what the basic cost covers and what may be extra.

◆ Ask others for help in making the right choice. The decision of what sort of retirement community is right for you—or for that matter, a loved one—doesn't have to happen in a vacuum. Ask your physician for guidance. Community-based geriatric care managers—both in community agencies or private practice—can also lend a hand in choosing the facility that's right for you.

Retire Right

One tip to help you get the community you want—move before you have to. Not only do some better spots have waiting lists, others require that newcomers be reasonably healthy and active.

When a Nursing Home Is Necessary

Nursing homes provide comprehensive, round-the-clock care for people with a host of ongoing needs. In addition to providing care from a staff of physicians and nurses, nursing homes develop and implement comprehensive care plans incorporating medication, physical therapy, nutrition, and a variety of other services.

Depending on the facility, a nursing home may also incorporate pharmaceutical, laboratory, and radiological services as well as occupational and speech therapy. Certain types of nursing homes may also specialize in particular conditions such as Alzheimer's disease and related conditions of dementia, care for Parkinson's disease, kidney dialysis, and other issues.

Like other sorts of retirement living arrangements, it's essential to gauge a person's needs and level of care and match those with a facility geared to meet those requirements. As with other community options, try to visit several nursing homes to compare cleanliness, atmosphere, staff characteristics, and other features.

Paying for Nursing Home Care

A nursing home may be few people's idea of the ideal living arrangement. But it's nothing compared with the potential expense of living in one—particularly for a long period of time.

Estimates vary, but a reasonable rule of thumb holds that nursing home stays run an average of $70,000 a year. And, depending on where you live and the level of care required, that annual expense can easily top $100,000.

Moreover, need for long-term care doesn't happen exclusively within the confines of a nursing home. Long-term care can also take place in your home, at an assisted living facility, or in *adult day care*.

def•i•ni•tion

Adult day care involves day programs in a group setting. They offer social and health-related services to support frail, impaired, elderly, or other disabled adults.

Here, let's insert some comforting news. Although nursing home costs are justifiably disturbing, the good news is only a small fraction of elderly people live in a nursing home. According to a national nursing home survey conducted by the National Center for Health Statistics, only slightly more than 3.5 percent of all persons age 65 and older lived in a nursing home in 2004. Moreover, other estimates hold that the length of stay generally isn't particularly long—usually about three years or thereabouts (due in part to lower disability rates, greater financial resources, and options other than nursing homes).

Still, even the possibility of facing the enormous financial burden of long-term care can be sobering—where will the money to pay for such services come from?

The first consideration might be personal savings. Trouble is, unless you have substantial assets at the ready, it's very possible that you may spend down what you have in a great hurry.

> **Retirement Reality**
>
> Why the small nursing home population? Two possible explanations are improving levels of health and a range of other living options.

The second option is Medicare, which is designed to pay for some long-term care costs. However, there are significant limitations. For instance, Medicare pays only for medically necessary skilled nursing facilities or home health care. Medicare will not pay for "custodial care"—assistance with support services such as activities of daily living like dressing, bathing, and using the bathroom. Additionally, large deductibles take effect within a few weeks.

A third—and for many, the least palatable—option is Medicaid, the federal program designed to pay for health care for the poor. Here, the scenario is that you've virtually exhausted all other sources to pay for long-term care.

And an extreme scenario it is. You meet a state-determined poverty level and certain health-related criteria. Generally, that means you may keep only the house in which your spouse or some other dependent lives, furniture, a car, a burial plot and funeral funds, and a small amount of cash—often as little as $2,000.

> **Retirement Reality**
>
> It may not be the most appealing choice, but many retirees in long-term care situations pay down what assets they have as quickly as possible to qualify for Medicaid.

Enter Long-Term Care Insurance

Long-term care insurance is as straightforward as most any other type of insurance (a rather loaded statement). You pay a premium which varies according to your age, the extent of the coverage you buy, and other factors. In turn, should the need arise, this coverage helps pay for the expense of long-term care.

Moreover, the coverage can apply in several sorts of living situations. For instance, long-term care insurance can pay for long-term care, either in an institution (such as a nursing home) or in a residence, such as an assisted living facility or in one's own home.

That unto itself may suggest that long-term care insurance is a good idea. However, there are a number of serious caveats to bear in mind. For one thing, unlike health insurance, which you're likely to use at some point in your life, you may never actually turn to long-term care coverage to pay for applicable expenses. That means you've spent money on premiums for coverage that hasn't done you a lick of good.

And those premiums can add up quickly. For instance, a 50-year-old choosing a fairly modest long-term care plan (covering three years with a total maximum benefit of roughly $109,000) would pay about $42 a month in premiums. Up that to the top of the line (unlimited benefit period, unlimited total benefits) and the monthly bill jumps to $156.

The wrinkle with this is that the earlier you buy the coverage, the lower your premiums will be. For instance, a 35-year-old opting for the complete coverage package we just mentioned would only pay $93 a month. The downside, of course, is that a 35-year-old is starting to pay those premiums 15 years earlier than the 50-year-old—and, again, those premiums are going for coverage that he or she may never actually use.

One offsetting element to the expense of long-term care coverage is that you may get a tax break. However, there are significant restrictions. For instance, if you're 40 or younger, your deduction is an exceedingly paltry $260, although the amount you can deduct increases as you get older.

Is It Worth It?

Long-term care coverage is a hotly debated topic for a variety of reasons, including expense, applicability, and the financial stability of insurers.

That said, the question of whether long-term care insurance makes sense depends on a variety of factors. Here are several to help you make the right choice:

Retire Right

The *Consumer Reports* website offers a succinct, stinging assessment of long-term care coverage: "Long term care insurance may be a lousy deal, but right now it's about the only deal."

- ◆ **Consider how much you're worth.** As a rule, long-term care insurance tends to make the most sense for people caught in a sort of financial no man's land—those with insufficient assets to pay for long-term care and those with so little that Medicaid will quickly come to the rescue. How this area breaks out depends on whom you ask. Generally speaking, if you have between $200,000 and $1.5 million, long-term care insurance may be worth a look.

◆ **Consider your health history.** If you come from a family with a history of debilitating diseases, such as Alzheimer's or Parkinson's disease, long-term care insurance may be more viable than someone whose family has a record of living independently well into old age.

◆ **Can you afford it?** Should you consider long-term care insurance, many financial pros urge that premiums account for no more than 5 to 6 percent of your income. Remember, after you retire, your income often drops by a significant amount. You should never get to the point where premiums become a financial burden, forcing you to consider dropping the coverage altogether.

◆ **It may not pay for everything you need.** Depending on the policy you buy, you still may end up having to pay for certain services and supplies on your own, such as medications. Moreover, long-term care policies only pay a portion of the overall expense of in-home care.

◆ **Consider if there's an estate you wish to pass on.** If you have assets that you hope to pass along to someone else, long-term care insurance may be worth the money, as it can prove an effective tool in preserving assets.

◆ **Consider that all policies have limitations.** For one thing, all long-term policies have waiting periods—as long as 100 days—that you have to pay for out of pocket until the policy kicks in. The higher the waiting period, the lower your premium. And, with the exception of lifetime coverage policies, long-term care generally mandates a maximum coverage period as well as a maximum financial benefit the policy will pay. In effect, you're betting that you won't need more coverage than you can afford to pay for.

How to Shop for Long-Term Care Insurance

If, after considering all the pluses and drawbacks of long-term care insurance, you figure that it's worth investigating, here are some shopping tips and guidelines:

◆ Don't buy it until you reach age 60 or thereabouts. Organizations such as *Consumer Reports* urge people not to consider buying long-term care coverage until age 65 or so (the exception being someone with a chronic illness that will likely mandate long-term care). The premiums will be more expensive than if you bought earlier, but you won't have spent a dime on premiums to that point—something of a financial wash.

◆ Check the long-term stability of the company selling you the insurance. Research by *Consumer Reports* has found that a number of long-term care insurers are suffering from rather shaky finances. If your company goes broke, you may lose your coverage as well as at least a portion of the premiums you already paid. Additionally, you may be forced to deal with significantly more expensive premiums if your company is bought out by another carrier.

Use company rating services such as Moody's (www.moodys.com) and Standard and Poor's (www.standardandpoors.com) to assess the financial stability of any insurer you may be considering. In particular, *Consumer Reports* suggests that you only buy coverage if the company receives a strong rating from at least two of the ratings services.

◆ Find out where you can receive benefits. Some policies limit where you can receive care, such as a nursing home. Others are more flexible, including home care or assisted living. Make sure your policy covers where you're likely to be living.

◆ Review the policy to see if it covers any specific long-term care conditions, such as Alzheimer's or Parkinson's.

◆ Check to see how coverage starts. Insurers will not begin providing payment for long-term care until the insured is unable to perform what are referred to as a certain number of "activities of daily living." These include bathing, dressing, preparing meals, and the like. *Consumer Reports* recommends that you only consider policies that require an inability to perform two such activities.

Moreover, check to see what sort of involvement by a physician may be necessary. Some policies mandate that you be examined by a company physician before you're eligible to receive benefits (not surprisingly, this is designed to hold down the number of applicable claims). If possible, look for coverage that lets your own doctor sign off on eligibility.

◆ Consider daily benefits. How much your policy will pay depends on how large a premium you're willing to spend. Maximum daily benefits range from as low as $50 to as much as $200 a day. To get a feel for what level of coverage you may need, call a few nursing homes in the area to see what the going daily rate might be.

◆ Consider the maximum life of the policy's coverage. As we discussed earlier, how long the coverage remains in place also dictates the size of your premium. Although you can opt for policies that have unlimited terms of coverage,

Consumer Reports suggests that a four-year benefit plan should address most circumstances. The reasoning: the average length of stay in a nursing home doesn't exceed that and, if it looks as though you will stay in longer than four years, you have a cushion of time to investigate other financial options.

Additionally, *Consumer Reports* recommends a 30-day waiting period. Opting for a longer waiting period may trim premiums a bit, but you may end up paying a good deal more in actual costs if you have to pay for additional care out of pocket.

◆ If appropriate, consider inflation adjustment features. Even the best long-term care policy may be of little good if, over time, inflation strips the policy's ability to cover your costs. As a result, many policies offer inflation adjustment (usually 5 percent) to bolster your coverage's long-term financial strength. The downside to this is that inflation adjustment can significantly increase the size of your premiums—up to as much as 50 percent.

One strategy: forgo the inflation protection if you're buying the coverage at age 70 or older. Between age 65 and 70, inflation protection may be worth it, since you won't be paying the additional premiums as long as you would have had you bought the coverage at an earlier age.

◆ If you live in the right spot, investigate "partnership programs." Four states— New York, California, Connecticut, and Indiana—let you buy a "partnership plan" that allows you to protect some of your assets and still qualify for Medicaid for long-term care. For instance, in California, Indiana, and New York, you buy coverage that will pay the equivalent of the amount of assets you want to protect. Once that's paid out, you're Medicaid-eligible but you still have some assets protected. By contrast, in New York, you buy nursing home and home health care coverage. You're eventually Medicaid-eligible after all benefits are paid out and your remaining assets are protected.

The Least You Need to Know

◆ There are a variety of retirement communities from which to choose. Shop for one that meets your social as well as your medical needs.

◆ Consider both individual services as well as more group-oriented programs and facilities. Ask friends and family members for referrals and be sure to visit several communities.

◆ Nursing home care is required by a relatively small segment of the adult population but, if necessary, it can prove exceedingly expensive.

◆ Long-term care insurance can also prove expensive. As a rule, don't consider it unless you have less than $200,000 or more than $1.5 million in assets.

◆ Don't consider long-term care coverage until you're 65 or so, except for people with chronic conditions.

◆ Shop for coverage carefully. Consider the financial strength of the insurer, any limitations the coverage may have, and whether you can genuinely afford it (premiums that are no greater than 5 to 6 percent of your income).

Chapter 20

Other Insurance Issues

In This Chapter

- ◆ What life insurance does
- ◆ How term life insurance works
- ◆ Inside cash value life insurance
- ◆ Disability insurance—get it now, not later
- ◆ Other forms of insurance
- ◆ Insurance you can live without

Up to this point, we've covered two aspects of insurance that can have a significant impact on the quality of your retirement—health insurance and long-term care coverage.

But they're by no means the only insurance issues that are important to address. In this chapter, we move on to cover some remaining forms of insurance that, depending on your situation, can prove critical elements of your overall retirement financial plan. We'll also hit on some types of insurance that you should avoid—coverage that is not merely redundant but likely unnecessary and most assuredly a waste of money.

The Role of Life Insurance

To put it bluntly, the issue of life insurance can make particle physics seem simple and straightforward by comparison. Not only does life insurance come in a variety of forms with all sorts of bells and whistles, it can also prove a highly contentious topic—one where enthusiastic supporters and equally ardent detractors seem equally divided.

But, in its essence, life insurance is simple. It's a form of financial protection designed to provide your beneficiaries with sufficient funds should you die. End of story.

Well, not quite. First is the issue of determining whether you need it at all. Next is the question of how much coverage you need. From there, we'll have a look at what form of life insurance might best fit your situation. And, last, we'll tackle the topic of how life insurance may prove of benefit in your retirement years.

Do You Need It?

As we just mentioned, life insurance in its essence is a form of protection for other people—not you. And that raises the first issue—do you need it at all?

Financial considerations aside, the answer is likely no if there's really no one else you need to protect. Unless a spouse, child, or some other relative relies on you financially, it doesn't make sense to spend money on protection that protects no one.

The same argument can also be made for a member of a household who doesn't contribute a substantial percentage of a family's income. So, if you're single or a stay-at-home parent, it's difficult to make the case for you to buy life insurance—in any form.

However, if there is someone who does rely on you financially, life insurance is an essential element of your overall financial plan. However macabre the notion may be, it's critical that you have adequate financial protection in place should you no longer be in the picture.

How Much Coverage Do You Need?

If someone is relying on you financially, the next issue to consider is how much coverage you need.

When you start shopping for life insurance coverage, you'll encounter rounded-off numbers. Life insurance companies are fond of offering coverage in somewhat global terms, such as $50,000, $100,000, and so on.

That may be handy, but it doesn't necessarily address your coverage needs. Instead, you need to work through a variety of issues and calculate a more specific financial target.

Certified Financial Planner Dustin LaPorte provides the following breakdown (for a complete worksheet that offers these steps in detail and in worksheet form, refer to Appendix B):

1. First, determine how much money you would want your survivors to receive on an annual basis.

2. Calculate how many years you would want them to receive this annual amount. Multiply results of question 1 by question 2.

3. Add to this total funeral costs, medical bills, cost of college (if applicable), and various forms of debt including mortgage and credit card debt. Add the total from question 3 to the total from question 2.

4. From this amount, subtract Social Security benefits, pension payout, any other life insurance coverage, and other assets. The result is your life insurance coverage requirements.

Let's work through a scenario to see what this can all add up to. Let's say you're 45 years old, married, with two children ages 10 and 15. You earn $50,000 a year. Your thinking is to provide coverage until the younger child graduates from college. That's 11 years.

Retire Right

A reminder: to get a sense of what your Social Security benefits might be, use Social Security's online benefits calculators located at www.ssa.gov/planners/calculators.htm.

First, you want to replace income. That's $550,000 right there. Add on, say, $100,000 in college costs (rather low, admittedly, for two kids, but you don't plan on going into hock completely to pay for school). Tack on a $75,000 mortgage and roughly $10,000 in funeral expenses.

Under this scenario, you would need a total of $735,000 in coverage.

Now that you've picked yourself up off the floor, let's add a bit of healthy reality to this scenario. First, you've set aside some $200,000 in retirement benefits. Additionally, according to Social Security, your family would have a maximum monthly survivors benefit of roughly $2,500. That's an additional $27,500. Finally, your aging father has told you that you can expect some $150,000 in inheritance once he passes away.

The total offset: $377,500. End result: you should shop for insurance coverage in the vicinity of $357,000.

There are also a number of online calculators where you can work through your life insurance needs. They include:

◆ www.smartmoney.com/insurance/life/index.cfm?story=intro

◆ www.ipipeline.com/iquote/e-needs.htm

◆ www.bankrate.com/brm/insurance-advisers/life-insurance.asp

Types of Coverage

Now that we've got a handle on whether you need insurance at all and, if so, how much, we turn to the two main forms of life insurance available—term life and whole life.

Term Life Insurance

Term life insurance provides the most basic form of protection. The policyholder pays an annual amount of money known as the premium. That keeps the coverage in place for that one year.

The size of the premium depends on your age when you buy the policy, the amount of coverage, and your overall health. As a point of illustration, our healthy 45-year-old looking to buy $357,000 in coverage can expect to pay anywhere from $460 all the way up to $1,300 or so per year (the premiums are largely based on the financial rating of the company issuing the insurance and, in part, on how long the company guarantees that the annual premium won't change).

Retire Right _____

To get an idea of what you might pay for term life coverage, check out www.intelliquote.com.

Term carries no savings component. It is life insurance in its most basic form—you pay the premium and you're covered. As we briefly noted previously, most policies have guaranteed premiums for an established amount of time—generally 20 to 30 years. After that, the premiums start to go up. Most policies guarantee that you can keep the policy so long as you keep paying the premiums. As such, avoid any policy that doesn't specify guaranteed renewal.

Term's greatest attributes are its simplicity and relatively inexpensive cost when compared with cash value options. It also fits into the well-known financial maxim of buying term and investing the difference. Put another way, protect yourself in the most cost-effective means possible and invest whatever funds you may have left over.

Cash Value Life Insurance

The other major form of life insurance is known as cash value insurance. The name represents the product nicely—unlike term, where all you have is the protection of the insurance itself, cash value has a cash component in addition to the coverage.

Cash value life insurance comes in four primary forms: whole life, universal life, variable life, and variable universal life.

Whole Life

This is the most straightforward form of cash value. Here, the life insurance incorporates a savings mechanism. Part of whole life's premiums goes toward the actual insurance protection, while the remainder is placed in a reserve account.

The reserve performs two functions. One is to meet increasing insurance costs as the policy owner gets older. The other part of the reserve is invested, with the policy owner guaranteed a certain rate of return.

There are also a variety of payment forms with whole life plans. With a modified life program, you pay lower premiums when you're younger and higher ones as you age. Additionally, there are single premium programs, in which the entire cost of the insurance is met with a single payment.

Proponents of whole life applaud the insurance's "forced" savings component. Whether you like it or not, if you want the insurance, part of what you pay is going to be set aside on your behalf. Of course, that's not exactly a windfall—for instance, one insurance company says on its website that it paid the equivalent interest of the average corporate bond interest (as of this writing, in the vicinity of 5 percent). What makes that a bit better is the returns on whole life are tax-free.

Another plus is that you can take out a loan against the cash value of the policy with no effect whatsoever on the monetary value of the insurance itself.

Finally, unlike term, whole life insurance premiums don't necessarily go on forever. Some policies can be fully paid up in as few as 10 years. After that the policy remains in force without the policyholder having to shell out another penny.

There are, however, significant issues with whole life. First, whole life is more expensive than term, pure and simple—one estimate obtained for the $357,000 coverage example we used earlier came in at about $5,800 a year.

def•i•ni•tion

Surrender value refers to the amount you receive if you cash out a life insurance policy prematurely. It takes into account a fee levied by the company—in effect, a penalty for cashing in the policy prematurely.

Moreover, much of the early premiums you pay go toward sales commissions and other costs rather than building up cash value. In fact, upwards of 100 percent of your first year's premiums may go to costs rather than any sort of cash value. That can make whole life a bad choice if, by chance, you cash out the policy or "surrender" it after owning it for only a few years. In those cases, the *surrender value* may not even equal the amount of premium you paid into the policy.

Universal Life

A wrinkle on straight whole life insurance is known as universal life. Here, you have minimum premiums which you must pay—anything you pay above and beyond those are invested by the company, usually in mortgages and other relatively stable choices. The money generated by this goes into a cash account, which can be used to help pay your premiums or build cash value in the policy.

One nice feature about universal life is its flexibility. Premiums can be adjusted depending on how much of the cash value may be used to pay them. Additionally, the amount of protection afforded by universal can be changed to meet shifting coverage needs.

Variable Life

This is similar to universal, except that it's potentially much more aggressive. It's also more self-directed—rather than the insurance company, the policyholder decides how the cash value of the policy is invested. You can choose investments ranging from stocks, mutual funds, or bonds.

Although that may generate greater returns for the policy, it's also much more risky, since the cash value of the policy depends on the performance of the investments chosen by the policyholder. However, variable life policies incorporate a minimum death benefit—no matter how the cash value performs, the death benefit can never fall below this guaranteed minimum.

Variable Universal Life

Like the name implies, this is a hybrid combining features of variable and universal life. On the one hand, like universal life, assets in the cash value portion of the policy may be invested in a variety of options. And, like variable life insurance, there is a degree of flexibility in the year-to-year premiums paid by the policyholder.

Choosing Between Term and Whole Life

Now comes the central question: how do you choose between term and the varying products covered by whole life?

The first consideration is the simplest. If cost is a factor, it's best to go with term. This is particularly important for people who are already having difficulty setting aside sufficient funds for retirement in other vehicles, such as a 401(k) or an IRA. That's all the more important with a Roth IRA which, like cash value life insurance, grows on a tax-deferred basis and may be withdrawn tax-free.

Term also makes sense from a supposed advantage to cash value—asset growth. Here, the maxim of investing the difference comes to the fore. As we mentioned earlier, although cash value can be construed as a form of forced savings, the returns can be rather paltry, depending on the policy you choose.

From a financial standpoint, you can come out far better if you take the money saved by buying term and invest it in a vehicle that pays better than cash value life. Let's use the numbers we quoted earlier for a $357,000 policy—erring on the high side, let's use the $1,300-per-year quote for term versus $5,800 for whole life.

If you invest the difference between the two amounts—$4,500—and get an 8 percent return the first year, that's a $360 return right off the bat (while, as likely as not, the first year of a whole life premium would produce little or no cash value). Although the cash value policy would eventually start producing cash value, it would still be playing catch-up to the strategy of investing the difference between the two premiums. And, although the life insurance offers tax advantages, there is the issue of surrender charges, which could potentially cut the cash available to you even more.

Another issue that argues for term is your increasing wealth as the years go on. For instance, by the time you reach age 60 or so, you may have accumulated sufficient assets to make life insurance coverage unnecessary. With term, you can simply cancel the policy at this point, having invested relatively little when compared with cash value coverage.

Still, there are some arguments in favor of some form of cash value coverage. It can be suitable for people who simply have a terrible time saving in any other manner (although, granted, you better be really savings challenged to make this a viable option). It's also advantageous if you wish to have insurance for your entire life (term policies are generally only renewable until age 75).

Another plausible strategy works for persons of high wealth who can use whole life in estate planning. Proceeds of the policy can be used to pay taxes and other expenses.

No matter which form of life insurance you're interested in, be sure to shop aggressively. With both term and cash value, be sure to check out the company's financial stability with one of the major ratings services.

> **Retirement Reality**
>
> A.M. Best (www.ambest.com) and Standard and Poor's (www.standardandpoors.com) are two sources of financial ratings information.

With term, make certain that your policy stipulates guaranteed renewability. This means your policy can't be canceled if you experience a streak of bad health and chalk up a lot of medical expenses. And, as we indicated earlier, compare premiums, as they can differ from one carrier to the next.

That's also the case with cash value. What one company charges for a certain amount of coverage can be drastically different from another, so be certain to shop. Additionally, investigate the specific features of each policy, such as rate of return.

Disability Insurance—Often Overlooked, Always Crucial

We mentioned this earlier but, no matter where you happen to be in your move toward retirement, disability insurance is an essential form of protection. That's for a simple reason: odds are reasonable that, sometime during your working life, you're going to become disabled and unable to continue working and earning a living.

And that can run roughshod over your finances—not only in your ability to meet your current living expenses but also in your capacity to set aside savings for retirement.

That makes disability insurance a central element of your overall retirement savings plan. In a nutshell, disability protects your income in case you're hurt or sick and unable to earn a paycheck through your regular form of employment.

At first glance, you may think that's what Social Security's disability provisions are for. But, remember, Social Security has some tough guidelines. You must be unable to do any sort of substantial work—any work, not merely what you've been trained to do or have done in the past. Moreover, your condition has to have lasted—or be expected to last—at least one year or, even worse, expected to result in your death.

Your employer may also offer disability coverage. If so, check out several issues, including how much disability coverage you may be eligible for, how soon benefits begin following the disabling injury or illness, and how long the benefits continue.

Even if your workplace does offer disability coverage, problems can persist. For one thing, many policies are limited in how long benefits continue. And, like your conventional income, employer-provided disability coverage is taxable.

That can make a good argument for buying disability insurance on your own. As a general rule, you should look to replace between 60 to 80 percent of your salary. Obviously, the more coverage you choose, the higher your premiums will be.

And the unfortunate news is that disability insurance can be expensive. One quote obtained from an insurance company cited an example of a 40-year-old man with an annual salary of $50,000. A policy paying $2,900 a month (roughly 69 percent) would cost about $1,700 a year. Moreover, the coverage would be good for five years for a covered disability.

That's a fair chunk of change. Fortunately, there are ways to trim the expense. One way is through opting for a longer *waiting period*.

Most policies come with a 90-day waiting period. Increasing that to 180 days can save you several hundred dollars a year in premiums. However, be sure that you have enough cash on hand to see you through the additional wait time. One tip is to take the money saved as a result of the longer waiting period and put it into an emergency fund.

def•i•ni•tion

Waiting period refers to the time between the onset of the disability and when benefits begin.

Another issue to bear in mind when shopping for disability coverage is how long a particular policy will continue to pay benefits. The best (and most expensive, of course) policies will keep paying you until you're able to return to work full-time or, in the case of severe disability, until you reach age 65 (there, the reasoning goes, Social Security benefits would pick up the slack).

You can lower your premiums even further by limiting the amount of time disability benefits will continue. But that can prove financially dicey if your benefits end but you're unable to return to work. Examine what other assets you may have to determine whether a shorter benefits period is a reasonable chance to take.

Other Forms of Insurance

Think we're done with insurance? Not quite. We'd like to mention a couple more types of insurance that you may do well to consider. From there, in something of a turnaround, we'll hit on a few forms of insurance that you need not waste your hard-earned dollars on.

Umbrella Insurance

We might as well face facts—we Americans have something of a love affair with lawsuits, often over incidents that, looked at in a different light, might seem somewhat trivial.

But the fact remains that we're litigious by nature. And that makes umbrella insurance an essential element of your overall insurance protection program. Umbrella insurance is liability coverage that provides an additional form of protection over whatever might be offered by homeowner's, automobile, and renter's insurance. That protection can prove critical if, say, the mailman slips and falls on your icy steps and a generous jury awards him a hefty cash award.

Moreover, relative to other forms of insurance, umbrella coverage is a bargain. Policies offering upwards of a million dollars in coverage cost only a couple hundred dollars a year in premiums. It's a cheap and potentially pivotal form of protection—one that can further shield your retirement nest egg.

Vision and Dental Insurance

Neither of these types of insurance are particularly pricey. Dental, for instance, can run anywhere from $15 or so per month on up, depending on the policy.

Dental and vision insurance can be handy if you or family members have a history of dental or vision problems (and expect to carry them into retirement). If that's the case, shop carefully—for instance, plans differ as to whether they cover pre-existing conditions. Moreover, you may have some trouble qualifying for coverage if you have a substantial history of medical issues.

Check, too, for the size of deductibles and how much a particular plan will pay in a given year. If, for instance, a plan only pays for a certain amount and you exceed that, you're on your own until the next year of coverage begins.

If, however, your vision and dental expenses are rather run of the mill, consider investing the money you would have spent on premiums. That way, if significant dental or vision problems crop up in the future, you'll have funds set aside to meet them.

Insurance You Don't Need

Let's wrap up the chapter with an overview of some forms of insurance that, for most people, are unnecessary:

♦ **Cancer insurance.** Granted, it's a very frightening disease. But there are all sorts of reasons to skip this specific form of coverage. For one thing, premiums can run as high as $300 a year. Moreover, some policies have rather strict limitations—some will only pay for hospital care (outpatient care comes out of your pocket) while others only offer benefits of a couple years or so. Instead, invest in a comprehensive health care plan.

♦ **Mortgage insurance.** This is designed to pay off your mortgage in the event you pass away. That's fine, but a solid life insurance policy is designed to do the same thing. On top of that, mortgage insurance can be far more expensive than a good term life insurance policy.

♦ **Accidental death insurance.** Here, your loved ones receive a death benefit, but only if you die in some type of accident. Trouble is, only a small fraction of the population dies in these sorts of mishaps. Stick with life insurance, which pays regardless of the cause of death.

The Least You Need to Know

♦ Life insurance is important, but only if someone else is relying on your income.

♦ Term life insurance is the most straightforward and least expensive. You pay the premium and you're covered.

♦ Cash value insurance in its varying forms offers a savings component in addition to insurance coverage.

♦ Don't overlook disability insurance. This covers you when you are ill or injured and unable to work.

♦ Umbrella insurance provides an additional layer of liability coverage. It's an inexpensive yet useful addition.

♦ Cancer insurance, mortgage protection, and accidental death insurance are unnecessary types of insurance.

Chapter 21

Estate Planning

In This Chapter

- ◆ Estate planning essentials
- ◆ How to draw up a will
- ◆ The basics of living wills
- ◆ All about trusts
- ◆ Should you preplan or prepay a funeral?
- ◆ The importance of turning to professionals

Planning for the financial solvency of retirement goes beyond saving and investing prudently. It also involves taking those steps that are necessary to ensure the safety of what you own—and, when the time comes, to make certain that your assets pass along in the manner and to whom you wish.

In this chapter, we'll introduce you to a number of salient estate planning issues and topics. We'll provide an overview of how they are developed and implemented as well as offer a sense of how they work together to protect the assets and other elements of your working life that you worked so diligently to obtain.

The Basics of Estate Planning

Some may think of what they own as being too modest to qualify for the term "estate," but that's just what it is. Your estate is everything you own. And estate planning ensures that your financial goals and the needs of your family are addressed after you pass away.

Although one estate plan may vary considerably from another, a number of features are common to estate plans (we'll discuss these in greater detail later in this chapter):

- A will
- A living will
- Powers of attorney
- Trusts of various types

A well-thought-out estate plan will fashion each of these and other elements so that they work in concert with one another. Not only can that make things happen more smoothly when the time comes, it can also eliminate a good deal of confusion and anxiety among surviving family members.

Retire Right _____

We'll make a greater point of it later in this chapter, but it bears an early mention. It's generally a good idea to involve a number of professionals in the development of your estate plan, including an attorney, tax professional, and others.

First Steps

On the surface, it may seem that a visit to an attorney—one preferably experienced with estate planning issues—would be the first thing you should do to get your estate planning process underway.

But before you do that, it's important to take some time to organize the materials you will need to get the process started—not to mention addressing a few questions with regard to your estate.

Inventory all your assets to know precisely what you have and what they are worth. This should include the following:

❏ Your home. If you're not certain as to its current value, refer to your property tax appraisal. To get a sense of the home's true market value (which can often differ considerably from a government tax assessment), consult a real estate agent.

❏ Values of your investments, including stocks, bonds, annuities, mutual funds, 401(k)s, pensions, Individual Retirement Accounts, and other holdings.

❏ Cash value of any whole life insurance policies.

❏ Assets in checking accounts, savings accounts, certificates of deposit, savings bonds, and other vehicles.

❏ Values of cars, trucks, boats, and like items.

❏ Value of any interest in investment real estate or other business interests.

❏ Amount of any outstanding debts.

❏ Any documents that may impact the estate, such as prenuptial agreements, divorce decrees, and recent tax returns.

❏ Location and contents of any safe deposit boxes.

Other information that can be helpful when preparing to draw up an estate plan include

❏ Names, addresses, and birthdates of people you expect to include in your will.

❏ Name, address, and birth date of the planned *executor* of your will.

❏ Information on minor children and guardians.

def•i•ni•tion

An **executor** is charged with overseeing the execution of a will.

Your Beneficiaries

Beneficiaries are the people and organization to whom you wish to leave your worldly goods. For many people, that seems a straightforward choice. Spouses, children, grandchildren, and other family members are often clear-cut choices as beneficiaries.

But sometimes the overall lineup of beneficiaries is not quite so obvious. For instance, people in second and third marriages may face challenges determining who among the panoply of children, stepchildren, and others should get what. If you own a business, the line of who is most deserving can often be blurred depending on whom you ask.

Another issue relevant to beneficiaries is deciding alternate beneficiaries. These are people or groups who would receive your assets and property should a primary beneficiary predecease you. This can also eliminate the need for last-minute changes to wills, trusts, and other documents should a primary beneficiary die unexpectedly.

That makes talking about your estate plans with your heirs another central first step. However uncomfortable such a discussion may make some, it's essential that you let everyone who may be involved know what your intentions are. That, like other elements of the estate planning process, can help head off any sort of confusion or conflict later on.

Other Ways Estate Planning Helps

Making sure your family and loved ones receive your property and assets as you wish is only one of the primary objectives of estate planning. Other potential advantages include:

- **Distributing assets quickly.** A well-drawn estate plan can help ensure that your assets are distributed to beneficiaries as quickly as possible.

- **Cutting costs.** A solid estate is cost-efficient, limiting the expense to execute it and distribute assets.

- **Targeting worthy causes.** As we've mentioned, family members are not the only potential beneficiaries. Depending on how you draw up your estate plan, you can also distribute assets to religious, educational, and charitable groups and organizations.

- **Cut taxes.** Proper estate planning is geared to limit tax liability as much as possible. That leaves more money for you to give to the people and groups you want to get it.

- **Address possible incapacity.** As we will see later, estate planning features such as living wills and power of attorney can prove invaluable if you become ill or incapacitated and need someone else to make critical decisions.

- **Keep a business going.** If you own or have a significant holding in a business, an estate plan can address how you want your share handled.

Writing a Will

A will is at the heart of many estates. In its essence, a will is a written document that delineates how you want your property distributed after you die. A will can go into as much detail as you wish—you essentially have complete control over who receives what property, how much each person gets, and when they can take ownership.

Anyone over the age of 18 can draft a will. You must also show that you're mentally competent and are aware of the decisions you're spelling out in your will. You also have the right to amend your will at any time. In fact, it's a solid idea to review your will periodically. That way, any updates or changes can be handled without any undue time pressures.

When drafting a will, another important decision is the choice of your executor.

Being an executor generally involves paying bills and relevant taxes and other expenses, taking care of property and, ultimately, making sure assets are distributed according to your wishes. An executor may be paid for his or her services.

Although a suitable executor doesn't have to be a legal or financial expert, choose an executor carefully. The person should know you well, know where important documents and other materials are located, and be willing and able to invest the time that may be needed to carry out your wishes to the letter.

Many people use an attorney to draft their will. This is generally the safest, most reliable route, as an attorney can identify issues and concerns with your estate that you may have not even been aware of. This is particularly the case if your estate is involved or complicated. A less expensive option is to draw up a will using software or online will-drafting services.

After a will is drawn up, you finish this process of estate planning by executing the will. This involves at least two witnesses who have no relationship at all to you or your estate. The witnesses watch you sign and then sign the will themselves to document that you signed of your free choice.

> **Retirement Reality**
>
> According to AARP, 60 percent of adults age 50 and older have wills. That percentage jumps as people get older—testimony to a will's importance.

> **Retire Right**
>
> Some people have a video will filmed to accompany a written will. This can help address any concerns about mental incompetence and help establish that the person drafting the will was fully aware of its implications.

Dying intestate can cause numerous and prickly problems. If you don't have a legal document specifying how you wanted your assets handled after you die, your estate is effectively turned over to the state for handling.

def•i•ni•tion

The legal term that refers to lack of a will or a trust that provides instructions is known as **dying intestate.**

Without a will, the local probate court in your area will designate someone as your estate's administrator. This person will direct the legal distribution of property—effectively operating on assumptions on where they thought you wanted your money to go.

Not only can the absence of a will potentially leave your loved ones without the assets you wanted them to have, dying intestate can be expensive. The administrator must be paid for his or her services (in fact, the administrator must be paid before any property is distributed). Any other costs associated with distribution of assets must also be borne by your estate.

Living Wills

A will is designed to let your wishes be known after you die. But what happens if you're medically incapacitated and unable to communicate with those around you?

That makes a living will another important part of estate planning. A living will (which also goes by the name of an advanced medical directive) is a document that outlines your decisions about any sort of life-sustaining treatment. Put another way, if you become terminally ill and unable to talk or otherwise communicate, your living will lets those around you know what sort of medical care you want—and don't want.

That can take in any number of variables. For instance, some people may ask that they not receive any sort of significant medical intervention such as artificial life support.

One challenge to living wills is that different states have a variety of laws regarding advanced medical directives. For instance, some states may restrict the kinds of medical procedures that a living will can address.

Retirement Reality

Power of attorney can be assigned to address other areas. For instance, financial power of attorney lets someone make financial decisions on your behalf.

To help ensure that your wishes are carried out, it can be helpful to have a predesignated advocate who is able to speak on your behalf. As a result, many with living wills also assign what is referred to as medical power of attorney.

Medical power of attorney involves signing a document that gives someone else the legal right to make medical decisions on your behalf when you're incapable of doing so. Medical power of attorney can address all sorts of situations when you're incapacitated (a living will, by contrast, is used when someone is terminally ill).

Trusts

The notion of a trust may connote blue bloods scheming to keep their cache of cash intact. But the fact is trusts can be a helpful estate-planning tool for a large number of families, not merely the super rich.

A trust is basically a legal vehicle in which one person—known as the trustee—holds property for another person (known as the beneficiary). This trustee can be a person or a trust company.

The person providing the property for the trusts—which can include money, real estate, stocks, and other assets—is known as the grantor. To receive the various sorts of protection a trust can provide, the assets are retitled in the name of the trust.

A trust offers a variety of advantages. For one thing, it allows you to establish guidelines as to how and when you wish to have your assets distributed after you die. It also provides solid protection if you're concerned about creditors and potential lawsuits that may be filed against your estate. Depending on the sort of trust used, it can also help reduce gift and estate taxes.

Another significant advantage is that trusts can be used to avoid *probate*.

Probate is designed to identify the rightful heirs to an estate (and their appropriate shares) and to legally transfer title of the property to the heirs. Not only can probate lead to a loss of privacy—probate procedures are all public, often with newspaper notices—but it can be time-consuming and exceedingly expensive. Average costs for probate can run anywhere from 6 to 10 percent of the value of the estate.

def•i•ni•tion _____

> **Probate** is the legal process that the state must go through should you die with property still in your name.

A trust also allows you to direct the specific chronology of the distribution of your assets. For instance, if your children and grandchildren stand to inherit money, you can break down the payments into several steps that are met as the beneficiaries reach a certain age. It can also be useful when someone's mental competency is in question.

One form of trust is known as a testamentary trust. This, created under a last will and testament, becomes effective only after the grantor dies and the will admitted to probate.

Another popular form of trust is known as a living trust. This trust becomes effective immediately—hence, the "living" portion of the name. Living trusts can be either revocable or irrevocable. A revocable trust can be changed or eliminated completely during a person's lifetime. By contrast, an irrevocable trust can't be changed in any way during the grantor's lifetime.

Other more specific types of trusts include

> ### Retirement Reality
>
> Why would anyone choose an irrevocable trust that's locked in place for a lifetime? The answer is almost always due to tax advantages.

- ◆ **Bypass trust.** Also known as a credit shelter or family trust, this helps you protect your spouse financially. If you have a great deal of assets, this lets you set aside a certain amount of money for the trust, which is then used to benefit your spouse after you die. The remainder of your assets—now considerably smaller—may be able to pass directly to your spouse tax-free.

- ◆ **Generation-skipping trust.** This is designed to move assets to generations further removed than just your children.

- ◆ **Irrevocable life insurance trust.** This takes life insurance out of your estate.

- ◆ **Qualified personal residence trust.** This takes the value of your primary or vacation home out of your estate.

- ◆ **Qualified terminable interest property trust.** This is often used in families with divorces and stepchildren. It allows you to earmark your assets for your children while your surviving spouse benefits from the trust as well.

Of course, trusts in their varied forms are not without their drawbacks. For one thing, they can prove pricey—up to several thousand dollars paid to an attorney to draw up the trust, depending on how complex the trust is.

> ### Golden Years Gaffes
>
> If a trust seems appealing, consult a qualified attorney and/or tax professional. They're often too involved to do them yourself.

Nor does a trust remove the necessity of a will. Although you may try to be as thorough as possible, chances are good that something will not be placed in a trust. That means that has to be handled by the directives in a will.

Last, there are other ways to pass funds along to heirs without the necessity of a trust. For instance, you can give gifts up to $12,000 a year annually to as many people as you wish. Additionally, you can pay expenses such as college tuition for someone else's benefit, provided that you pay the school directly rather just giving the cash to your intended beneficiary.

Preplanning/Prepaying a Funeral

One final element to the topic of estate planning is indeed final: the issue of whether you should preplan or prepay for your funeral.

Granted, it's not the cheeriest topic, but it does warrant some discussion—if for no other reason than that an increasing number of people are opting for this advanced sort of planning. In some instances, it is an issue of simple planning. People give some thought as to where they'd like to be buried (or cremated), what sort of service they would prefer, and literally any other decision they care to specify.

Others take that a step further by prepaying for funeral services. This involves a contract—usually with a funeral home—where they prepay for goods and services, often long before they expect to pass away. A third party may hold the funds until they are needed.

Although it may not be a pleasant chore, preplanning and prepaying offer significant advantages. Perhaps most significant is the reduction of burden on your family. Since you've laid out your wishes in advance, that's a host of concerns they no longer will have to worry about during a time of emotional turmoil.

Additionally, if you prepay, there's the issue of rising costs. Since you may buy funeral services and goods many years in advance, you're likely to save a good deal of money as prices continue to rise.

If preplanning or prepaying seem a reasonable consideration, take some issues into account:

◆ If you preplan, write down your wishes and provide copies to family members and your lawyer.

◆ If prepaying, know precisely what you're getting. Does it include services as well as certain goods, such as a casket?

◆ Contact your state office that oversees funeral professionals and see what laws are on the books regarding prepaying. For instance, does your state require that prepaid funds be held by a third party?

- Does the money just sit there or does it earn interest?

- Can you get your money back if the company goes out of business? What if you change your mind about the whole arrangement?

The Importance of Professionals

One final word about estate planning. As you can no doubt tell, it's a complicated, often convoluted topic. What we've done here is offer an introduction.

That said, when considering issues and steps with regard to estate planning, it's never ill-advised to work with an experienced, competent professional. That can mean everything from working with an experienced estate attorney to a tax professional well versed in crafting an estate plan that can help save on tax liability.

As we've seen, that can prove a somewhat expensive proposition, particularly if vehicles such as trusts come into the picture. But as we've also discussed, those sorts of vehicles and an estate plan that is prudent and well thought out and executed can prove invaluable, both in emotional and financial terms. And that comes out as money well spent.

The Least You Need to Know

- Estate planning, which includes elements such as wills, medical directives, and other things, is an important part of retirement planning.

- When beginning an estate plan, start with a complete inventory of all your assets.

- A solid will lays out your wishes in direct, concrete terms. It's often best to use an attorney to draft one.

- Living wills and power of attorney can also be helpful if you're somehow incapacitated and unable to communicate.

- Trusts come in a variety of forms and can be useful in passing your estate along in the most efficient manner possible.

- Consider preplanning or prepaying for a funeral to save on costs and to spare your survivors the emotional burden of having to do so.

Part 5

When It's Not Enough

Not every retirement begins with a pile of cash and the time to enjoy it to the full. Part 5 explores the issue of inadequate savings and steps you can take to counteract a lack of cash. Strategies include trading down, working after retirement, and considering a variety of alternate living arrangements that are not only cost-effective but may offer valuable social connections to boot. Financial challenges need not ruin your retirement. Rather, a few modest steps and ideas can often turn a cash-strapped retirement into a financially viable one.

22

Retiring on a Shoestring

In This Chapter

- ◆ What can you do without?
- ◆ Work part-time or work longer
- ◆ Manage what you have
- ◆ Tapping into your home's equity
- ◆ It's more than just money

Sometimes, despite all your best intentions ….

It happens—a lot. Many people reach retirement age with, to put it mildly, inadequate savings. How they got there can derive from any number of reasons, but the fact remains—money is tight, and it's going to stay that way.

There are a number of ideas and strategies that you can put to use should you be looking at retirement with less than what you once hoped for in financial assets.

That doesn't mean that retiring on a shoestring is necessarily easy. But it doesn't have to be the trial by fire that it first might appear to be. This chapter is here to help.

Just How Tight Are Things?

If you expect your retirement to be a cash-strapped one, the first step is to determine just how much of a challenge you're facing. From there, you can determine what steps will help make up as much of the shortfall as possible.

First, tally up all assets and potential sources of income. As we outlined in Chapter 15, these can include personal savings, company pensions, and Social Security benefits.

Next, compile a list of your expected expenses to compare with your available assets. Be as exhaustive as possible, including not only major expenditures (mortgage payments, insurance premiums, and similar costs) but lesser obligations as well, such as entertainment, clothing, and other items.

From here, it's time to calculate how long your money will last if you used every source of income to meet your list of obligations. Again, we did this in Chapter 15. The difference here is to pinpoint just when your savings would be exhausted if you were to withdraw them without any concern for exhausting them—or, by the same token, which expenses would not be met even if you limited withdrawals.

Here's an example. Say you were able to save only $75,000 toward your retirement. You estimate you'll need about $30,000 a year in a retirement that could last upwards of 20 years. Social Security kicks in about $1,400 a month, or $16,800 a year. If your $75,000 nest egg earns 7 percent a year in return, that allows for a payout of roughly $5,300 a year. That totals to some $22,000, resulting in an $8,000 shortfall—a good-size deficit, but certainly not beyond your ability to make up.

Cutting Back

A cash-strapped retirement doesn't necessarily equate with desperate poverty. Often, a few small cutbacks—perhaps implemented in concert—can make up the difference.

One place to start is your expenses. Since you compiled a fairly exhaustive list of these to examine your overall financial health, you should have them in hand. Study the list carefully and see where you might be able to tighten things up.

This may not be the make or break to a solid financial retirement, but it can prove a contributing factor. Some ideas that can help trim your expenses include:

- ◆ **Discretionary spending.** Necessary expenses include such items as housing, food, insurance, and similar costs. Items such as health-club memberships, vacations, and magazine subscriptions aren't so necessary. If you can live without some of these, you can save a good chunk of change right off the bat.

- **Housing.** If you own your own home, see if refinancing may cut your monthly mortgage payment. Flip back to Chapter 6 for additional details and considerations with this option.

- **Transportation.** If you don't own your car outright, is it possible to trade it in for a less expensive model? In these days of soaring gas prices, is a more fuel-efficient model possible? Do you have more than one car when one would prove adequate? Do you shop aggressively for the best possible gasoline prices?

- **Food.** Keep an eye out for sales whenever possible. If you have adequate storage space, bulk warehouses sell certain items in quantity, which can offer significant savings. See if there's a food co-op near where you live.

Retire Right _____

If you live in an area with extensive public transportation, consider using that more often. Not only is it cheaper, but older people often get discounts.

- **Telephone services.** Shop aggressively for the lowest-cost cellular phone and other sorts of telephone services. This is a competitive market, with deals galore.

- **Prescription drugs.** If you pay for prescription drugs, make it a habit to see if a less expensive generic equivalent is available.

- **Charitable giving.** Prioritize charitable giving and other gifts. This may be a difficult area to address, particularly if you value your support of a particular organization or cause. But, if cash is tight, consider at least paring back your contribution levels.

- **Travel.** Not every trip needs to be aboard a luxury ocean liner. Investigate inexpensive travel options, such as online travel services that let you bid for travel, accommodations, and other expenses.

Consider Working Part-Time

We cover this option in detail in Chapter 23, but taking on some sort of paying work after you retire can often prove a big difference in making ends meet.

It helps in two ways. First, since you're bringing in a paycheck, you're generating cash necessary to meet ongoing expenses. Second, you hold off on withdrawing your savings, letting it grow that much more with time.

Retirement Reality

A post-retirement job is becoming more common all the time. A Merrill Lynch study found that most retirees expected to begin a second career or start a business after they retired.

Here's an illustration. Say you take a part-time job paying $10,000 a year. Naturally enough, that's $10,000 you don't have to take out of an IRA, 401(k), or other retirement vehicle every year. Even better, if you can stay that course for 10 years and your retirement savings account earns an average of 8 percent a year, you end that 10-year period with roughly $152,000. And all thanks to a part-time job paying a modest $10,000 a year.

Nor does a job necessarily mandate some sort of mindless drudgery. For instance, Kent Donley, a financial adviser for Edward Jones, advises clients to consider "hobby jobs"—part-time jobs that clients enjoy rather than consider a chore. Even some clients with sufficient retirement savings are choosing a hobby job just to stay active and socially engaged.

But if a job is as much an issue of income as it is activity, be sure it doesn't affect your Social Security benefits. There's more about this and other details about working after you retire in Chapter 23.

Work a Bit Longer

If you've yet to retire but it seems clear that your finances aren't quite what they ought to be, there's always the option of delaying your retirement and working longer than you initially planned.

Retirement Reality

Like a part-time job after you retire, you're not alone if you decide to work a bit longer. The National Association of Professional Employer Organizations found in a survey that nearly one fifth of small businesses had workers who were remaining on the job past 65.

The benefits can be numerous. First, naturally enough, you're pulling a paycheck to help meet your financial obligations. And, like a part-time job, you're leaving your retirement savings intact, promoting further growth.

But there are other pluses. If you receive health benefits through your employer, that's an important—and often expensive—financial obligation that you don't have to meet yourself.

Even better, as we discussed in Chapter 8, working longer can also boost your Social Security benefits.

Remember—if you were born anytime after 1943, you can expect to receive an annual bonus of 8 percent in Social Security benefits for every year you work beyond full retirement. (Note: Chapter 8 includes a chart that outlines what full retirement age means.)

Nor do your benefits increase simply through the 8 percent annual bonus. The longer you work, the greater the overall income Social Security calculates to determine your benefit. That, too, can boost the payments from Social Security which you eventually receive.

Manage What You Have Carefully

Implicit in our discussion about trimming expenses is the importance of keeping as close an eye on your money as possible. Although a financial slam dunk may be hard to come by, small efforts brought together as part of a concerted whole can go a long way toward making your retirement as financially comfortable as possible.

That means careful management of your money beyond trying to trim expenses at every opportunity. Some additional money-smart ideas include:

- **Aim for 4 percent annual withdrawals.** As we worked out earlier in this chapter, drawing down as little as possible from saved assets—and, as a result, relying on other sources to pick up the financial slack—offers you the best opportunity to stretch what you have been able to save. Recall that experts recommend retirees withdraw no more than 4 percent of their saved assets in any given year. Aim to hit that objective as best you can, and look to alternatives for additional sources of cash.

- **Shop for the best savings returns.** Conventional savings and checking accounts often offer paltry interest rates. Investigate money market accounts and other vehicles that offer better returns.

- **Watch your tax bill.** The last thing you need in a cash-strapped retirement is an unnecessarily high tax bill. While that's likely less of a concern with income taxes, don't overlook other sorts of taxes such as your property taxes. Check back to Chapter 17 to see what you can do to trim your property tax bill.

- **Keep tax-deferred and tax-free savings intact for as long as possible.** The longer they remain untapped, the longer they can grow—and, in the case of the tax-deferred savings, the longer you can put off any resulting tax bill.

- **Avoid consumer debt whenever possible.** Credit card debt can strangle even the best efforts to live within your means. If you have credit card debt, pay it down as quickly as you can without unduly straining other areas of your budget.

If you find it difficult not to use a credit card, don't be shy about slicing it up and instead using a debit card, which withdraws funds directly from a checking account.

◆ **Take a long-term view.** Although retiring on a shoestring may be challenging and at times frustrating, it need not be a life of deprivation. If you know you want to spend a significant amount of money in the future, begin earmarking a regular series of savings to meet the expense. That way, you can enjoy yourself without having to slough the expense off on a credit card or force your budget to take a singularly large hit.

Trading Down

Up to this point, many of the ideas and strategies we've covered have been designed to make small changes to help address the issue of inadequate savings. Now, we'll hit on two strategies that, while involving a good deal more legwork and effort, can often make a significant difference in making a cash-strapped retirement a good deal less burdensome.

The first option is trading down, or choosing to live in a smaller, less expensive home than the one you live in now. Given the way real estate prices have trended over the past several decades, this can be a virtual lifesaver for someone who otherwise may have been unable to set aside any significant amount of savings toward retirement.

On the surface, it seems simple. You now live in a house with more space than you possibly need—not to mention a bigger mortgage payment than you can comfortably continue to meet in retirement. You sell your existing home and pocket the (hopefully) substantial profits.

From there, two primary options exist. You could buy a less expensive house outright, eliminating the burden of a mortgage altogether. Or you could put a down payment on a smaller home, hanging on to a greater amount of cash for other purposes, and opt for a much less expensive mortgage than your first home carried.

Until 1997, you were required to reinvest all the proceeds in a new home. If you didn't, you owed taxes on the profit. And, even if you did reinvest all the gains on your prior home, it didn't eliminate a tax bill—it merely postponed it.

Nor did laws up to that point cut older people that much slack. Under former guidelines, owners age 55 and older could enjoy up to $125,000 in gains from the sale of a home tax-free. On top of that, the tax break was a one-shot deal—use it once and it was gone for good.

Happily, that has all changed for the better. Homeowners selling their homes are no longer effectively obligated to buy a more expensive home. No matter how old you are, as much as $250,000 of profit from the sale of a home is tax-free if you're single (or a couple who files separately). For couples who file joint tax returns, you can pocket as much as $500,000 tax-free.

Moreover, it's no longer a "use it once and it's done" proposition. Federal law now allows you to take the tax-free break every two years. That means all you have to do is stay in a home for a minimum of 24 months and you're once again eligible for the tax break.

Retire Right _____

If you're still a long way from retirement, the relaxed federal guidelines let you trade down without tax implications. If you're concerned you're not saving enough, that can free up funds you can put toward your retirement.

Reverse Mortgages

Maybe the idea of selling your home and relocating doesn't appeal to you. The size of your house still fits your needs and, if nothing else, you feel too much of a sense of attachment to take your life elsewhere.

Still, the need for additional cash to fund your retirement persists. In these situations, many people consider a reverse mortgage. (We covered this briefly in Chapter 5, but it's particularly pertinent in cash-strapped situations.)

A reverse mortgage allows you to take advantage of the equity in your home. In effect, you turn that equity into an income source. You can receive payments in a variety of ways, including a monthly check, lump sum, and other options.

You must be at least 62 years of age to apply for a reverse mortgage. Additionally, you can generally take one out from what is considered your primary residence, meaning that reverse mortgages are not available for properties such as vacation homes. The overall amount you're eligible for depends on your age, the value of the house, and the interest rate the lender charges.

As you continue to access the reverse mortgage, as the name implies, your loan balance actually increases rather than decreases. The loan becomes due when you sell your house, die, or otherwise vacate the property.

On the surface, reverse mortgages may seem like the answer to a prayer for retirees who face a dearth of available cash. That's particularly so if they've owned the house for a considerable amount of time and, as a result, have built up a substantial amount of equity.

Unfortunately, there are a number of issues and caveats when it comes to reverse mortgages. For one thing, they can be complicated. On top of that, they can prove pricey in terms of interest rates and fees.

Golden Years Gaffes

HECM counselors cannot charge a fee for their consultation—something that some counselors who were less than above board tried to do in the past.

Retire Right

Additional information—including a calculator to estimate how much cash a reverse mortgage may offer you—can be found at the National Reverse Mortgage Lenders Association (www. reversemortgage.org).

Additionally, although reverse mortgages are offered by a number of sources—banks, mortgage companies, and other private sorts of lenders—the only one that is insured by the federal government is known as a home equity conversion mortgage (HECM). Not only are these federally backed, they often offer lower consumer costs than other competing loans.

To receive an HECM, federal law mandates that you meet with a counselor who has been approved by the federal Department of Housing and Urban Development. This counseling session is designed to better acquaint you with HECMs and to help address any concern or confusion you may have regarding them.

Reverse mortgages are also akin to refinancing in that you need to consider how long you plan to remain in your home. Since fees and other expenses are significant, it doesn't make sense to lay out substantial cash when you only plan to stay in the house for a year or two. In those instances, it may be a better play to investigate a home equity loan.

Home Equity Loans

The name says it all, as these derive from the amount of equity you have in your home. In a nutshell, you are able to borrow against that equity. Depending on the bank or other lending source with whom you work, you may be able to borrow up to 80 percent of your home's equity, minus whatever balance you owe on your mortgage.

Home equity loans offer a variety of advantages. For one thing, they're exceedingly flexible. Once you have the loan in place, you can use it when you see fit to do so. Repayment plans can also be flexible, with options such as interest-only programs available. Moreover, unlike conventional consumer debt, interest on home equity loans is usually fully tax-deductible on loans as large as $100,000.

In terms of interest, home equity loans are a downright bargain relative to interest levied by consumer loans such as credit cards. As of this writing, a home equity loan could be had with an interest rate in the vicinity of 8 percent. Compare that with credit cards, whose interest rates can easily reach into the mid- and high teens.

Additionally, like other elements of the financial world, competition for home equity loans has become exceedingly fierce. That has made their up-front costs and time needed to obtain a loan to be far more consumer-friendly than they may have been in the past.

Still, shop carefully for home equity loans. Like any other loan, different loans will contain a variety of up-front costs and expenses, including closing costs, other fees, and *points*.

Overall, the best strategy for using a home equity loan may be to pay down bills that would otherwise prove more expensive, such as credit card debt and auto loans. Although home equity may seem an attractive source of ready cash, it is nonetheless a loan that will eventually have to be repaid in some manner. That means that if you pass away and your home goes on the market, the balance on the home equity loan will be subtracted from the proceeds.

def•i•ni•tion

Points represent an up-front interest payment to the lender. One point is equivalent to 1 percent of the amount borrowed.

Look Beyond Money

At this point, it's obvious what the overriding premise of this book is all about—the importance of solid financial planning and execution to help you enjoy the sort of retirement you want and deserve.

But it's also essential (and healthy) to interject another justifiably important point that we raised earlier in the book—however important, money need not be the make or break to anyone's retirement.

That's a valuable point to raise, particularly within the context of retirees who are facing cash-flow challenges in retirement. And that can make a focus on things other than a dearth of cash a valuable ally in building a solid and satisfying retirement.

One helpful resource is Ralph Warner's book *Get a Life: You Don't Need a Million to Retire Well* (Nolo Press, 2004). In it, Warner features interviews with nine seniors whom he describes as "energized" and "life embracing." The bottom line: money may be important, but it's not necessarily what retirees obsess about when retirement time actually rolls around.

Granted, says Warner, some of the retirees with whom he spoke had saved an ample amount and, as a result, had few financial concerns. But, writes Warner in an *Inc. Magazine* piece: "But many others, with more typical middle class incomes, also don't give money much thought. Some have chosen to live fairly frugal lives; others are so busy thinking and doing interesting things they simply don't have the time or desire to focus a large amount of energy on their finances."

To conclude, Warner asked retirees what they would advise younger people to do to prepare for retirement. Here's what they said:

- Learn new things.
- Develop lots of interests.
- Find useful ways to connect with the world.
- Cultivate important family relationships and friendships.
- Take steps to protect your health.

What to take away from Warner's ideas? Is money completely irrelevant? Of course not. Not even the most socially connected, healthy retiree stands much of a chance of enjoying his or her post-working years if he or she can't pay the mortgage month after month.

Still, it's a powerful message to remember that money, in the end, is just one vehicle to a happy retirement. If you don't have enough, perhaps a focus on issues other than money can be helpful.

The Least You Need to Know

- If you're retiring with less money than you had planned on, the first step is to determine just how financially short you are. From there, you can institute steps to make up the difference.

- Working part-time in retirement can provide extra income and save you from tapping into what savings you have.

- Working longer before retiring also provides extra income and can boost your Social Security benefits.

- Trading down to a smaller home can provide your retirement with a significant cash infusion.

- Reverse mortgages and home equity loans are two means of tapping into your home's equity in retirement.

- Money is important to your retirement, but other issues—your health, activities, and connection with others—are also critical to a happy retirement.

Chapter 23

Retire–Then Go to Work

In This Chapter

- How to decide if you should work
- Where to start looking
- How to market yourself
- Watch out for age discrimination
- How to start your own business
- The impact on Social Security and Medicare

Estimates hold that, by 2010, 1 of every 10 workers in the United States will be at least 50 years old. Studies also show that, as the pool of experienced employees continues to dwindle, companies of all sorts will be increasingly interested in hooking up with older employees who possess that level of knowledge and practical experience.

Maybe you didn't save enough money to retire in the manner you wanted to. Or, on a more positive note, even though you're no longer at what once might have been a lifetime career, you're not ready to get out of the game. Whatever the reason, if the notion of pursuing some sort of work after you retire captures your interest, this chapter will provide some solid, practical ways to help you identify and enjoy the job you want.

How to Decide If You Need to Go Back to Work

The reasons behind going back to work after you retire can be varied. As we discussed in prior chapters, people derive all sorts of benefits from work that supersede a mere paycheck. For many, work is a source of achievement, respect, satisfaction, companionship and, ideally, fun.

That may be all well and good but, for some retirees, working after retirement isn't simply a matter of personal fulfillment. It may be an issue of money, an unexpected shortfall in the amount of assets you need to retire as you want to.

> ### Retirement Reality
>
> According to an AARP study, four out five baby boomers said they planned to work in some capacity after they retire.

Let's work through some math to see if it's a money issue for you—and what you can do about it. Let's say you retired at age 62 with savings totaling $300,000. You invest that and earn an average of 7 percent a year. If you've calculated that you'll need $30,000 a year to live on, that $300,000 sum is only going to last about 12 years—likely not nearly long enough.

Let's push the time horizon out a bit and say you hope your assets will stay in place for 23 years (you have a history of family longevity). With that time frame, your $300,000 nest egg at 7 percent gives you $19,416 a year. Granted, Social Security may pick up some of the slack but, with the effects of inflation kicking in, you may still come up short.

That illustrates a positive element to many retirement scenarios. While your overall situation may benefit from working after you retire, you may not need a cache of cash to make up the shortfall. In the example we just worked through, our retiree would be on track with just a few thousand dollars of income a year. That shows that even modest amounts of supplementary income can make a big difference in a retirement that's enjoyed rather than merely endured.

Nor for that matter does work have to be a particularly long-term proposition. Consider another scenario. Let's say we have the same $300,000 nest egg—still a bit short at age 62. Rather than looking at a long-term balance between working and drawing down retirement assets, our retiree and his wife both land post-retirement jobs paying a bit more than $12,000 a year—$25,000 between the two of them. Tack on a prorated contribution from Social Security (we'll cover this aspect of post-retirement work later in this chapter) and they've made their $30,000-a-year goal.

Even better, their retirement assets continue to grow untouched. In just five years' time at an annual return of 7 percent, that initial $300,000 amount has blossomed into more than $420,000—a substantially better financial position since the initial $300,000 remained intact throughout.

Nor is income necessarily the sole financial reason for returning to some form of employment after retirement. For many people, health insurance is an equally popular lure. Since Medicare doesn't begin until age 65, health insurance can be a valuable add-on to workers who retire prior to that age and don't want—or have the means— to seek out their own coverage.

Where to Begin Looking

So, you've determined that working after retirement may be both financially and mentally rewarding. Where do you start to look?

Before you dust off your resumé, it's wise to take a few minutes to consider some essential questions—issues that may have a profound effect on where you look for work and what sort of work you might choose to pursue. Consider:

- How much do I want (or need) to work?

- What do I want to do?

- What sort of specific skills can I offer an employer?

How Much Do I Want (or Need) to Work?

The answer to this depends in large part on your financial situation. If work is something of a necessity, you may have to opt for as many hours as you can get (at least initially, as we illustrated earlier by pulling a paycheck while leaving your retirement assets untouched).

However (and hopefully), you may have an element of flexibility in determining how much you wish to work. If that's the case, build your thinking around other elements of your retirement. For instance, would you prefer to work weekends, leaving a chunk of weekdays free for travel and other opportunities? How about nights? Consider, too, a job where time off is available for more extended activities.

Whatever you decide, it's important that the time you spend working complement your other retirement pursuits, rather than limiting them in any way. Through that, you can achieve whatever financial goals may be necessary while still getting the most out of your retirement off-hours.

What Do I Want to Do?

This can be the real fun part of working after you retire—deciding just what it is you wish to do with your working time.

For many of us, working after retirement seems a natural segue from our pre-retirement career. Perhaps you'd like to continue work in a similar vein—perhaps in a consulting capacity or other type of work where your experience and savvy can prove valuable.

Retire Right _____

If you like what you did before you retired, ask your former employer if they offer part-time employment to retirees.

On the other hand, working after you retire can follow a completely different path. Perhaps you didn't particularly care for your "first" career. Maybe you liked it fine, but always felt drawn to doing something else.

Now may be the time to do just that. Many retirees find that a completely fresh form of work can prove stimulating and challenging. Perhaps a hobby or some other form of avocation provides work opportunities, particularly if you're willing to start your own business along those lines (we'll get into that later).

What Sort of Specific Skills Can I Offer an Employer?

Knowing what you'd like to do is one thing—recognizing that you have the means to succeed is another. Consider carefully all the skills, experience, and working attributes you've acquired over the years. What sort of employer or business might they lend themselves to? Are there certain sorts of skills that you lack or could stand to polish? If that's the case, we'll hit on that later.

Retire Right _____

If you're having trouble getting a grip on what sorts of skills you may be able to bring to a position, consider hooking up with a career coach to hone your thinking.

Start Your Search

Now that you've tackled some elementary issues having to do with work after retirement, you can begin to take some tangible steps toward achieving your employment goals. Here are some ways to do that:

◆ We already talked about asking your former employer about part-time work. Don't forget to ask about filling in for vacationing employees, flex-time work, and project specific assignments.

◆ Check your local paper to see what sorts of jobs are available. You can do this every day or opt for the extra listings afforded by Sunday editions. In particular, look for the sort of background, education, skills, and other experience they require (that, again, may hint at additional training).

◆ Network. Chances are good that you have a lengthy list of friends and colleagues still in the working world or not far removed. Hook up with them not only to pursue leads but to solicit their feedback on ways to search effectively. Consider joining professional and community organizations to further your contacts.

◆ Contact temp agencies. Temporary employment agencies actively look for retired workers with a range of job skills and experience. Not only can temping provide excellent work settings with a good deal of flexibility, temporary positions sometimes turn into permanent ones.

◆ Volunteer. Like temp positions, volunteer positions at companies and other organizations can occasionally lead to paid employment.

◆ Take advantage of the Internet. If you're comfortable going online, the Internet affords a wide variety of job-hunting information and options. Courtesy of AARP, here are a few sites that may be worth a gander or two:

   ❑ RetirementJobs.com (www.retirementjobs.com)—Provides job leaders for people 50 and older. Positions range from accounting to marketing sales jobs.

   ❑ Jobs 4.0 (www.jobs4point0.com)—For job seekers 40 and older.

   ❑ Senior Job Bank (www.seniorjobbank.org)—Geared specifically to job seekers 50 and up.

   ❑ Retired Brains (www.retiredbrains.com)—A site suited to older boomers, seniors, and retirees.

   ❑ Seniors4Hire (www.seniors4hire.com)—For job seekers 50 and over.

   ❑ YourEncore (www.yourencore.com)—This site is designed to bring older scientists, engineers, and product developers together with interested technology companies and other concerns.

At many of these and other similar sites, not only can you sort through available job listings, you can also post a profile of yourself that prospective employers can access.

Other employment-related sites that may prove helpful include:

❑ AARP National Employer Team (www.aarp.org/money/careers/findingajob/
featuredemployers)—These employers have hooked up with AARP to actively
seek out older workers with experience and leadership skills.

❑ AARP Best Employers for Workers Over 50 (www.aarp.org/money/careers/
employerresourcecenter/bestemployers)—This annual compilation lists the top
50 companies in the United States that, by their practices and policies, provide
some of the best places for people aged 50 and up to work.

❑ AARP Foundation Senior Community Service Employment Program (www.aarp.
org/money/careers/findingajob/jobseekers/a2005-01-03-job_training_placement.
html)—This program helps people with lower income with training and job
placement.

Marketing Yourself

With a road map of resources and opportunities in place, now it's time to, shall we say,
go to work on yourself so you present yourself in the best possible light to any prospective employer. Here are some tips.

Upgrade and Hone Your Resumé

If you worked at the same job for a number of years, you may not even know where
your resumé is, let alone how relevant or up-to-date it is.

A resumé remains a central element to a successful job hunt. If you have one already in
hand—or need to build one from scratch—here are some guidelines and suggestions:

◆ **Craft your information to address the needs of particular employers.** If you
know a certain company is looking for people experienced in marketing, highlight that element in your background.

Retire Right _____

If you know someone who
already works at a company
you're interested in, ask
them for suggestions of topics to
emphasize in your resumé.

◆ **Emphasize skills or experience that can apply
to a number of companies or industries.**
This is especially important if you're looking to
enter a specific type of work for the first time, as
opposed to one particular company.

◆ **Have several resumés at the ready.** These first two bits of advice suggest that no one resumé is right in all situations. Craft several resumés, each of which plays up different features and elements of your background.

◆ **Showcase your achievements—but take it further than that.** Granted, a resumé should show where you've been. But also use your achievements to indicate what new things you might be able to bring to a job. To illustrate—a consistent record of sales success naturally suggests a continued ability to sell. In addition, it also positions you as a valuable training resource for younger sales-people.

◆ **Keep it on point.** Mentioning elements such as unrelated hobbies or pastimes can skew the focus of a resumé. That goes for personal information such as age, race, religion, and other details.

◆ **School is optional.** If you have an arm's length of degrees from prestigious universities or a host of some other sort of academic achievements, putting them in your resumé may build you up in the eyes of your prospective employer. Otherwise, consider keeping education out of your resumé (after all, it was likely some time ago).

◆ **Keep it short.** The old rule of thumb that resumés should never exceed one page has pretty much gone the way of a buck-per-gallon gas—particularly with older workers with an ample work history to document. But do try to keep it within two pages—anything longer starts to read like the telephone book.

◆ **If you have one, include an e-mail address in addition to a physical address and telephone number.** Companies are increasingly contacting prospective employees via e-mail, so if you have one, let them know what it is.

Improve Your Skills

As we discussed earlier, a fair assessment of your job skills is an important element contributing to your eventual job hunting success. In fact, depending on the type of position you're after, job skills may actually be of greater importance than whatever experience you may be able to bring to the job.

That said, if you find you're lacking in certain skills, it may behoove you to get some additional training or education. One likely candidate is computer skills, such as word processing, spreadsheets, Powerpoint presentations, and other functions. High schools, community colleges, and other community-based institutions frequently offer computer training of all sorts.

Additionally, investigate other sorts of training programs that can bolster your overall appeal to a possible employer. Courses on business management, customer service, personnel and human services, and other similar topics can all contribute to your roster of skills and abilities.

Learn the Art of the Interview

Resumés and other credentials are one thing, but little can replace or supersede the face-to-face importance of a job interview. It's your opportunity to showcase your skills and, at the same time, find out critical information about an employer to ensure you're a good fit.

In fact, there are really two types of interviews that happen during the job hunting process—the informational interview and the job interview itself.

The Informational Interview

This type of interview can be as much about gaining important insight and information as about actually landing a job.

In one instance, you may be interested in a position at a particular company but don't know if one actually exists. In another, you're trying to get information about a particular field or line of work, along with some guidelines and suggestions on how to proceed from there.

To start the process, contact the appropriate person within an organization (the president, if it's a small firm, or perhaps human resources if it's large) and ask to schedule an interview. Let them know that it's an informational meeting and that you would welcome both their time and assistance.

Some ideas for informational interviews:

❑ Bring along a resumé and give the person a chance to review it.

❑ Mention any person who may have referred you.

❑ Keep the discussion on track. Don't go off on tangents that waste time.

❑ Keep the interview short—say, no more than a half an hour.

It can be helpful to prepare a list of questions. These might include:

❑ "I'm looking for a particular job (mention it here). Do you have any current openings or expect any openings that may match what I'm looking for?"

❑ "Can you refer me to other companies or organizations that may be hiring for the sort of position I'm looking for?"

❑ "Can you suggest any other places I might look, such as professional groups or civic organizations?"

❑ "Can you suggest any additional training or education that may help me?"

❑ "I have extensive experience in (name your area of experience) and am looking to move into (identify your target job). Do you have any ideas or suggestions that may prove helpful to me?"

 Retire Right

Be sure to take complete notes during an informational interview. Also, leave all pertinent contact information.

The Job Interview Itself

Congratulations! You've landed an interview for a job opening. And, like you did for the informational interview, the more you can prepare beforehand, the better the results are likely to be.

Interestingly enough, interviewers who conduct job interviews on an ongoing basis say there are 10 basic rules to help ensure a successful interview. They are:

1. Show up when you're supposed to.

2. Dress appropriately.

3. Be polite.

4. Express enthusiasm for the job.

5. Stick to past experiences that relate to the job you're applying for.

6. Show how you'll be a good fit.

7. Don't say anything bad about past employers, jobs, or colleagues.

8. Don't tell your prospective employer how he or she could do things better.

9. Ask questions.

10. Follow up with a thank you note or e-mail.

That's basically it, although there are a few additional ideas that may help:

❑ Emphasize your willingness to learn and your ability to get along with people from differing backgrounds and age groups.

Retirement Reality

If the topic of age does present itself during an interview, simply tell your interviewer that you are fully qualified to do whatever the job requires. In a nutshell: make age a moot point.

❑ Never, ever say you're looking for a job because you need the money. Instead, say you feel you have something to contribute, miss the camaraderie of the workplace, or some other reason. Money motivation may smack of desperation.

❑ Instead of defending your age, leverage it. Cite your work ethic, ability to solve problems or come up with fresh solutions, and other ways your experience can be of advantage to the company.

Keep an Eye Peeled for Age Discrimination

It may be a convenient turn of phrase to say "respect your elders," but that doesn't always play out—particularly in the workplace.

Passed in 1967, the Age Discrimination in Employment Act prohibits any employer from refusing to hire, discharge, or discriminate in any way based on a person's age. More specifically, the law applies to workers and job applicants age 40 and over and to employers with 20 or more employees. (Some individual states also have laws on the books covering smaller businesses.)

Unfortunately, it's often hard to tell whether an employer turns an older person down for a job due to age. For one thing, it's technically not against the law to ask about age. On top of that, if push comes to shove, it's awfully easy for an employer to concoct some other, more legal rationale.

If, however, you think you may have been discriminated against in a hiring decision because of age, you can file a complaint with the Equal Employment Opportunity Commission (EEOC). Call the EEOC at 1-800-669-4000 or go to www.eeoc.gov for directions on how to file and the EEOC office nearest to you.

Retirement Reality

In fiscal year 2006, the EEOC resolved 14,146 age discrimination cases and recovered $51.5 million in monetary benefits.

You need to file a complaint within 180 days of the time you felt you were discriminated against. It will be up to you to gather evidence of your claim. The EEOC may attempt to mediate the claim to come to a mutually satisfactory settlement. If that doesn't occur, the EEOC may investigate further, consider further legal action, or just close the case.

Start Your Own Business

There's one place where you can be guaranteed to never encounter a shred of discrimination based on your age. That would be a business you start yourself.

A growing number of retirees are opting to start their own business rather than hooking up with an existing one. According to the Cornell Retirement and Well Being Study we cited extensively earlier in the book, nearly half of all retirees participating in the study were self-employed.

Small wonder. With a business of your own, you can pursue the business activities of your dreams, set your own hours, and pretty much call every shot that may have something to do with the business.

But it's also an opportunity wrought with uncertainty. By one estimate, some 40,000 small businesses worldwide will be declared insolvent in 2007, up 8 percent from the prior year.

The reasons for that sort of carnage vary significantly from one situation to the next. However, if you're thinking about starting out on your own, consider these guidelines:

- ◆ **Draw up a business plan.** Far too many businesses fail because they haven't been carefully thought out. To avoid that, draw up a business plan that identifies your potential customers, marketing strategy, budgetary guidelines, and other important considerations. There are a number of software programs and websites that will walk you through this in detail.

- ◆ **Know where the money will come from.** Businesses also fail because they lack adequate financing, particularly at the outset. Consider your funding sources. Will you use a line of credit, savings, or some other source? Project how long it will last before sufficient income kicks in to keep the business going. You may want to have a financial pro review your projections to see if they're reasonable.

- ◆ **Set a point to call it quits.** Don't sacrifice your retirement at the feet of a failing business. As part of your planning, determine at what point you'll cut your losses and close things down. Unpleasant planning it may be, but it's essential to know just when a struggling business becomes too much of a financial drain.

Effects on Social Security and Medicare

One final element having to do with working after you retire is its impact on Social Security benefits and Medicare.

With regard to Social Security, yes, there is an impact. First, revisit the federal government's definition of "full retirement age" as summarized in the chart in Chapter 8.

Here's the deal. If you're at full retirement age or older, you can earn as much as you want without affecting your Social Security benefits. However, if you're younger than full retirement age, $1 in benefits is withheld for every $2 you earn over the limit of $12,960. (Note: that's as of 2007. The limit increases every year.)

If, by chance, you reach full retirement age in 2007, $1 in benefits is withheld for every $3 over the limit of $33,240. That holds true until the month you reach full retirement age.

Since Medicare only kicks in at age 65, working after retirement has no affect at all on that particular program.

The Least You Need to Know

◆ Look in your local newspaper, scan the Internet, and network with friends and colleagues to get a sense of available jobs.

◆ Upgrade you resumé to emphasize your skills and breadth of experience.

◆ If need be, get additional training to improve your work skills.

◆ In additional to conventional interviews, use informational interviews to search for potential jobs and contacts.

◆ Know that you cannot be refused a job due to your age.

◆ If you earn above a certain level before you reach full retirement age, your Social Security benefits will be affected.

Chapter 24

Alternate Living

In This Chapter

- ◆ Staying put
- ◆ Senior co-ops, cohousing, and shared housing
- ◆ The ECHO alternative
- ◆ How to choose an affordable place to live
- ◆ Living outside the U.S.

In Chapter 19, we discussed the range of retirement communities. Here, we'll take the topic a few steps further and examine some other housing options for retirees, covering various sorts of living arrangements as well as locations.

Sure, you can opt for an old tried-and-true housing arrangement and be as happy as a clam. But, if your needs are different—or your taste runs to something a bit more unusual—there is an ample array of options from which to choose.

Staying Where You Are—With a Difference

In the past, as someone aged and living on one's own grew less able to work, the standard solution was to relocate—to an assisted living facility or a nursing home.

Not any more. Programs are springing up throughout the country that allow retirees to remain in their own homes longer—and, as a result, remain attached to the elements of the communities that they may have bonded with for much of their lives.

Beacon Hill Village in Boston is one such program. Beacon Hill Village is a nonprofit association designed to let aging residents of the community remain in their homes. Founded in 2001, the program provides rides to grocery stores and access to health care and exercise programs. Beacon Hill Village also prescreens service providers and, in turn, makes them available to residents at upwards of a 50 percent discount.

The program is open to neighborhood residents age 50 and older. Membership runs $780 a year for households and $550 for singles (deep discounts are offered to lower-income residents). Similar programs are being set up in a number of other American cities, including Washington, D.C., and Denver.

Retire Right

If the Beacon Hill Village concept appeals, find out more at www.beaconhillvillage.org.

Other programs are gearing up elsewhere. For instance, the state of New York is supporting what it terms "naturally occurring retirement communities" in some 50 areas throughout the state. By providing social workers, health care providers, and other services, the program is allowing residents of neighborhoods, housing projects, and apartment complexes to continue to live in their homes.

For instance, the program has provided an on-site nurse and support staff to Depdale Garden Co-Op, a Queens apartment complex where more than half the residents are at least 60 years old. The program has taken in everything from routine medical screenings to fixing unsafe cracked sidewalks. Cities and towns in some 20 other states are kick starting similar programs.

Senior Co-Ops

Not every retiree abandons home because he or she is forced to. Some aggressively look for options other than staying in their existing home. While expense may be an issue, equally compelling are the responsibilities and frequent headaches of home ownership, from routine maintenance to keeping the driveway clear of snow in the winter.

For retirees eager to chuck the headaches of home ownership, senior co-ops can prove an answer to a prayer. The first senior co-ops began appearing in the 1970s but enjoyed a rejuvenation in popularity in the late 1990s.

Like other forms of cooperative living, senior co-ops own both the building in which they live as well as the land. The co-op is effectively a corporation, with stock owned by residents (value of the stock is adjusted to the size of their homes).

Although each co-op unit is individually owned, the co-op elects a board of directors who are charged with policy decisions regarding the co-op. The mix is something of a cross between individual and communal living. While residents maintain their own homes, cook their own meals, and the like, the overall facility provides a variety of group facilities and events, from exercise equipment to planned group outings.

There are, however, slight differences between senior co-ops and other more conventional cooperative living arrangements. For one thing, they have age requirements. Generally, you have to be 55 or older to be eligible to live in a senior co-op (or be married to someone who is).

Pricing and equity appreciation arrangements can also differ. Some senior co-ops have what's known as a limited-equity principle, meaning that value appreciation is controlled by the cooperative. That, in turn, makes the co-op more affordable to a broader number of prospective buyers.

Other co-ops maintain what's known as a market equity arrangement, where share prices can go up or down along with the conventional housing market. While the owner may potentially pocket more cash at resale, the added cost may make the unit more of a challenge to sell.

In fact, there are some co-ops geared specifically to low-income seniors. For instance, Chatham Park South Cooperative in Chicago has 112 units. Membership fee is $666 and monthly charges are prorated to equate to 30 percent of the resident's income.

However, other co-ops are a good deal more pricey. For instance, at Silver Glen, a senior cooperative located in Bellevue, Washington, a 1,536-square-foot unit is priced at $292,000. Added on are monthly property taxes of $102 and maintenance fees of $625.

Moreover, senior co-ops are not exactly a nationwide phenomenon. According to the Senior Cooperative Foundation, the lion's share of senior co-ops are located in Minnesota and other parts of the Midwest, with a smattering of other co-ops located in the South and on either coast.

But that's not to say it will always stay that way. For one thing, the federal Department of Housing and Urban Development provides funding assistance earmarked specifically for senior co-op projects. Another plus for prospective developers: senior co-ops historically have very low turnover rates.

Then there is the array of advantages cited by senior co-op residents. Among them:

◆ Homeowner tax advantages

◆ Lower maintenance costs

◆ A supportive and safe community

◆ The opportunity to remain in their communities (it's often the case that retirees move only a short distance when choosing a co-op)

◆ Services such as maintenance, repair, landscaping, housekeeping, transportation, and shopping assistance become less of a problem

Retire Right

For more information on senior cooperatives, including a list of senior cooperative properties throughout the country, go to www.seniorcoops.org.

Senior Cohousing

Introduced in Denmark in the 1970s, cohousing is a sort of semicommunal living arrangement. Separate units which are individually owned—often attached as condos might be—are arranged around a "common house." The common house has a kitchen, a dining area, and possibly other space for gathering and activities.

But the concept is more than just logistics. The idea behind cohousing is to promote neighbors' involvement in the lives of those around them. Cohousing residents not only share meals and chores, but also help out when a resident is sick or laid up in some way.

Retirement Reality

The first senior cohousing development in the United States, called Glacier Circle, opened in Davis, California, in 2005.

But cohousing differs from other sorts of alternate living arrangements in several ways. One way is through residents' involvement in the design of the facility. Cohousing often starts through newspaper advertisement, word of mouth, or the common interest of a group of friends. They then will meet with an architect, developer, financing sources, and others involved in the project to work up a design that will specifically meet the group's needs.

The eventual design of a cohousing project reflects the overriding sense of community. Individual residences are clustered on the project site, typically facing each other. The common house is generally at the center of the arrangement.

Retirement Reality

Cohousing is not for the impatient: estimates hold it usually takes upwards of two years to complete a project.

Unlike co-ops, which have a greater sense of autonomy, the common house emphasizes the community built around it. Typical features include a common kitchen, dining space, library, exercise facilities, and even a library and a workshop. And, while co-ops may have personnel to do chores and perform other responsibilities in the co-op, cohousing residents perform much of the work needed to maintain the property.

Cohousing can also be significantly smaller than other group-living arrangements. Most cohousing communities in the United States take in between 20 to 40 units, while the number can go as high as 75 or so. Co-ops and apartment houses, by comparison, can run significantly larger.

Another distinction is cost. Although expense varies from one development to another, supporters of elder cohousing argue that it's a cost-effective alternative to many other housing options, particularly assisted living and nursing homes. For instance, in ElderSpirit, an elder cohousing community in Abingdon, Virginia, one-bedroom units have sold in the vicinity of $100,000 (two-bedroom units are slightly more expensive).

In addition, unlike co-ops, cohousing often offers rental opportunities rather than outright purchase. For instance, 16 of ElderSpirit's units are federally subsidized rentals costing upwards of $350 a month for a one-bedroom unit and $484 for two-bedroom digs.

However, similarities do exist between co-ops and cohousing facilities. Both facilities emphasize internal management, with residents of both co-ops and cohousing developments meeting as a group to develop policy and make other communitywide decisions.

But other elements of elder cohousing remain a bit unclear. For one thing, it can make estate planning a bit dicey—current residents will want to ensure that their heirs maintain the continuity of the community.

Additionally, since the phenomenon of cohousing is relatively new, it has generally attracted

Retirement Reality

One appeal of cohousing to baby boomers, say authorities, is that, in many ways, they recreate the communes and communal living of their youth.

Retire Right _____

For more information on cohousing, check out the Cohousing Association of America at www.cohousing.org.

a rather predictable population of retirees who are active and healthy. While that raises concerns about what might happen when an increasing number of residents become older and more sickly, supporters counter that cohousing's emphasis on community support and shared commitment will be ideal to meet those sorts of situations.

Shared Housing

Often, the most effective alternative living arrangement can be one of the most simple. That's the case with shared housing—a viable option for many seniors.

The arrangement is, indeed, straightforward. Someone has a home or apartment and decides to invite an unrelated person to live with them. The actual workings are also generally simple. Most of the home or apartment is shared space, with each person having access and responsibility for that space. At the same time, everyone in the home has a private space—usually a bedroom—that affords complete privacy when necessary.

The reasons for home sharing are varied. For many people—such as widows, widowers, and divorcees—the loneliness and isolation of living alone is more than they can comfortably handle. In these instances, they're likely looking for companionship and friendship.

Others take a more empirical approach to home sharing. Perhaps they're tired of having to pony up a substantial mortgage or rental payment every month and are looking to mitigate the cost. Others may be tired of the demands of the upkeep of a home and are looking for someone to share the responsibility.

Either arrangement can work. The important thing is to know what your primary motivation is for home sharing and, in turn, what the other person (or, depending on the circumstances, people) hope to get out of it.

The National Shared Housing Resource Center offers the following tips to determine if home sharing might work for you and, if so, what sort of arrangement might be best:

❑ Draw up a list of every pro and con you can think of regarding home sharing. Include things such as money, loss of some privacy, shared responsibility, and other issues. In what ways would home sharing represent an improvement over where you are now? In what ways would things be less so?

❑ Assess yourself honestly and go over whatever past experiences you may have had with sharing a living space with others. What worked? What did not? Are you assertive enough to ask for what you need and, at the same time, are you flexible enough to accommodate others? Do you talk about your feelings easily and are you sensitive to others' feelings? (The Resource Center suggests that, if the answer to any of these questions is negative, home sharing may not be your cup of tea.)

❑ Figure out the financials. What is your price range if you're looking to move into someone else's home? Do you have allergies? Do you only want to live in certain areas? If it's your home, do you want a 50/50 split or would you be willing to accept less for someone who seemed particularly compatible?

❑ Look for a home sharer who would complement your situation. For instance, if you have a large yard but find it difficult to take care of, look for an avid gardener. Don't like to cook? An accomplished chef may be just the ticket.

❑ Don't commit unnecessarily to the arrangement. If you find someone whom you think may be a suitable home sharer, set up a trial period to see how things go. Whether it's just a week or a month, earmark a specific time to see just how well the arrangement might work if it became more permanent. Once the trial period is done, have a frank discussion about whether you think home sharing is a solid idea.

Retire Right _____

Don't limit your home sharing to other retirees. For instance, if you're looking to pay off a mortgage, a young couple hoping to save for a down payment for their own home may be ideal.

For more information on shared housing, check out the National Shared Housing Resource Center at www.nationalsharedhousing.org.

The ECHO Option

Often, children can play a role in an alternate means of retirement housing. For some, the best choice is to have their parents maintain their autonomy and pay for (often with their children's help) necessary geriatric care. These services, which can range from for-profit social workers to nurses specializing in elder issues, can help with any number of responsibilities—seeing to doctor's appointments, overseeing medication and nutrition, and similar responsibilities.

Trouble is, this choice can prove pricey—anywhere upwards of $200 an hour—and is generally not covered by insurance. Moreover, depending on the condition of the parent, it can prove a slippery financial slope that can go on for a long time.

The other option is having retired parents move in with their kids—often an ideal solution. Unfortunately, moving back home with the kids can often raise more issues than it solves—among them loss of privacy and the responsibility of caring for a parent, not to mention the emotional powder keg that can result when parents and offspring reunite under one roof.

There is, however, an alternative known as ECHO (an acronym for Elder Cottage Housing Opportunities). This is usually a separate, small manufactured home that is added onto the side or backyard of an existing home. In effect, this can become the retired parent's new home.

ECHO offers a variety of advantages. For one thing, elderly adults in need of assistance on some occasion are physically close to family members who can provide it. But that proximity doesn't come at the expense of privacy. Since the parent lives in a separate space, no one in the overall family needs to feel any sort of undue invasion of privacy.

There are additional benefits for retirees. ECHO allows them a greater sense of independence than they might have with other living arrangements that foster more contact. At the same time, if children are in the picture, it affords the opportunity for closer relationships without the potential strain of constant contact.

Families also enjoy benefits. For one thing, the need to travel long distances to provide necessary care and support is eliminated. And the cottages can be low-cost alternatives to other arrangements (in fact, ECHO housing can often be leased rather than bought outright).

Retire Right _____

Additional information on ECHO housing and other options can be found at www.seniorresource.com.

However, there are a number of considerations to take into account. First, check with any local zoning ordinances that may pertain. Some communities don't allow them, while others may stipulate that the unit be attached to the existing home rather than freestanding.

Additionally, some communities have age limitations as to who can occupy an ECHO unit. For example, in some places no one under the age of 62 can legally live in an ECHO facility.

Choosing an Affordable Place to Live

Affordability of a particular retirement spot is as important as many other factors. But no matter how important affordability may be, don't choose a retirement spot solely because it's dirt cheap.

As we outlined in Chapter 3, draw up a list of those issues and parameters that matter the most to you. Include such factors as climate, crime, health care, and any other issue that you believe will genuinely affect the quality of your retirement.

Now that you have your list, it's time to start paring it down according to affordability. One way to proceed is to contact the chambers of commerce, tourism boards, housing offices, and other pertinent organizations in each of those places. They can provide reams of information on the cost of living, from the cost of groceries to property taxes.

Be sure to take as many factors into consideration as possible. In fact, some places' cost of living can be deceiving. Although it's important to find affordable housing, it's also essential to make sure that affordability isn't offset by some other crippling expense.

If that seems more legwork than you feel like taking on, once again the Internet rides to the rescue with a variety of websites offering calculators geared to comparing the cost of living at various places around the country. Here are a few helpful websites:

- www.bestplaces.net

- http://cgi.money.cnn.com/tools/costofliving/costofliving.html

- www.homefair.com/calc/salcalc.html

In most cases with these websites, all you have to do is enter the name of one or more cities (and possibly some additional information, such as available funds) and the calculator will indicate which place is better, at least from the standpoint of cost of living.

Other sources of information include the following sites:

- www.retirementliving.com/RLtaxes.html

- www.bestretirementspots.com/cost_of_living.htm

As you get further into your search for affordable places to retire, consider the following additional tips:

◆ If your work situation affords it, consider selecting and moving to an affordable spot before you retire. You'll save money and get to know the location before you actually stop working.

◆ Don't bypass smaller communities. While larger towns and cities can offer more cultural amenities and possibly better health care, smaller communities are becoming increasingly popular, in part due to lower housing expenses. To illustrate, a study of Census Bureau data by the Brookings Institution identified the following 10 small towns with the greatest population growth in ages 55 and up: Gillette, Wyoming; Silverthorne, Colorado; Juneau, Alaska; Edwards, Colorado; Jackson, Wyoming; Bozeman, Montana; St. Marys, Georgia; Rock Springs, Wyoming; Taos, New Mexico; and Evanston, Wyoming.

◆ Even if money isn't such a critical issue, don't completely bypass the topic of affordability. Even if you have scads of money with which to retire, that only means those funds will go that much further in a cost-effective spot. And you'll be better positioned to meet unexpected expenses, such as substantial medical bills.

Living Abroad

For a growing number of retirees, the United States is by no means the sole option for a retirement destination. According to the Migration Policy Institute, as of 1970, some 97,229 U.S.–born persons lived in Mexico; by 2000 that number had jumped to 358,614, many of them retirees. Similarly, Panama saw an increase of 136 percent in U.S.–born seniors age 55 and older.

Granted, there are likely a variety of reasons for some retirees' decision to bid the United States adieu, but affordability is certainly one of them. For instance, in Belize, retirees enjoy tax-free status on their first $75,000 of income. Property taxes are downright paltry. Moreover, Social Security retirement benefits remain unchanged, unless you live in Cuba, North Korea, and certain other parts of the world.

Is retiring abroad right for you? Again, like other aspects of alternative retirement, don't start by making money your first and overriding priority. Instead, outline those elements of expatriate retirement that you think might be appealing—getting to know a new culture, a new language, a different pace of life, and other issues.

There are a host of Internet websites, newsletters, and other publications geared to retirement outside the United States. Although they can be helpful in honing your thinking or generating new ideas, take some with a grain of salt, as more than a few are geared to pushing certain retirement spots rather than providing completely objective information.

If you know someone who's retired overseas, contact them and ask them to share the experience. See what they enjoyed about their choice and what they didn't like or, at the very least, didn't expect.

Other tips:

♦ **Do it on a trial basis.** Like any retirement relocation, start short-term. Rent a place to live for a few months and see how it pans out.

♦ **Be prepared to be open-minded.** Anyone who's been overseas and has experienced what some might perceive as a lack of pervading efficiency had better be flexible if they plan to live there. Tasks such as banking, Internet connections, and other common elements of daily life might not necessarily happen at a U.S.–style pace—be ready to wait longer.

♦ **You may need to learn a new language.** This, of course, depends on where you go, but English isn't predominant in many places. If that's the case, you'll be best served by taking on the local language.

♦ **Say adios to Medicare.** Although Social Security trucks on no matter where you live, Medicare is useless once you cross the border. That means you'll need private insurance or to buy into the local health care system (which may be terrific or dreadful). Know before you go what sort of health care options are available.

♦ **You can come home again.** In this case, Thomas Wolfe had it wrong. Don't take living overseas as a no-change deal. Set aside funds to bring you back home if need be (if, for instance, your health takes a turn for the worse). If you're on a trial basis overseas, don't sell your home back in the States. If things don't fly in your new country, you can always fly right back to what may possibly prove a much happier home.

The Least You Need to Know

♦ Programs that allow retirees with health and other issues to remain in their homes are being developed throughout the country.

- Senior co-ops are another option that bring seniors together into a community.

- Cohousing is still another choice designed to foster community and camaraderie among seniors.

- Shared housing—where you bring someone else into your home or you move into theirs—can provide companionship and cut expenses.

- If affordability is a particularly important issue, do extensive homework to determine a community's overall cost of living—including housing costs, property taxes, and other expenses.

- Living abroad is becoming more popular for retirees due to affordability, among other factors. But research any potential destination carefully to ensure that it fits you in other ways as well.

Appendix A

Glossary

adult day care   Programs in a group setting that offer social and health-related services to support frail, impaired, elderly, or other disabled adults.

Age Discrimination in Employment Act   Passed in 1967, this act prohibits any employer from refusing to hire, discharge, or discriminate in any way based on a person's age.

annuity   A financial contract. You buy an annuity with the guarantee that the company—usually an insurance company—will provide a series of regular, fixed payments in exchange. Annuities come in a variety of forms.

assisted living   A kind of housing that provides a modest amount of assistance, including bathing, dressing, and cooking meals.

baby boomers   People born in a flourish of family-boosting activity that followed World War II and continued into the 1960s.

board and care   Another type of assisted living that generally offers group meals and other activities for residents who want to spend time with friends and neighbors.

bonds   A form of loan. In buying a bond, you're effectively entering into a contract with the issuer of that bond to pay whatever money you invested, plus interest. Bonds come in a variety of forms.

book value   The real value of a company. It's calculated by totaling all assets and subtracting debt and liabilities.

call provision   Bonds that are paid off prior to their prearranged maturity.

career average plans   Similar to final pay programs, but based on the average of all the years you work for a company. You may get a percentage of your salary for every year you were in the plan. In other cases, you may get an average for all years you were in the plan.

cash value life insurance   A form of life insurance that builds an accompanying cash value. These come in several different forms.

catastrophic coverage   Health insurance with exceedingly high deductibles.

Certificates of Deposit (CDs)   A form of promissory note; the lender effectively promises to pay you a certain interest rate if you let them hold your money for a specified amount of time.

COBRA   The Consolidated Omnibus Budget Reconciliation Act requires companies with 20 or more employees to allow you to stay on your health plan for an additional 18 months after you leave your job.

cohousing   A semicommunal living arrangement where separate living units are arranged around a "common house."

compounding   The effect of money earning interest which, in turn, results in a larger sum that earns even more.

congregate housing   A variant of assisted living, offering both a level of assisted care as well as private living space.

continuing care retirement communities   This involves several sorts of housing and living arrangements, including independent living facilities, assisted living, and nursing homes. Retirees can remain in the same retirement community, with the option to change the level of care they receive as their individual needs mandate it.

conventional IRA   The first Individual Retirement Account introduced, this defers any tax impact until you begin to withdraw money from the account.

custodian   The institution that holds your IRA. It can be a bank, brokerage house, or similar place.

deductibles   The amount you have to pay before insurance coverage begins.

deep discount broker   An investment house that sells stocks and funds very inexpensively.

defined benefit program   A pension payout based on your salary and number of years of service.

defined contribution programs   A program in which money is automatically deducted from your salary before you take possession of it. From there, the money is put into an investment vehicle of your choosing, including mutual funds, company stock, and other options.

disability insurance   Insurance that provides income if you become disabled or temporarily unable to earn a living.

discount brokers   Brokers that charge less than full-service brokers to execute trades.

dividends   Payments to shareholders authorized by a company's board of directors. They can be in cash or additional shares of the company's stock.

dollar-cost averaging   A stock-buying strategy in which you invest a set amount of money on a regular basis, regardless of whether the stock is going up or down.

Dow Jones Industrials   A stock index made up of 30 of the largest publicly held companies traded on the New York Stock Exchange.

dying intestate   The legal term that refers to lack of a will or trust that provide instructions after someone dies.

ECHO   An acronym for Elder Cottage Housing Opportunities. This is usually a separate, small manufactured home that is added onto the side or backyard of an existing home.

employee stock ownership plan (ESOP)   A program that allows employees to buy company stock, often with little or no commission.

enrolled agent   A financial professional who specializes in taxes.

equity   The difference between the value of your home and the amount you owe on your mortgage.

executor   The person charged with overseeing the execution of a will.

expense ratio   This takes in all expenses incurred by a fund's operations and expresses them in terms of percentages.

face value   The principal; the amount of money you invested when you bought a bond. It's also known as par value.

fee for service   A form of health insurance that lets you choose any doctor or health care provider you like. Generally, the coverage pays 80 percent of any costs you accumulate. You are obligated to pick up the remaining 20 percent.

final pay plan   Pension plans that can offer the biggest payout, as they average your salary over the last several years you're employed at a company.

flat benefit plan   The most simple and straightforward pension payout. You receive a set monthly amount based on how long you worked for a company.

flexible spending account   A program that allows you to set aside money from your salary tax-free. These funds can then be used to help pay for medical expenses that are not covered by your employer's health plan.

401(k) plan   A workplace retirement program that lets you save by automatically deducting a certain portion of salary before you take possession of your paycheck.

full retirement age   The age at which you can receive your full retirement benefit from Social Security.

fund family   A company that maintains several different mutual funds. These are usually set up for different financial objectives.

fundamental analysis   A stock analysis involving examination of a company's operating statistics and numbers.

guaranteed investment contracts (GICs)   A contract involving a guaranteed rate of return.

home equity line of credit   Credit based on the amount of equity you have in your home.

individual 401(k)s   A retirement savings program best suited for someone who works on their own and has no plans to bring on any employees in the future.

Individual Retirement Accounts (IRAs)   Savings accounts for retirement. They come in two forms—conventional IRAs and Roth IRAs.

inflation   The effect of rising prices on the value of money to buy goods and services.

irrevocable trust   A trust that can't be changed in any way during the grantor's lifetime.

Keogh plans   A tax-deferred retirement plan that lets small business owners and the self-employed save money for retirement.

limit orders   A stock purchase system that lets you establish prices at which you wish to buy or sell.

living will   Also known as an advanced medical directive, this is a document that outlines your decisions about any sort of life-sustaining treatment.

long-term care insurance   Insurance you buy to pay for nursing home care and other sorts of long-term, comprehensive care.

managed care   Also known as health maintenance organizations, this is less expensive than fee for service. However, you have a limited choice of health care providers.

Medicaid   The federal program designed to pay for health care for the poor.

Medicare   The United States' health care program for persons age 65 and up. It is subdivided into four parts, offering different forms of coverage.

Medigap insurance   Supplemental insurance to cover any gaps in Medicare coverage.

minimum distribution   The amount you must begin withdrawing from a conventional IRA at age 70½. This is calculated by dividing the balance of the IRA account by the person's life expectancy.

money market deposit accounts   Accounts that pay slightly higher interest than conventional savings.

money market funds   Funds offered by brokerage houses and mutual fund families. They invest in relatively safe choices such as government securities.

mutual fund   An investment company that pools funds from many investors and, in turn, invests them in a broad array of stocks, bonds, and other types of securities. Mutual funds come in a variety of types.

net unrealized appreciation   The difference in value between the average cost that you paid for stock and its current market value.

points   These represent an up-front interest payment to a lender. One point is equivalent to 1 percent of the amount borrowed.

power of attorney   Allows someone to make decisions when you're incapable of doing so yourself. Examples include medical and financial power of attorney.

price-earnings ratio (P/E)   A popular stock ratio that illustrates how much an investor would be willing to spend in return for $1 in company earnings.

price/book ratio (P/B)   A ratio that compares a stock's price to what a company is worth.

price/sales ratio (P/S)   A ratio that is calculated by dividing a current stock price by a company's earnings per share.

primary insurance amount (PIA)   All your Social Security cash benefits, including your monthly benefit as well as benefits for dependents and survivors.

probate   The legal process that the state must go through should you die with property still in your name.

qualified   A term that means a pension program has to adhere to certain governmental guidelines for tax purposes.

real estate investment trusts (REITs)   Funds that invest in property, including shopping centers, apartment buildings, and similar commercial operations.

reverse mortgage   A mortgage that lets you tap the accumulated equity in your home. In doing so, your loan balance increases rather than going down.

revocable trust   A trust that may be changed or eliminated completely.

risk tolerance   The amount of uncertainty and volatility with which an investor feels comfortable.

Roth IRA   A newer version of an IRA, this offers none of the potential tax deductions of a conventional IRA, but all funds can be withdrawn tax-free after you retire.

self-insured   Having sufficient assets to make life insurance unnecessary.

shared housing   Someone has a home or apartment and decides to invite an unrelated person to live with them.

shares outstanding   The total number of shares owned by investors.

Sharpe ratio   Devised by Nobel Prize–winner William Sharpe, this ratio weighs the risks of an investment against its potential return.

SIMPLE IRA   An acronym for Savings Incentive Match Plan. This type of IRA is particularly suited to someone whose self-employment income is relatively modest—$30,000 annually or less.

Simplified Employee Pensions   A retirement plan available to employers and the self-employed. All contributions are tax-deductible.

Social Security   Formally known as the Federal Old Age, Survivors and Disability Insurance program, this program provides retirement funding and other benefits.

stocks   A share of ownership in a company. Stocks come in a variety of types, with different features and objectives.

stop loss orders   A method of stock buying specifically designed to limit your losses and protect whatever profit you may have earned from a stock.

surrender value   The amount you receive if you cash out a life insurance policy.

teaser cards   Credit cards with very low interest rates that last only for a limited amount of time.

technical analysis   A stock analysis on which a company's trading patterns are charted.

term life insurance   The most simple form of life insurance, as it involves no cash value.

testamentary trust   A trust, created under a last will and testament, that becomes effective only after the grantor dies and the will is admitted to probate.

Treasury securities   Securities that are issued and backed by the federal government. They come in various forms, including securities, notes, savings bonds, and other formats.

trusts   A legal vehicle in which one person (known as the trustee) holds property for another person (known as the beneficiary). This trustee can be a person or a trust company. Trusts are useful in distributing the assets of an estate.

umbrella insurance   An additional form of liability insurance coverage.

unearned income   Income you don't earn. Common examples are pension and annuity payouts, dividends, and interest and proceeds from life insurance.

value averaging   A variant on dollar-cost averaging that takes into account stock price movement.

waiting period   The time between the onset of a disability and when benefits begin.

will   A written document that delineates how you want your property distributed after you die.

work credits   A system to determine Social Security eligibility. You become formally eligible once you have accumulated 40 "work credits."

yield   The effective rate of interest that a bond pays to investors.

Retirement Planning Worksheets

When it comes to calculating your retirement needs, it's always helpful to have some prearranged questionnaires at the ready. Following are several such worksheets, along with a risk profile questionnaire you can take to determine what sort of investor you are. Finally, we offer a spending and age report to help you gauge how much you might expect to spend on certain items when you retire.

Budget Worksheet

Use this worksheet to see how your budget matches up with your spending.

A Monthly $PENDING PLAN

To make it easy to budget, calculate in monthly amounts. For weekly expenses multiply it by 4.5 to estimate the monthly expenditure. Divide annual expenses by 12 to get monthly amounts.

MONTHLY GROSS INCOME
Salary & Earned Income $ _____
Child Support & Alimony $ _____
Pension & Social Security $ _____
Rental Income $ _____
Other _____ $ _____

LIABILITIES
Mortgage Payment or Rent $ _____
Residence Real Estate Taxes $ _____
Vacation Home Mortgage $ _____
Vacation Home taxes $ _____
Automobile Loan(s) $ _____
Personal Loans/Charge Accts $ _____
Child Support & Alimony $ _____
Other _____ $ _____

TAXES
Federal Income Taxes $ _____
State & Intangible Taxes $ _____
Other _____ $ _____

FICA & MEDICARE WITHHOLDING
You $ _____
Spouse $ _____

INSURANCE
Life Insurance $ _____
Health Insurance $ _____
Disability Income Insurance $ _____
Auto Insurance $ _____
Home Owners Insurance $ _____
Other _____ $ _____

TRANSPORTATION
Gas and Oil $ _____
Maintenance and Repair $ _____
License, Registration $ _____
Public Transportation $ _____
Other _____ $ _____

MONTHLY SAVINGS FOR GOALS
Emergency Funds $ _____
Savings Account $ _____
Retirement Funds $ _____
College Funds $ _____
Vacation Fund $ _____
Other _____ $ _____
Other _____ $ _____
Other _____ $ _____
Other _____ $ _____

MONTHLY CHARITY CONTRIBUTIONS
Tithes & Offerings $ _____
Charitable $ _____

HOUSEHOLD EXPENSES
Food $ _____
Clothing $ _____
Doctor & Dentist $ _____
Prescription Drugs $ _____
Professional Fees $ _____
Education Expenses $ _____
Day Care $ _____
Personal Care $ _____
Electricity, Gas, Fuel $ _____
Telephone $ _____
Water & Water Conditioners $ _____
Garbage and Pest Control $ _____
Home Maintenance & Repair $ _____
Pool Maintenance & Repair $ _____
Security Systems $ _____
Home Furnishings $ _____
Recreation, Entertainment, Hobbies $ _____
Veterinarian & Pet Care $ _____
Books, Magazines $ _____
Club Dues $ _____
Vacation and Travel $ _____
Children's Allowances $ _____
Gifts $ _____
Other _____ $ _____

Take GROSS INCOME and subtract the other categories to determine if you are balancing the budget.

(Courtesy of Dustin LaPorte, CFP)

Budget Calculator

This calculator automates your budget calculations (Excel required). Go to www. dustinlaporte.com/worksheets.html and click on "Budget Calculator."

Spending Plan

GROSS INCOME
Salary & Earned Income _____
Rental Income _____
Pension & Social Security _____
Dividends, Interest, CapGain _____
Other _____ _____

TAXES
Federal Income Taxes _____
State & Intangible Taxes _____
Client - FICA & Medicare Taxes _____
Spouse - FICA & Medicare Taxes _____
Property Taxes _____
Local Taxes _____
Other _____ _____

LIABILITIES
Mortgage Payment or Rent _____
Residence Real Estate Taxes _____
Vacation Home Mortgage _____
Vacation Home taxes _____
Automobile Loan(s) _____
Personal Loans/Charge Accts _____
Child Support & Alimony _____
Other _____ _____

INSURANCE
Life Insurance _____
Health Insurance _____
Disability Income Insurance _____
Auto Insurance _____
Home Owners Insurance _____
Other _____ _____

TRANSPORTATION
Gas and Oil _____
Maintenance and Repair _____
License, Registration _____
Public Transportation _____
Other _____ _____

SAVINGS AND INVESTMENTS
Payroll Deductions
Credit Union
Mutual Funds
Stocks and Bonds
Real Estate
Annuities
Certificates of Deposit
Qualified Retirement Plans
Other _____

CONTRIBUTIONS
Charitable
Other _____

HOUSEHOLD EXPENSES
Food
Clothing
Doctor & Dentist
Prescription Drugs
Professional Fees
Education Expenses
Day Care
Personal Care
Electricity, Gas, Fuel
Telephone
Water & Water Conditioners
Garbage and Pest Control
Home Maintenance & Repair
Pool Maintenance & Repair
Security Systems
Home Furnishings
Recreation, Entertainment, Hobbies
Veterinarian & Pet Care
Books, Magazines
Club Dues
Vacation and Travel
Children's Allowances
Gifts
Other _____

TOTAL INCOME: $0
TOTAL OUTFLOW: $0
NET INCOME: $0

(Courtesy of Dustin LaPorte, CFP)

Life Insurance Worksheet

Use this life insurance worksheet to calculate your life insurance needs.

Life Insurance Worksheet

To find out how much coverage you need, total up the costs of your needs and subtract them from your current coverage, Social Security (to get an estimate visit the Social Security Administration website www.ssa.gov/pubs/deathbenefits.htm or call 1-800-772-1213), pension, and other assets that will be used to cover expenses. When you died your life insurance proceeds can help eliminate your debt; thus, reducing your family's required income needs.

NEED: If I or my spouse died to day, I would want to make sure …

_____ □ my family would receive a yearly income of $_____ for _____ years (for an estimate, take the year income amount and times it by the number of years). This does not factor in inflation or interest made from investing your life insurance proceeds.

_____ □ funeral and administration costs and estate taxes are paid.

_____ □ all medical bills from the accident or illness will be paid.

_____ □ the children's college education will be fully funded.

_____ □ our family will be debt free (mortgage, credit cards, loans, etc.).

_____ □ _____

TOTAL NEED: _____

SUBTRACT   _____
(Social Security, Pension,
Life Insurance Coverage,
and other Assets)

RESULTS: _____

(Courtesy of Dustin LaPorte, CFP)

Retirement Planning Chart

This handy chart gives you an idea of how much you'll need to save—based on your age and income—to be able to spend 75 percent of your current income in retirement.

Retirement Planning

Current Salary Age	$20,000	$40,000	$60,000
20	$1,252,000	$2,606,000	$3,963,000
25	1,010,000	2,120,000	3,233,000
30	813,000	1,722,000	2,633,000
35	651,000	1,395,000	2,142,000
40	511,000	1,116,000	1,724,000
45	409,000	897,000	1,395,000
50	326,000	719,000	1,128,000
55	258,000	572,000	905,000
60	195,000	442,000	712,000

Salary Age	$80,000	$100,000	$120,000
20	$5,322,000	$6,681,000	$8,541,000
25	4,347,000	5,460,000	6,575,000
30	3,546,000	4,459,000	5,373,000
35	2,890,000	3,637,000	4,386,000
40	2,334,000	2,944,000	3,555,000
45	1,894,000	2,393,000	2,893,000
50	1,534,000	1,942,000	2,351,000
55	1,238,000	1,572,000	1,906,000
60	983,000	1,253,000	1,524,000

Most people in retirement want 75% of their preretirement income. This table will help you estimate the total nest egg you will need to provide 75% of your current salary for a 25-year retirement that begins at age 65. Select your current age and current salary that best fit your situation.

Calculations assume a 4% inflation rate and 8% investment return. Principal will be depleted after 25 years. No tax consequences were considered. All returns and inflation rate are hypothetical and are not intended to represent the performance of any specific investment. As always investing involves risks and you may incur a profit or a loss.

(Courtesy of Dustin LaPorte, CFP)

Investor Risk Profile Questionnaire

This questionnaire can help you get a feel for what sort of investment risk might be most appropriate for you.

Client Information and Investment History

1. **Name(s) of individual(s) in which your account(s) should be registered:**

   Name: _____ Date of Birth: ___/ ___/ ___
   Occupation (former occupation, if retired): _____

   Name: _____ Date of Birth: ___/ ___/ ___
   Occupation (former occupation, if retired): _____

2. **Have your ever made any investments (i.e. purchased stocks, bonds or mutual funds)?**

   ☐ Yes   ☐ No

3. **Have you ever used an investment adviser, financial planner, or other professional to manage your investments?**

   ☐ No   ☐ Yes

   If yes, please specify adviser or planner or other professional: _____

4. **What was your tax bracket for the current year or last year?** _____ %

5. **Approximate annual income(s) of registrant(s):**

   Name: _____ Annual Income: $ _____
   Name: _____ Annual Income: $ _____

6. **Approximate net worth (excluding primary residence) of registrant(s):**

   Name: _____ Net Worth: $ _____
   Name: _____ Net Worth: $ _____

7. **What percentage of your total investable assets (excluding primary residence) will be represented by your account?**

   ☐ 0% - 25%   ☐ 26% - 50%   ☐ 51% - 75%   ☐ 76% - 100%

8. **Over what time frame do you believe it is reasonable to evaluate the performance of your investment adviser?**

   ☐ 1 to 3 years   ☐ 3 to 5 years   ☐ 5 to 7 years

9. **Additional information:**

   Is there any additional information you wish to make us aware of regarding your financial or investment situation?

   _____

   _____

Investor Risk Profile Questionnaire
(Courtesy of Mark J. Snyder Financial Services Inc.)

Investor Risk Profile Questionnaire

1. TIME FRAME

Take a look at how many years you can let your money grow before you'll need to tap into your nest egg. (This is important because a "fully-invested" investor must be able to withstand down cycles).

If the working time frame for
your investment portfolio is...   Give yourself:

1-2 years ....…..……...... 1 point ☐
3-5 years …....................…........ 2 points ☐
6-10 years ….................…..…....... 3 points ☐
more than 10 years …......….…....... 4 points ☐

2. YEARS UNTIL RETIREMENT

Where are you in relation to retirement? The farther you are from retirement, the more risk you may take.

If the number of years between
now and retirement is...   Give yourself:

0 years ……………...….......…..…… 1 point ☐
3-5 years ………………....…...….......... 2 points ☐
6-10 years ……………………….…....... 3 points ☐
more than 10 years ....…..…........ 4 points ☐

3. FINANCIAL CUSHION

Take a look at your total financial position and the cushion you have set aside for emergencies. This will help you decide how much risk you may prudently take in your investing.

If you have...   Give yourself:

Little outside savings set aside,
hence preservation of principal
is very important....................…....… 1 point ☐

Reasonable savings set aside and
are willing to take moderate risk
for moderate returns....................…..... 2 points ☐

Ample savings set aside (house paid off, CDs, insurance, etc.), hence you feel comfortable taking large risks for maximum return potential .... 3 points ☐

4. NEED FOR INCOME

How important is current income to you in the near term? Will you depend on income from your investment account for living expenses?

If current income is...   Give yourself:

Critical…………….................…............ 1 point ☐
Needed to a large degree................ 2 points ☐
Needed to a minor extent................ 3 points ☐
Not important................…................ 4 points ☐

5. INVESTING ATTITUDE

Your current attitude toward investing over the next decade will help dictate what type of strategy you could adopt and how much risk your investments could entail.

If your current attitude is...   Give yourself:

I cannot afford any significant loss of capital regardless of potential return... 1 point ☐

If I can get ample income from bonds, it is not worth suffering through the ups and downs of the stock market.......... 2 points ☐

If I can get a moderate return on my money, I am willing to sit through some fluctuations in my investments... 3 points ☐

Higher risk investments tend to earn higher returns than lower risk investments, and I want higher returns so I am willing to take higher risks….................…........ 4 points ☐

6. SPECIAL CIRCUMSTANCES

Are there any circumstances you can envision (college tuition, home purchase, retirement, etc.), outside the usual contributions and withdrawals, that might necessitate the immediate liquidation of a major portion of your portfolio?

If you can envision...   Give yourself:

Full portfolio could be liquidated....... 1 point ☐
Major liquidations.........................… 2 points ☐
Some small liquidations................... 3 points ☐
No liquidations planned. .... 4 points ☐

7. PRIMARY OBJECTIVE

Think about your personal investment goals.

If you would generally categorize your primary objective as... Give yourself:

Capital preservation - emphasis on maximizing principal stability; future growth of income and principal are of minor importance; short investment time horizon and low tolerance for big fluctuations in current income......... 1 point ❏

Current income - emphasis on providing a high level of current income; future growth of income and principal are secondary objectives..................................... 2 points ❏

Balanced - approximately equal emphasis on current income and potential for future appreciation and income growth....................... 3 points ❏

Long-term Growth - emphasis on future appreciation, not current income; year-to-year principal stability is not important................................…...... 4 points ❏

8. OVER THE PAST 70 YEARS, THE INVESTMENT VEHICLES BELOW RETURNED THE FOLLOWING AVERAGE YEARLY GAINS:

Stocks	11.0%
Bonds	5.2%
Cash (T-bills)	3.7%
Inflation	3.7%

Knowing this, what would you consider to be a reasonable average annual return for your portfolio?

Give yourself:

Less than 5% .... 1 point ❏

5-8% .... 2 points ❏

9-12% .... 3 points ❏

13 or more .... 4 points ❏

Note: We can make no assurances that this result will be achieved.

9. THE TABLE BELOW INDICATES HOW MUCH THE STOCK MARKET HAS FALLEN IN ANY GIVEN YEAR SINCE THE TURN OF THE CENTURY:

	How Often to Expect This
Routine Decline (5% or more)	About 3 times a year
Moderate Correction (10% or more)	About once a year
Severe Correction (15% or more)	About once every 2 years
Bear Market (20% or more)	About every 3 years

Past performance does not guarantee future results.
Source: Ibbotson

Assume you have a $100,000 invested and that sum represents your entire savings. Given the information in the table above, what is the maximum level of decline you can comfortably accept for your $100,000 investment?

Give yourself:

$95,000 .... 1 point ❏

$90,000 .... 2 points ❏

$85,000 .... 3 points ❏

$78,000 .... 4 points ❏

Investor Risk Profile

SCORECARD

	Points
1. Time Frame	
2. Years to Retirement	
3. Financial Cushion	
4. Need for Income	
5. Investing Attitude	
6. Special Circumstances	
7. Primary Objective	
8. Return on Your Investment	
9. Risk Tolerance	

Your Total Score [ ]

What Your Score Means

If your total score is:	This is the amount of risk you could take:	This is the type of investment plan you could follow:
9-13	Low Risk	**Income:** This objective is most suitable for the needs of more conservative investors desiring greater total return from their fixed-income portfolio.
14-22	Medium Risk	**Balanced:** This objective is most suitable for the needs of clients desiring moderate growth of capital.
23-31	High Risk	**Growth:** This objective is most suitable for the needs of aggressive investors who are willing to accept greater risk in search of higher returns.
32-35	High Risk	**Aggressive Growth:** This objective is an equity mutual fund-based service for aggressive growth investors with a 3-5 year time horizon and little sensitivity to tax considerations. Aggressive Growth accepts larger interim losses in the pursuit of growth returns. This Centurion Capital Management's least defensive service.

CLIENT AGREEMENT

The score reached by tabulating your answers is only one tool used by your Investment Consultant in evaluating the suitability of various investment alternatives. The choice of which investment strategy you invest in may be influenced by other investments in your portfolio. You should review your investments with your Investment Consultant on a regular basis.

I have answered the questions in the risk profile questionnaire based on my current financial situation and needs. Whenever my circumstances or investment attitude changes, I will contact my Investment Consultant to discuss what, if any, changes would be appropriate at such time. Circumstances that would trigger a reevaluation of my portfolio may include, but are not limited to; retirement, loss of employment, change in income, marriage, birth of a child or child entering college.

_____	_____
Signature	Signature
_____	_____
Print Name	Print Name
_____	_____
Date	Date

Spending and Age Report

The data in this report can prove handy when calculating what you might spend for certain goods and services in retirement.

Item	All consumer units	Under 25 years	25-34 years	35-44 years	45-54 years	55-64 years	65 years and older	65-74 years	75 years and older
Number of consumer units (in thousands)	117,356	8,543	19,635	23,835	24,393	18,104	22,847	11,505	11,342
Consumer unit characteristics:									
Income before taxes	$58,712	$27,494	$55,066	$72,699	$75,266	$64,156	$36,936	$45,202	$28,552
Income after taxes	56,304	27,120	53,257	69,619	71,442	61,068	36,007	43,976	27,924
Age of reference person	48.6	21.5	29.5	39.7	49.3	59.3	75.2	69.1	81.4
Average number in consumer unit:									
Persons	2.5	2.1	2.8	3.2	2.7	2.1	1.7	1.9	1.5
Children under 18	.6	.5	1.1	1.3	.6	.2	.1	.1	(^{1})
Persons 65 and over	.3	(^{1})	(^{1})	(^{1})	(^{1})	.1	1.4	1.4	1.3
Earners	1.3	1.4	1.5	1.7	1.7	1.3	.5	.7	.2
Vehicles	2.0	1.3	1.8	2.1	2.4	2.2	1.6	1.9	1.2
Percent distribution:									
Sex of reference person:									
Male	47	47	48	48	48	49	44	48	39
Female	53	53	52	52	52	51	56	52	61
Housing tenure:									
Homeowner	67	19	48	69	75	82	80	83	78
With mortgage	43	12	42	59	58	46	19	28	11
Without mortgage	25	6	6	11	17	36	61	55	67
Renter	33	81	52	31	25	18	20	17	22
Race of reference person:									
Black or African-American	12	11	14	13	13	10	9	11	7
White, Asian, and all other races	88	89	86	87	87	90	91	89	93
Hispanic or Latino origin of reference person:									
Hispanic or Latino	11	14	17	14	10	7	5	6	4
Not Hispanic or Latino	89	86	83	86	90	93	95	94	96
Education of reference person:									
Elementary (1-8)	5	3	3	4	4	5	11	9	13
High school (9-12)	36	37	31	34	34	35	44	42	47
College	59	60	66	62	62	60	44	49	40
Never attended and other	(^{2})	(^{3})	(^{2})	(^{2})	(^{2})	(^{2})	(^{2})	(^{2})	(^{2})
At least one vehicle owned or leased	88	75	89	91	91	91	84	89	79
Average annual expenditures	$46,409	$27,776	$45,068	$55,190	$55,854	$49,592	$32,866	$38,573	$27,018
Food	5,931	3,933	5,639	7,359	6,980	6,202	4,163	4,899	3,388
Food at home	3,297	1,917	2,945	4,121	3,807	3,487	2,605	2,967	2,222
Cereals and bakery products	445	273	387	564	499	465	366	405	326
Cereals and cereal products	143	106	138	183	159	139	106	114	97
Bakery products	302	167	249	381	340	326	261	291	229
Meats, poultry, fish, and eggs	764	449	654	963	918	827	569	691	440
Beef	228	149	189	293	283	250	150	189	108
Pork	153	79	121	199	179	167	126	152	98
Other meats	103	59	95	133	117	107	79	92	65
Poultry	134	83	137	170	162	134	85	104	65
Fish and seafood	113	59	82	131	140	132	102	124	79
Eggs	33	21	30	38	37	36	28	30	25
Dairy products	378	214	348	479	433	377	308	344	269
Fresh milk and cream	146	90	139	191	159	139	119	128	109
Other dairy products	232	124	209	288	274	238	189	216	160
Fruits and vegetables	552	298	461	663	614	626	490	553	424
Fresh fruits	182	87	145	218	201	211	170	192	146
Fresh vegetables	175	90	144	202	202	214	147	172	122
Processed fruits	106	69	91	132	114	104	101	106	96
Processed vegetables	89	51	82	111	98	97	72	83	61

See footnotes at end of table.

(Courtesy of U.S. Department of Labor's Bureau of Labor Statistics)

— Continued

Item	All consumer units	Under 25 years	25-34 years	35-44 years	45-54 years	55-64 years	65 years and older	65-74 years	75 years and older
Other food at home	$1,158	$684	$1,094	$1,452	$1,342	$1,192	$871	$974	$762
Sugar and other sweets	119	60	91	144	142	129	107	118	95
Fats and oils	85	43	76	99	99	94	71	79	64
Miscellaneous foods	609	381	613	777	688	594	449	488	408
Nonalcoholic beverages	303	186	281	389	366	317	203	238	167
Food prepared by consumer unit on out-of-town trips	41	13	32	42	47	58	40	51	29
Food away from home	2,634	2,015	2,694	3,238	3,173	2,715	1,558	1,933	1,166
Alcoholic beverages	426	401	478	511	458	454	248	325	167
Housing	15,167	8,940	15,516	18,482	17,258	15,769	11,058	12,474	9,612
Shelter	8,805	5,538	9,491	10,835	10,281	8,686	5,836	6,423	5,240
Owned dwellings	5,958	1,263	5,206	7,936	7,686	6,650	3,903	4,664	3,132
Mortgage interest and charges	3,317	835	3,535	5,169	4,493	3,076	1,060	1,570	542
Property taxes	1,541	287	1,027	1,760	1,940	1,883	1,524	1,659	1,387
Maintenance, repairs, insurance, other expenses	1,101	140	645	1,006	1,253	1,692	1,320	1,435	1,204
Rented dwellings	2,345	4,085	4,043	2,473	1,826	1,290	1,492	1,140	1,850
Other lodging	502	190	241	427	770	747	440	619	258
Utilities, fuels, and public services	3,183	1,755	2,909	3,569	3,693	3,427	2,813	3,091	2,531
Natural gas	473	191	396	524	536	521	489	504	474
Electricity	1,155	645	1,047	1,290	1,332	1,255	1,029	1,151	905
Fuel oil and other fuels	142	36	65	137	172	172	195	199	192
Telephone services	1,048	744	1,099	1,208	1,229	1,077	733	845	619
Water and other public services	366	140	302	410	425	402	367	392	341
Household operations	801	387	1,004	1,145	668	689	650	677	623
Personal services	322	237	651	666	132	71	113	95	130
Other household expenses	479	151	354	479	536	618	538	582	100
Housekeeping supplies	611	242	504	716	717	736	534	644	418
Laundry and cleaning supplies	134	63	127	161	154	150	106	122	89
Other household products	320	110	253	385	389	383	271	326	212
Postage and stationery	157	69	123	170	174	203	157	195	116
Household furnishings and equipment	1,767	1,018	1,608	2,216	1,899	2,231	1,225	1,640	800
Household textiles	132	58	136	155	159	153	91	114	66
Furniture	467	297	537	626	423	527	306	442	168
Floor coverings	56	17	41	55	91	83	28	34	21
Major appliances	223	95	184	247	239	298	204	217	192
Small appliances, miscellaneous housewares	105	68	89	100	124	140	95	120	68
Miscellaneous household equipment	782	483	621	1,033	863	1,031	503	713	285
Apparel and services	1,886	1,577	2,082	2,365	2,318	1,784	957	1,313	584
Men and boys	440	316	468	598	573	397	191	276	101
Men, 16 and over	349	279	353	405	478	359	169	241	94
Boys, 2 to 15	91	37	115	193	95	38	21	35	7
Women and girls	754	678	728	927	955	709	448	629	257
Women, 16 and over	633	636	587	671	821	650	423	593	244
Girls, 2 to 15	121	42	141	256	135	59	25	36	14
Children under 2	82	97	172	106	52	58	22	31	13
Footwear	320	297	384	397	369	298	159	189	128
Other apparel products and services	290	189	330	336	368	323	137	188	85
Transportation	8,344	5,987	8,798	9,945	9,795	8,908	5,171	6,568	3,754
Vehicle purchases (net outlay)	3,544	2,721	3,949	4,407	3,945	3,756	2,007	2,608	1,398
Cars and trucks, new	1,931	720	1,877	2,381	2,160	2,370	1,370	1,761	973
Cars and trucks, used	1,531	1,907	2,001	1,852	1,723	1,296	630	833	424
Other vehicles	82	95	71	175	62	90	[4]7	[4]13	([3])
Gasoline and motor oil	2,013	1,538	2,123	2,379	2,424	2,101	1,208	1,567	843

See footnotes at end of table.

— Continued

Item	All consumer units	Under 25 years	25-34 years	35-44 years	45-54 years	55-64 years	65 years and older	65-74 years	75 years and older
Other vehicle expenses	$2,339	$1,536	$2,361	$2,669	$2,850	$2,513	$1,594	$1,926	$1,257
Vehicle finance charges	297	199	402	395	331	289	110	167	52
Maintenance and repairs	671	444	618	727	810	738	542	657	427
Vehicle insurance	913	626	888	1,008	1,159	944	658	737	577
Vehicle rental, leases, licenses, and other charges	458	267	452	539	550	542	284	366	201
Public transportation	448	191	366	490	576	537	362	467	256
Healthcare	2,664	704	1,522	2,272	2,672	3,410	4,193	4,176	4,210
Health insurance	1,361	377	822	1,160	1,283	1,585	2,307	2,352	2,260
Medical services	677	197	399	665	771	979	769	733	805
Drugs	521	99	237	354	494	713	977	956	998
Medical supplies	105	31	63	93	124	134	140	134	146
Entertainment	2,388	1,393	2,455	2,765	3,034	2,429	1,593	2,143	1,032
Fees and admissions	588	249	489	753	753	633	416	548	282
Audio and visual equipment and services	888	631	943	1,029	1,046	862	642	797	484
Pets, toys, hobbies, and playground equipment	420	184	443	468	539	526	233	327	137
Other entertainment supplies, equipment, and services	492	328	580	516	697	408	301	471	129
Personal care products and services	541	337	504	627	627	550	462	495	427
Reading	126	49	89	121	143	167	143	154	132
Education	940	1,359	779	931	1,769	733	211	256	165
Tobacco products and smoking supplies	319	308	307	357	427	336	165	228	102
Miscellaneous	808	263	697	791	949	981	839	1,037	635
Cash contributions	1,663	393	1,080	1,735	2,076	1,960	1,889	1,925	1,852
Personal insurance and pensions	5,204	2,133	5,123	6,929	7,348	5,909	1,775	2,580	959
Life and other personal insurance	381	45	219	397	474	541	403	449	357
Pensions and Social Security	4,823	2,088	4,903	6,532	6,874	5,368	1,372	2,132	601
Sources of income and personal taxes:									
Money income before taxes	58,712	27,494	55,066	72,699	75,266	64,156	36,936	45,202	28,552
Wages and salaries	46,291	24,041	50,468	65,224	65,522	46,563	10,522	15,947	5,018
Self-employment income	3,772	953	2,782	4,579	5,468	4,533	2,421	4,070	750
Social Security, private and government retirement	6,147	204	342	798	2,106	9,582	20,534	21,892	19,157
Interest, dividends, rental income, other property income	1,379	312	267	882	897	2,539	2,845	2,592	3,102
Unemployment and workers' compensation, veterans' benefits	203	65	173	235	303	259	97	151	[4]43
Public assistance, supplemental security income, food stamps	343	373	355	366	364	404	227	268	186
Regular contributions for support	382	973	383	500	390	167	196	206	185
Other income	194	572	295	114	217	109	94	77	111
Personal taxes	2,408	373	1,809	3,080	3,824	3,088	929	1,226	628
Federal income taxes	1,696	200	1,189	2,190	2,794	2,192	612	862	357
State and local income taxes	534	161	509	739	823	631	97	113	81
Other taxes	177	13	111	151	208	264	220	250	190
Income after taxes	56,304	27,120	53,257	69,619	71,442	61,068	36,007	43,976	27,924

See footnotes at end of table.

— Continued

Item	All consumer units	Under 25 years	25-34 years	35-44 years	45-54 years	55-64 years	65 years and older	65-74 years	75 years and older
Addenda:									
Net change in total assets and liabilities	- $9,495	- $2,966	- $10,770	- $17,003	- $9,829	- $4,658	- $6,485	- $7,891	- $5,059
Net change in total assets	10,661	8,617	19,181	15,400	10,097	10,843	-381	79	-847
Net change in total liabilities	20,157	11,583	29,951	32,403	19,926	15,501	6,105	7,970	4,213
Other financial information:									
Other money receipts	530	99	448	289	521	1,110	563	603	522
Mortgage principal paid on owned property	-2,092	-307	-1,572	-2,748	-3,012	-2,722	-1,040	-1,667	-404
Estimated market value of owned home	164,800	33,327	102,020	178,366	200,096	223,763	169,355	190,381	148,026
Estimated monthly rental value of owned home	833	182	570	928	980	1,025	891	987	794
Gifts of goods and services	1,091	367	482	903	1,855	1,595	878	1,071	676
Food	111	16	35	105	195	205	60	85	33
Alcoholic beverages	14	27	10	20	16	8	7	10	4
Housing	233	98	121	215	344	365	177	243	108
Housekeeping supplies	31	22	24	31	39	52	19	30	7
Household textiles	13	[4]5	10	12	17	21	11	10	12
Appliances and miscellaneous housewares	24	15	19	14	26	38	27	35	19
Major appliances	7	[4]4	[4]3	4	9	10	11	17	[4]5
Small appliances and miscellaneous housewares	17	[4]11	16	10	17	28	16	19	14
Miscellaneous household equipment	66	22	25	106	73	101	43	58	28
Other housing	98	35	52	189	154	77	110	43
Apparel and services	205	128	116	226	233	292	166	255	73
Males, 2 and over	48	23	27	55	61	64	43	73	12
Females, 2 and over	77	33	40	90	90	103	78	121	32
Children under 2	37	30	46	41	35	50	20	26	13
Other apparel products and services	42	42	32	40	46	74	26	35	15
Jewelry and watches	22	28	14	23	21	43	10	11	8
All other apparel products and services ...	21	[4]14	19	18	26	31	16	24	[4]7
Transportation	58	5	46	64	84	67	46	68	24
Health care	44	[4]4	[4]4	25	50	28	119	15	225
Entertainment	74	32	51	57	111	126	47	63	30
Toys, games, arts and crafts, and tricycles	25	12	16	22	26	48	23	33	12
Other entertainment	49	21	35	35	85	78	24	30	17
Personal care products and services	16	21	10	20	19	14	16	23	[4]8
Reading	1	([2])	1	([2])	1	1	2	2	2
Education	247	[4]6	14	109	678	360	134	140	129
All other gifts	88	30	45	63	124	130	104	166	42

[1] Value less than 0.05.
[2] Value less than or equal to 0.5.
[3] No data reported.
[4] Data are likely to have large sampling errors.

Index

a bond rating, 145
aa bond rating, 145
aaa bond rating, 145
AARP (American Association of Retired Persons)
  Tax-Aide program, 218
  travel deals, 200
accidental death insurance, 255
accounts
  401(k)s, 53-54
  CDs (certificates of deposit), 73
  IRAs (Individual Retirement Accounts), 52, 103
    advantages of, 105
    choosing, 108-109
    contribution levels, 105
    custodians, 111
    deductibility, 105
    importance of, 169-170
    introduction of, 104-105
    investing assets, 112-113
    limitations of, 106
    minimum distributions, 106
    moving funds, 111-112
    rollovers, 111
    Roth IRAs, 106-110
    transfers, 111
    withdrawal penalties, 106
  Money Market Deposit Accounts, 72
  reviewing, 196
  savings, choosing, 71-73
Ada Comstock Scholars Program (Smith College), 10
adult day care, 238
affordable housing, choosing, 299-300
age discrimination, 288
Age Discrimination in Employment Act, 6

aggressive growth funds, 118
Alaska, retirement population, 22
alternative living, 291
  ECHO (Elder Cottage Housing Opportunities), 297-299
  retirement neighborhoods, 292
  senior co-ops, 292-294
  senior cohousing, 294-296
  shared housing, 296-297
A.M. Best, 60, 252
American Stock Exchange, 131
Amtrak, discount fares, 200
analysis, stocks
  analysts, 137
  technical analysis, 136-137
analysts, stocks, 137
annual growth rate, formulating, 42
annual reports, corporations, 132
annuities, 59-60
  joint and survivor monthly benefit, 80
  ten-year certain monthly benefit, 80
  ten-year certain/life annuity monthly benefit, 80
a rating (bonds), 145
Aristotle, elements of happiness, 49
Arizona, retirement population, 22
arthritic symptoms, in elderly, 19
assets
  inventorying, 258-259
  IRAs, investing, 112-113
  liabilities, converting from, 71
assisted living, 234
ATM activity, monitoring, 199
auto insurance, shopping for, 203
automatic-investment programs, mutual funds, purchasing from, 126
average retirement age, 16-17

B

b bond rating, 145
ba bond rating, 145
baa bond rating, 145
baby boomers, 16
balance sheets
    companies, 133-134
    cost of sales, 133
    current assets, 133
    current liabilities, 133
    EPS (earnings per share), 134
    income tax, 134
    net income, 134
    pretax income, 133
    total liabilities and equity, 133
    total revenue, 133
Bankrate.com, 248
banks, choosing, 71-73
Beacon Hill Village, 292
beneficiaries, estates, 259-260
benefits
    annuities, 59-60
    cash balance plans, 81
    defined benefit plans, 78-80
        career average plans, 79
        final pay plans, 79
        flat benefit plans, 79
    defined contribution plans, 78, 82
        401(k) plans, 82-84
        ESOP (Employee Stock Ownership
            Plan), 84
        profit sharing, 84
        stock bonus plans, 84
    individual 401(k)s, 86-87
    Keogh plans, 85
        money purchase plans, 86
        profit sharing plans, 86
    life insurance, 58-59
    pension equity plans, 81
    qualified retirement plans, 79
    SEPs (Simplified Employee Pensions),
        87-88
    SIMPLE IRAs, 87

Social Security, 56, 91-93
    calculating, 94-95
    disability benefits, 57-58, 92, 101
    financial solvency, 101-102
    intentions of, 93
    introduction of, 92
    late retirement, 98
    life expectancy, 99-100
    Medicare, 92
    modifications to, 92
    Personal Earnings and Benfit
        Statements, 96
    receiving, 96-97
    spousal benefits, 57, 100
    SSI (Supplemental Social Security), 92
    survivors benefits, 57, 100-101
    taxes, 213
    taking advantage of, 88
Best Employers for Workers Over 50
    (AARP), 284
Bestfares, 200
Bestplaces.net, 299
Bestretirementspots.com, 299
Better Business Bureau, 205
blue chip stocks, 131
board and care, retirement communities, 234
boards of directors, serving on, 9
bond mutual funds, 151
bonds, 143-144
    bond mutual funds, 151
    call provisions, 150
    corporate bonds, 144-146
    credit ratings, 152
    earnings, 148-149
    expenses, 152
    face values, 144
    GICs (Guaranteed Investment Contracts),
        153-154
    inflation, 150
    interest rates, 149
    intermediate bonds, 144
    international bonds, 148
    liquidity, 149
    loads, 152

long-term bonds, 144
minimum starting investments, 152
municipal bonds, 147-148
purchasing, 150-151
ratings, 145-146
risks, 149-150
shopping for, 152
short-term bonds, 144
tracking, 152-153
Treasury bonds, 146-147
yields, 145
zero coupon bonds, 147
book value, stocks, 135
broad plans, importance of, 61-62
brokerage houses
deep discount, 139-140
discount, 139, 150
full-service, 138-139, 150
mutual funds, purchasing from, 125
brokers, deep discount, 117
Budget Travel Online, 200
budgets
adjusting, 198-199
shoestring budgets, 270-278
businesses, starting, 9, 289
buying
bonds, 150-151
stocks, 138-140
bypass trusts, 264

C

c bond rating, 146
ca bond rating, 146
caa bond rating, 146
calculating
expenditures, 41-42
income, 41
Social Security benefits, 94-95
California, retirement population, 21
call provisions, bonds, 150
cancer, in elderly, 20
cancer insurance, 255
capital preservation, 162

career average plans, 79
cash balance plans, 81
cash value life insurance, 249-251
certificates of deposit (CDs), 73
charges, unnecessary charges, avoiding, 203
charitable giving, cutting, 271
charitable solicitations, scams, 204
Chatham Park South Cooperative, 293
checklists, retirement, 28
chronic health problems, retireees, 19-20
closed-end mutual funds, 123
closing costs, 69
clubs, joining, 10
CNBC Stock Screener, 138
co-ops (senior), 292-294
COBRA health insurance, 227
cohousing (senior), 294-296
college, returning to, 10
Colorado, retirement population, 22
community-based programs and services,
retirement communities, 235-236
companies
annual reports, 132
balance sheets, 133-134
fundamental analysis, 133
company-sponsored retirement
cash balance plans, 81
defined benefit plans, 78-80
career average plans, 79
final pay plans, 79
flat benefit plans, 79
defined contribution plans, 78-82
401(k) plans, 82-84
ESOP (Employee Stock Ownership
Plan), 84
profit sharing, 84
stock bonus, 84
individual 401(k)s, 86-87
Keogh plans, 85
money purchase plans, 86
profit sharing plans, 86
pension equity plans, 81
qualified retirement plans, 79

recent developments, 78-79
SEPs (Simplified Employee Pensions), 87-88
SIMPLE IRAs, 87
taking advantage of, 88
compounding, 43-44
congregate housing, 234
consolidating credit card debt, 67
Consumer Credit Counseling Services, 202
continuing care retirement communities, 235
contribution levels (IRAs), 105
controlling
spending, 64-70
withdrawals, 189-190
converting traditional IRAs to Roth IRAs, 109-110, 211-213
corporate bonds, 144-146
corporations
annual reports, 132
balance sheets, 133-134
fundamental analysis, 133
cost of sales (balance sheets), 133
costs
health insurance, controlling, 225-226
mutual funds, 118, 122
couples, retiring at the same time, 32
coverages, life insurance, 246-252
credit card debt
consolidating, 67
detriments of, 66-67
credit cards
carrying, 67
teaser cards, 67
credit ratings, bonds, 152
credit risks, bonds, 149
current assets, balance sheets, 133
current liabilities, balance sheets, 133
custodians, IRAs, 111
cutting
charitable giving, 271
discretionary spending, 270
food costs, 271
housing costs, 271
prescription drug costs, 271
telephone service costs, 271
transportation costs, 271
travel costs, 271

D

debt
credit card debt, detriments of, 66-67
managing, 201-203
deductibility, IRAs, 105
deductions, itemizing, 215
deep discount brokerage houses, 117, 139-140
defined benefit plans, 78-80
career average plans, 79
final pay plans, 79
flat benefit plans, 79
defined benefit programs, 54
defined contribution plans, 55, 78, 82
401(k) plans, 82-84
ESOP (Employee Stock Ownership Plans), 84
profit sharing, 84
stock bonus plans, 84
Delaware, retirement population, 22
demographics, retirees, 16-18
dental insurance, 254
Depdale Garden Co-Op, 292
diabetes, in elderly, 20
disability benefits, Social Security, 57-58, 92, 101
disability insurance, 253
discount brokerage houses, 139, 150
discount purchase plans, bonds, 150
discounts, senior discounts, pursuing, 203
discretionary spending, cutting, 270
diversification, mutual funds, 117
dividend yield, stocks, 135-136
dividends, 119
dollar-cost averaging, stocks, 140
Dow Jones Industrials, 119
dying intestate, 262

E

E Savings Bonds, 146
early retirement
    choosing, 33-34
    health insurance, 227-228
earnings, bonds, 148-149
EAs (enrolled agents), 211
ECHO (Elder Cottage Housing
  Opportunities), 297-299
EE Savings Bonds, 146
Elder Cottage Housing Opportunities
  (ECHO), 297-299
emergency funds, 199
emotional buying, avoiding, 199
enrolled agents (EAs), 211
enrolling, Medicare, 229-230
EPS (earnings per share) (balance sheets),
  134
equity, 68
ESOP (Employee Stock Ownership Plan),
  55, 84
estate planning, 257-258
    advantages of, 260
    assets, inventorying, 258-259
    beneficiaries, 259-260
    funerals, preplanning/prepaying, 265-266
    professionals, 266
    trusts, 263-265
        bypass trusts, 264
        generation-skipping trusts, 264
        irrevocable life insurance trusts, 264
        qualified personal residence trusts, 264
        qualified terminable interest property
          trusts, 264
    wills
        living wills, 262
        writing, 261-262
estate planning professionals, 266
executor of will, 259
Expedia, 200
expenditures, calculating, 41-42
expense ratios, mutual funds, 122

expenses
    bonds, 152
    mutual funds, 122

F

face value, bonds, 144
Fastfa.com, 186
Federal Trade Commission, 205
fee-for-service health insurance, 223
fees, avoiding unnecessary, 203
final pay plans, 79
financial goals
    assessing, 173-188
    choosing, 181-182
    online calculators, 44
financial incentives, retirement, 7-8
financial planners, hiring, 192-193
Financial Planning Association, 193
financial portfolios, adjusting, 196-198
financial publications, mutual funds, 124-125
financial solvency, Social Security, 101-102
financial windfalls, saving, 71
flat benefit plans, 79
Florida, retirement population, 21
food costs, cutting, 271
formulas, annual growth rate, 42
Foundation Senior Community Service
  Employment Program (AARP), 284
four-percent rule, withdrawals, 187-190
Franklin, Benjamin, 29
full-service brokerage houses, 138-139, 150
Fuller, Ida Mae, 92
fund families, 126
fundamental analysis, stocks, 133
funds
    emergency funds, 199
    IRAs, moving, 111-112
    Money Market Funds, 72
    mutual funds, 115-118
        advantages, 117-118
        aggressive growth funds, 118
        choosing, 121-124

closed-end funds, 123
cost, 118
diversification, 117
drawbacks, 117-118
expense management, 117
expense ratios, 122
expenses, 122
fund families, 126
fund screens, 125
fund supermarkets, 125
growth and income funds, 119
growth funds, 118
index funds, 119, 122
international funds, 120
introduction of, 116
large-cap funds, 119
loads, 123
low investment risk, 117
management, 124
mid-cap funds, 119
NAV (net asset value), 116
open-end funds, 123
performance, 117, 121
portfolio turnover, 122
professional money management, 117
prospectus, 124
purchasing, 125-126
REITs (Real Estate Investment Trusts),
   120
researching, 124-125
risks, 121
sector funds, 120
shares outstanding, 116
sizes, 124
small-cap funds, 119
socially responsible funds, 120
taxation, 123
tracking, 126-127
withdrawing, 191-192
fund screens, mutual funds, 125
fund supermarkets, 125
funerals, preplanning/prepaying, 265-266

G

general obligations bonds, 147
generation-skipping trusts, 264
get-rich-quick schemes, avoiding, 204-205
*Get a Life: You Don't Need a Million to Retire
   Well*, 277
GICs (Guaranteed Investment Contracts),
   153-154
Glacier Circle senior cohousing, 294
goals
   financial goals
      assessing, 173-181, 184-188
      choosing, 181-182
   retirement, 31
   savings, 71
Golden Age Passport, 200
group-based programs and services, retirement communities, 235-236
growth and income funds, 119
growth funds, 118
growth stocks, 130
Guaranteed Investment Contracts (GICs),
   153-154

H

health, retirees, 19
   chronic conditions, 19-20
   mental health problems, 20-21
health insurance, 221-222
   costs, controlling, 225-226
   early retirement, 227-228
   fee-for-service insurance, 223
   importance of, 222
   job loss, 227
   long-term care insurance, 239-240
      choosing, 240-241
      purchasing, 241-243
   managed care plans, 223-224
   Medicare, 228-229
      enrolling in, 229-230
      parts, 229

needs, evaluating, 224-225
self-employment, 226
supplemental insurance, 231
heart disease, in elderly, 19
HECMs (Home Equity Conversion Mortgage), 61, 276
hiring financial planners, 192-193
HMOs (health maintenance organizations), 223-224
holidays, cutting costs, 199-201
home equity conversion mortgages (HECMs), 61, 276
home equity loans, 276-277
Homefair.com, 299
homes
closing costs, 69
equity, 68
scaling down, 202
Hotwire, 200
housing
choosing affordable, 299-300
costs, cutting, 271
hypertension, in elderly, 19

I

I Savings Bonds, 146
Idaho, retirement population, 22
Illinois, retirement population, 22
income
assessing, 40-43
steady income, importance of, 46-49
unearned income, 213
income stocks, 131
income tax, balance sheets, 134
income tax rates, 217-218
independent living arrangements, retirement communities, 234
index funds, 119, 122
individual 401(k)s, 86-87
Individual Retirement Accounts (IRAs). *See* IRAs (Individual Retirement Accounts)
individual services, retirement communities, 235

inflation, 45-46
bonds, 150
informational interviews, 286-287
insurance, 245
accidental death insurance, 255
annuities, 59-60
auto insurance, shopping for, 203
cancer insurance, 255
dental insurance, 254
disability insurance, 253
health insurance, 221-222
controlling costs, 225-226
early retirement, 227-228
fee-for-service insurance, 223
importance of, 222
job loss, 227
long-term care insurance, 239-243
managed care plans, 223-224
Medicare, 228-230
needs evaluations, 224-225
self employment, 226
supplemental insurance, 231
life insurance, 58-59, 246
cash value life insurance, 249-251
coverages, 246-252
needs assessments, 246
reevaluating, 203
surrender values, 250
term life insurance, 58, 248-252
universal life insurance, 250
variable life insurance, 250
variable universal life insurance, 251
whole life insurance, 58, 249-252
mortgage insurance, 255
umbrella insurance, 254
vision insurance, 254
interest, compound interest, 43-44
interest payments, points, 277
interest rates, bonds, 149
intermediate bonds, 144
international bonds, 148
international funds, 120

international stocks, 131
Internet fraud, avoiding, 204
interviews, employment, 286-288
inventorying assets, 258-259
investments
    after retirement, 188-189
    bonds, 143-144
        bond mutual funds, 151
        call provisions, 150
        corporate bonds, 144-146
        credit ratings, 152
        earnings, 148-149
        expenses, 152
        face values, 144
        GICs (Guaranteed Investment
            Contracts), 153-154
        inflation, 150
        interest rates, 149
        intermediate bonds, 144
        international bonds, 148
        liquidity, 149
        loads, 152
        long-term bonds, 144
        minimum starting investments, 152
        municipal bonds, 147-148
        purchasing, 150-151
        ratings, 145-146
        risks, 149-150
        shopping for, 152
        short-term bonds, 144
        tracking, 152-153
        Treasury bonds, 146-147
        yields, 145
        zero coupon bonds, 147
    compounding, 43-44
    deep discount brokers, 117
    Dow Jones Industrials, 119
    duration, 160-161
    IRA assets, 112-113
    long-term investments, 164-165
    mutual funds, 115-118
        advantages, 117-118
        aggressive growth funds, 118
        choosing, 121-124
        closed-end funds, 123

        cost, 118
        diversification, 117
        drawbacks, 117-118
        expense management, 117
        expense ratios, 122
        expenses, 122
        fund families, 126
        fund screens, 125
        fund supermarkets, 125
        growth and income funds, 119
        growth funds, 118
        index funds, 119-122
        international funds, 120
        introduction of, 116
        large-cap funds, 119
        loads, 123
        low investment risk, 117
        management, 124
        mid-cap funds, 119
        NAV (net asset value), 116
        open-end funds, 123
        performance, 117, 121
        portfolio turnover, 122
        professional money management, 117
        prospectus, 124
        purchasing, 125-126
        REITs (Real Estate Investment Trusts),
            120
        researching, 124-125
        risks, 121
        sector funds, 120
        shares outstanding, 116
        sizes, 124
        small-cap funds, 119
        socially responsible funds, 120
        taxation, 123
        tracking, 126-127
    rates of return, 190-191
    risk tolerance, 161-162
        approaching, 165-168
        investment returns, 162-164
        primary objectives, 162
    stocks, 129-131
        analysts, 137
        annual reports, 132

balance sheets, 133-134
blue chip stocks, 131
book value, 135
choosing, 132-138
comparing, 132
dividend yield, 135-136
dollar-cost averaging, 140
fundamental analysis, 133
growth stocks, 130
income stocks, 131
international stocks, 131
IPOs (initial public offerings), 131
limit orders, 140-141
long-term trends, 132
penny stocks, 131
purchasing, 138-140
ratios, 134-135
stock exchanges, 131-132
stock screens, 138
stop loss orders, 141
strategies, 140-141
technical analysis, 136-137
value averaging, 140
value stocks, 130
IPipeline.com, 248
IPOs (initial public offerings), 131
IRAs (Individual Retirement Accounts), 6,
103
advantages of, 105
assets, investing, 112-113
choosing, 108-109
contribution levels, 105
custodians, 111
deductibility, 105
funds, moving, 111-112
importance of, 169-170
introduction of, 6, 104-105
limitations of, 106
minimum distributions, 106, 214
rollovers, 111
Roth IRAs, 106-108
converting to, 109-110, 211-213
introduction of, 6
SIMPLE IRAs, 87
transfers, 111
withdrawal penalties, 106
IRAs (Individual Retirement Accounts), 52
irrevocable life insurance trusts, 264
itemizing tax deductions, 215

J-K-L

job loss, health insurance, 227
Jobs 4.0, 283
Johnson, Lyndon B., 229
joint and survivor monthly benefit (annuities), 80

Keogh plans, 85
money purchase plans, 86
profit sharing plans, 86

LaPorte, Dustin, 247
large-cap funds, 119
late retirement, Social Security benefits, 98
liabilities, assets, converting to, 71
life expectancy
increases in, 4-5
Social Security benefits, 99-100
life insurance, 58-59, 246
cash value life insurance, 249-251
coverages, 246-252
needs assessments, 246
reevaluating, 203
surrender values, 250
term life insurance, 58, 248-252
universal life insurance, 250
variable life insurance, 250
variable universal life insurance, 251
whole life insurance, 58, 249-252
lifestyle, retirement, 34-35
limit orders, stocks, 140-141
liquidity, bonds, 149
living abroad, 300-301
living wills, 262
Livingto100.com, 186

loads
   bonds, 152
   mutual funds, 123
loans, home equity loans, 276-277
locations, retirement, choosing, 35-37
long-term bonds, 144
long-term care insurance, 239-240
   choosing, 240-241
   purchasing, 241-243
long-term investments, 164-165
long-term trends, stocks, 132
lump sum distributions, 80

M

managed care health insurance plans,
  223-224
managing
   debt, 201-203
   mutual funds, 124
Martindell, Anne, 10
Massachusetts Investors Trust mutual fund,
  116
medical expenses, overlooking, 215
Medicare, 228-229
   enrolling in, 229-230
   introduction of, 92
   parts, 229
   post-retirement employment, 289-290
Medigap, 231
mental health problems, retireees, 20-21
Mexico, retirement population, 22
Michigan, retirement population, 22
mid-cap funds, 119
minimum distributions, IRAs, 106, 214
minimum starting investments, bonds, 152
money, assessing, 40-43
money management software, 64
Money Market Deposit Accounts, 72
Money Market Funds, 72
money purchase plans (Keogh), 86
Moneycentral.com, 186
Moody's bond ratings, 145
Morningstar, 138

Morrow-Howell, Nancy, 18
mortgage insurance, 255
mortgages
   closing costs, 69
   equity, 68
   HECM (Home Equity Conversion
    Mortgage), 61
   paying down, 68-69
   refinancing, 69-70, 202
   reverse mortgages, 60-61, 203, 275-276
moving IRA funds, 111-112
MSN Money Stock Screener, 138
MSN Money Tax Center, 219
municipal bonds (munis), 147-148
mutual funds, 115-118
   advantages, 117-118
   aggressive growth funds, 118
   bond mutual funds, 151
   choosing, 121-124
   closed-end funds, 123
   cost, 118
   diversification, 117
   drawbacks, 117-118
   expense management, 117
   expense ratios, 122
   expenses, 122
   fund families, 126
   fund screens, 125
   fund supermarkets, 125
   growth and income funds, 119
   growth funds, 118
   index funds, 119, 122
   international funds, 120
   introduction of, 116
   large-cap funds, 119
   loads, 123
   low investment risk, 117
   management, 124
   mid-cap funds, 119
   NAV (net asset value), 116
   open-end funds, 123
   performance, 117, 121
   portfolio turnover, 122

professional money management, 117
prospectus, 124
purchasing, 125-126
REITs (Real Estate Investment Trusts), 120
researching, 124-125
risks, 121
sector funds, 120
shares outstanding, 116
sizes, 124
small-cap funds, 119
socially responsible funds, 120
taxation, 123
tracking, 126-127

N

NASDAQ (National Association of Securities Dealers Automated Quotations System), 132
National Association of Personal Financial Advisors, 193
National Do Not Call Registry, 205
National Employer Team (AARP), 284
National Fraud Information Center, 205
national parks, Golden Age Passport, 200
National Reverse Mortgage Lenders Association, 276
National Shared Housing Resource Center, 297
NAV (net asset value), mutual funds, 116
net income, balance sheets, 134
net unrealized appreciation, stocks, 215
Nevada, retirement population, 22
New Jersey, retirement population, 22
new jobs, retirement plans, inquiring about, 168-169
New Mexico, retirement population, 22
New York, retirement population, 21
New York Stock Exchange, 131
nursing homes, 234
    choosing, 237-243

O

Ohio, retirement population, 22
online calculators, financial goals, 44
open-end mutual funds, 123
Orbitz, 200
organizations, joining, 10

P

P/B (price/book) ratios, stocks, 135
P/E (price/earnings) ratios, stocks, 134-135
P/S (price/sales) ratios, stocks, 135
Panama, retirement population, 22
part-time employment, attaining, 203, 271-272
parts, Medicare, 229
paying down mortgages, 68-69
payroll deductions, 71
Pennsylvania, retirement population, 21
penny stocks, 131
pension equity plans, 81
pensions, SEPs (Simplified Employee Pensions), 87-88
performance, mutual funds, 117, 121
Personal Earnings and Benefit Statements (Social Security), 96
planners (financial), hiring, 192-193
points, interest payments, 277
portfolio turnover, mutual funds, 122
portfolios, 127-128
    adjusting, 196-198
post-retirement employment, 279
    age discrimination, 288
    attaining, 271-272
    businesses, starting, 289
    choosing to, 280-281
    interviews, 286-288
    looking for, 281-284
    marketing yourself, 284-288
    Social Security, 289-290
power of attorney, 262

prepaying funerals, 265-266
preplanning funerals, 265-266
prescription drug costs, cutting, 271
pretax income (balance sheets), 133
primary objectives
    investment returns, 162-164
    risk tolerance, 162
probate, 263
profit sharing plans, 55, 84
    Keogh profit sharing plans), 86
property tax assessments, challenging, 216
purchasing
    bonds, 150-151
    long-term care insurance, 241-243
    mutual funds, 125-126
    stocks, 138-140
pyramid schemes, avoiding, 204

Q–R

qualified personal residence trusts, 264
qualified retirement plans, 79
qualified terminable interest property trusts,
    264

rates, income taxes, 217-218
rates of return, investments, 190-191
ratings, bonds, 145-146
ratios, stocks, 134
    P/B (price-book), 135
    P/E (price-earnings), 134-135
    P/S (price-sales), 135
Real Estate Investment Trusts (REITs), 120
receiving Social Security benefits, 96-97
refinancing mortgages, 69-70, 202
REITs (Real Estate Investment Trusts), 120
relocating, 36-37
resources
    mutual funds, 124-125
    taxes, 218-219
resumés, upgrading, 284-285
Retired Brains, 283

retirees
    demographics, 16-18
    health, 19
        chronic conditions, 19-20
        mental health problems, 20-21
retirement, 10-11
    affording, 23-25
    challenges, 11-13
    checklist, 28
    choosing, 28-31
    company-sponsored retirement
        cash balance plans, 81
        defined benefit plans, 78-80
        defined contribution plans, 78, 82-84
        Employee Stock Ownership Plan
            (ESOP), 55, 84
        individual 401(k)s, 86-87
        Keogh plans, 85-86
        pension equity plans, 81
        qualified retirement plans, 79
        recent developments, 78-79
        SEPs (Simplified Employee Pensions),
            87-88
        SIMPLE IRAs, 87
        taking advantage of, 88
    couples, 32
    dictionary definition of, 3
    early retirement, choosing, 33-34
    financial incentives, 7-8
    goals, 31
    lifestyle choices, 34-35
    locations, choosing, 35-37
    reasons for, 7
    recent developments regarding, 4-10
    shoestring budgets, 270-278
    stereotypes, 4
    strategies, 11-13
retirement age
    average retirement age, 16-17
    changes to, 5-6
    working past, 8-9
retirement benefits, Social Security, 56
retirement communities, 233-234
    adult day care, 238
    assisted living, 234

board and care, 234
choosing, 235-237
community-based programs and services, 235-236
congregate housing, 234
continuing care retirement communities, 235
group-based programs and services, 235-236
independent living arrangements, 234
individual services, 235
nursing homes, 234
    choosing, 237-243
retirement neighborhoods, 292
senior co-ops, 292-294
senior cohousing, 294-296
shared housing, 296-297
Retirement Confidence Survey (Employee Benefit and Research Institute), 172-173
RetirementJobs.com, 283
Retirementliving.com, 299
retirement locations, 21-23
retirement neighborhoods, 292
retirement plans
inquiring about, 168-169
retirement population, 5
retirement portfolios, 127-128
returns, investments, 162-164
rates of return, 190-191
revenue bonds, 147
reverse mortgages, 60-61, 203, 275-276
HEMCs (home equity conversion mortgages), 276
reviewing savings, 196
risks
bonds, 149-150
mutual funds, 121
risk tolerance
investing, 161-162
    investment returns, 162-164
    primary objectives, 162
investments, approaching, 165-168
"Rolling Lab" schemes, avoiding, 204

rollovers, IRAs, 111
Roosevelt, Franklin, 92
Roth IRAs, 106-108
assets, investing, 112-113
choosing, 108-109
converting to, 109-110, 211-213
custodians, 111
funds, moving, 111-112
introduction of, 6
rollovers, 111
transfers, 111

S

savings
401(k)s, 53-54
adjusting budgets, 198-199
choosing accounts, 71-73
CDs (certificates of deposit), 73
compounding, 43-44
forming habits, 71
setting goals, 71
IRAs (Individual Retirement Accounts), 52, 103
    advantages of, 105
    choosing, 108-109
    contribution levels, 105
    custodians, 111
    deductibility, 105
    importance of, 169-170
    introduction of, 104-105
    investing assets, 112-113
    limitations of, 106
    minimum distributions, 106
    moving funds, 111-112
    rollovers, 111
    Roth IRAs, 106-110
    transfers, 111
    withdrawal penalties, 106
maxing out, 166-168
Money Market Deposit Accounts, 72
Money Market Funds, 72
reviewing, 196
starting early, 45

Treasury Securities, 73
utilizing, 70-71
withdrawals, 187
controlling, 189-190
four-percent rule, 187-188
scams, avoiding, 204-205
schemes, avoiding, 204-205
school, returning to, 10
SCORE, 9
sector funds, 120
securities, Treasury Securities, 73
self-employed workers, Social Security, 92
self-employment, health insurance, 226
self-employment 401(k)s, 86
senior co-ops, 292-294
senior cohousing, 294-296
senior discounts, pursuing, 203
Senior Job Bank, 283
Seniors4Hire, 283
SEPs (Simplified Employee Pensions), 87-88
shared housing, 296-297
shares outstanding, mutual funds, 116
shoestring budgets, 270-278
short-term bonds, 144
Silver Glen senior cooperative, 293
Silver Wings program (United Airlines), 200
SIMPLE IRAs, 87
sinusitis, in elderly, 20
small-cap funds, 119
Smartmoney.com, 248
socially responsible funds, 120
Social Security, 55-56, 91-93
benefits
calculating, 94-95
disability benefits, 57-58, 92, 101
late retirement, 98
life expectancy, 99-100
Personal Earnings and Benfit
Statements, 96
receiving, 96-97
spousal benefits, 57, 100
survivors benefits, 57, 100-101
taxes, 213

financial solvency, 101-102
intentions of, 93
introduction of, 92
Medicare, 92, 228-229
enrolling in, 229-230
parts, 229
modifications to, 92
post-retirement employment, 289-290
retirement benefits, 56
self-employed workers, 92
SSI (Supplemental Social Security), 92
work credits, 56-57
software, money management software, 64
solicitations, scams, 204
spending, controlling, 64-70
spousal benefits, Social Security benefits, 57, 100
SSI (Supplemental Social Security), 92
Standard and Poor's, 60, 252
bond ratings, 145
steady income, importance of, 46-49
stock bonus plans, 84
stock bonuses, 55
stock exchanges, 131-132
stocks, 129-131
analysts, 137
annual reports, 132
balance sheets, 133-134
blue chip stocks, 131
book value, 135
choosing, 132-138
comparing, 132
dividends, 119
dollar-cost averaging, 140
fundamental analysis, 133
growth stocks, 130
income stocks, 131
international stocks, 131
IPOs (initial public offerings), 131
limit orders, 140-141
long-term trends, 132
net unrealized appreciation, 215
penny stocks, 131

purchasing, 138-140
ratios, 134
   dividend yield, 135-136
   P/B (price-book), 135
   P/E (price-earnings), 134-135
   P/S (price-sales), 135
stock exchanges, 131-132
stock screens, 138
stop loss orders, 141
strategies, 140-141
technical analysis, 136-137
value averaging, 140
value stocks, 130
stock screens, 138
stop loss orders, stocks, 141
strategies
   retirement, 11-13
   stocks, 140-141
supplemental health insurance, 231
surrender values, life insurance, 250
survivor benefits, Social Security benefits, 100-101
survivors benefits, Social Security, 57

T

T. Rowe Price, 190
Target Retirement 2010 Fund (Vanguard), 190
Tax Center (MSN Money), 219
Tax Counseling for the Elderly (TCE) Program (IRS), 218
tax professionals, consulting, 211, 214
Tax-Aide program (AARP), 218
tax-friendly states, moving to, 216
taxable assets, cashing in, 215
taxes, 209
   cutting after retirement, 214-217
   deductions, itemizing, 215
   importance of, 210
   income taxes, rates, 217-218
   mutual funds, 123

property tax assessments, challenging, 216
   resources, 218-219
   Roth IRAs, converting to, 211-213
   Social Security benefits, 213
   tax professionals, consulting, 211
Taxes About.com, 219
Taxmama.com, 219
teaser cards, 67
technical analysis, stocks, 136-137
telemarketing fraud, avoiding, 204
telephone service costs, cutting, 271
ten-year certain monthly benefit (annuities), 80
term life insurance, 58, 248-249
   whole life insurance, compared, 251-252
terms, bonds, 144
Texas, retirement population, 21
time, investments, 160-161
total liabilities and equity (balance sheets), 133
total revenue (balance sheets), 133
tracking
   bonds, 152-153
   mutual funds, 126-127
transfers, IRAs, 111
transportation costs, cutting, 271
travel, cutting costs, 199-201, 271
Travelocity, 200
Treasury bills, 146
Treasury bonds, 146-147
Treasury notes, 146
Treasury Securities, 73
TreasuryDirect, 151
trusts, 263-265
   bypass trusts, 264
   generation-skipping trusts, 264
   irrevocable life insurance trusts, 264
   qualified personal residence trusts, 264
   qualified terminable interest property trusts, 264

U

umbrella insurance, 254
unearned income, 213
United Airlines, Silver Wings program, 200
universal life insurance, 250
universities, returning to, 10
unnecessary fees and charges, avoiding, 203
Utah, retirement population, 22

V

vacations, cutting costs, 199-201, 271
value averaging, stocks, 140
value stocks, 130
Vanguard Target Retirement 2010 Fund, 190
variable life insurance, 250
variable universal life insurance, 251
vision insurance, 254
volunteer work, participating in, 9

W

waiting periods, disability insurance, 253
Wall Street Journal, mutual funds, tracking
  through, 127
Warner, Ralph, 277
Westegg.com, 46
Where to Retire magazine, 37
whole life insurance, 58, 249-250
  term life insurance, compared, 251-252
wills
  executors, 259
  living wills, 262
  writing, 261-262
withdrawal penalties, IRAs, 106
withdrawals
  funds, 191-192
  savings, 187
    controlling, 189-190
    four-percent rule, 187-188
work credits, Social Security, 56-57
workplace plans

cash balance plans, 81
defined benefit plans, 78-80
  career average plans, 79
  final pay plans, 79
  flat benefit plans, 79
defined contribution plans, 78, 82
  401(k) plans, 82-84
  ESOP (Employee Stock Ownership
    Plan), 84
  profit sharing, 84
  stock bonus plans, 84
individual 401(k)s, 86-87
Keogh plans, 85
  money purchase plans, 86
  profit sharing plans, 86
pension equity plans, 81
qualified retirement plans, 79
recent developments, 78-79
SEPs (Simplified Employee Pensions),
  87-88
SIMPLE IRAs, 87
taking advantage of, 88
workplace programs, 54
  401(k)s, 53-54
  defined benefit programs, 54
  defined contribution programs, 55
  ESOP (Employee Stock Ownership Plan),
    55
  profit sharing, 55
  stock bonuses, 55
writing wills, 261-262

X-Y-Z

Yahoo! Finance, 138
yields, bonds, 145
YourEncore.com, 283

zero coupon bonds, 147
Zweifler, Walter, 29

Check out these
BEST-SELLERS

READ BY MILLIONS!

Grammar and Style
SECOND EDITION
978-1-59257-115-4
$16.95

Buying & Selling a Home
FIFTH EDITION
978-1-59257-458-2
$19.95

FULL COLOR!

The Perfect Wedding
978-1-59257-566-4
$22.95

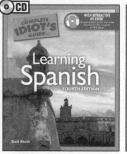
Learning Spanish
FOURTH EDITION
978-1-59257-485-8
$24.95

Investing
THIRD EDITION
978-1-59257-480-3
$19.95

Baby Sign Language
978-1-59257-469-8
$14.95

Total Nutrition
FOURTH EDITION
978-1-59257-439-1
$18.95

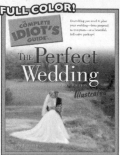
Positive Dog Training
SECOND EDITION
978-1-59257-483-4
$14.95

The Bible
THIRD EDITION
978-1-59257-389-9
$18.95

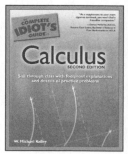
Calculus
SECOND EDITION
978-1-59257-471-1
$18.95

Music Theory
SECOND EDITION
978-1-59257-437-7
$19.95

The Perfect Resume
FOURTH EDITION
978-1-59257-463-6
$14.95

Playing the Guitar
SECOND EDITION
978-0-02864244-4
$21.95

Manga Illustrated
978-1-59257-335-6
$19.95

Knitting & Crocheting
THIRD EDITION
978-1-59257-491-9
$19.95

More than **450 titles** available at booksellers and online retailers everywhere

ALPHA
www.idiotsguides.com